That Book Is Dangerous!

That Book Is Dangerous!

How Moral Panic, Social Media, and the Culture Wars Are
Remaking Publishing

Adam Szetela

The MIT Press
Cambridge, Massachusetts
London, England

The MIT Press
Massachusetts Institute of Technology
77 Massachusetts Avenue, Cambridge, MA 02139
mitpress.mit.edu

The MIT Press would like to thank the anonymous peer reviewers who provided comments on drafts of this book. The generous work of academic experts is essential for establishing the authority and quality of our publications. We acknowledge with gratitude the contributions of these otherwise uncredited readers.

This book was set in ITC Stone Serif Std and ITC Stone Sans Std by New Best-set Typesetters Ltd. Printed and bound in the United States of America.

Library of Congress Cataloging-in-Publication Data is available.

ISBN: 978-0-262-04985-6

10   9   8   7   6   5   4   3   2   1

EU Authorised Representative: Easy Access System Europe, Mustamäe tee 50, 10621 Tallinn, Estonia | Email: gpsr.requests@easproject.com

There is more than one way to burn a book. And the world is full of people running about with lit matches.

Ray Bradbury, Coda to *Fahrenheit 451*

Contents

Introduction: Welcome to the Sensitivity Era

In 2019, Penguin Random House planned to publish the debut novel of young adult (YA) author Amélie Wen Zhao. A few months before the publication date, there was an uproar on Twitter. People who had never read *Blood Heir* proclaimed that it was racist because it was set in a fantastical world where oppression was not based on skin color. According to Zhao's critics, it was "cultural appropriation" and "antiblack" to depict slavery that was not African American slavery. The uproar was so loud that Zhao canceled the publication of *Blood Heir*. In a statement posted to Twitter, she apologized for the "pain" and "harm" her unpublished novel had caused the "readers" who never read it.

Later that year, the *New York Times* reported that *Blood Heir* would be published after all.[1] However, it would first be sent to sensitivity readers. These beta readers would help Zhao rewrite her book by vetting it for potentially offensive material. Around the same time, YA author Kosoko Jackson canceled his own debut novel, *A Place for Wolves*, after people on Twitter and Goodreads protested the inclusion of a Muslim villain. They claimed this fictional character was "offensive." He was "harmful." He was "dangerous." In an ironic twist, Jackson was one of the people on Twitter who went after Zhao. He is also a sensitivity reader for Big Five publishers. Literally, his job is to ensure that books are not offensive.

Around the same time, people organized an internet campaign to leave one-star reviews for Laurie Forest's debut YA novel *The Black Witch*, which one blogger and bookseller described as "the most dangerous, offensive book I have ever read."[2] Among other literary crimes, Forest's unpublished novel was pilloried for including characters who say and do prejudiced things, despite the fact that the novel itself is a strong critique of prejudice.

As Forest puts it, "Its message is that people who may have been raised with prejudiced views can change for the better." The campaign tanked the book's rating on Goodreads.

Other people compelled *Kirkus Reviews* to retract and then rewrite a starred review of Laura Moriarty's debut YA novel, *American Heart*, after it, too, was declared "harmful" and "dangerous." The book was accused of "silencing Muslim voices" because it focuses on a white protagonist who learns to overcome her prejudices.[3] For this reason, the novel was considered Islamophobic. However, Moriarty wrote *American Heart* to "highlight the existence of white privilege and the need for native-born Americans to acknowledge the plight of immigrants and people of color."[4] Before it was slammed, the *Kirkus* reviewer, who happened to be a Muslim woman of color, read it as a progressive and important YA novel.

As the publication date approached for Keira Drake's debut YA novel, *The Continent*, progressives burned advance reading copies of it. Like Zhao, Jackson, Forest, and Moriarty, Drake is a progressive who was found guilty of intolerance. Her novel included a "white savior." But it is not just debut authors who have seen their books burned by people who act like the firemen in *Fahrenheit 451*. At the end of 2020, *Newsweek* reported that videos of people burning *Harry Potter* books were "spreading like wildfire across TikTok."[5] Historically, *Harry Potter* has been burned by right-wing fundamentalists who accuse J. K. Rowling of promoting witchcraft. But these book burners accused Rowling and her novels of transphobia, fatphobia, and racism. One editor and sensitivity reader called on her Twitter followers to assault Rowling, a survivor of domestic violence, until her "nose breaks [and] it gushes all over her clothes."[6]

In March 2021, a petition targeted *The Adventures of Ook and Gluk* by Dav Pilkey because it includes "stereotypical Chinese proverbs," "dashes for eyes for the Asian characters," and a "white savior" storyline "that has the Kung Fu master rescued by the non-Asian protagonists."[7] Scholastic pulled the book. Some bookstores and public libraries wiped it clean from their shelves.[8] In the past, Pilkey's work had been banned by the right. That same month, Dr. Seuss Enterprises discontinued publication of six Dr. Seuss books. Within days, eBay responded, too. "eBay is currently sweeping our marketplace to remove these items," exclaimed a spokeswoman for the company.[9] For their part, some public libraries abandoned basic principles of literary freedom, as they barred their own patrons from checking these books out.[10] One of Dr. Seuss's titles depicts a slanty-eyed "China-man" who eats rice with chopsticks, whereas another includes an "Eskimo" in a fur-lined parka. In his time, Seuss was excoriated by the right for producing "dangerous" work that condemned Jim Crow, antisemitism, and other forms of intolerance. Today, his books are "dangerous" in the eyes of the left.

After Scholastic published *A Birthday Cake for George Washington* written by Ramin Ganeshram, illustrated by Vanessa Brantley-Newton, and edited by Andrea Davis Pinkney, progressives signed a petition demanding that Amazon remove this "racist" picture book from their website because it "whitewashes slavery."[11] Soon after, Scholastic pulled the book from distribution. Ganeshram is a woman of color who has won seven Society of Professional Journalist awards. Brantley-Newton is an African American woman and a past finalist for the NAACP Image Award for Outstanding Literary Work for Children. Pinkney, another African American woman, is a past winner of the Coretta Scott King Award. Among other contributions, she launched the first African American children's book imprint at Walt Disney. Nonetheless, the public was once again told that "racism" hides everywhere, and young readers need to be protected from their "dangerous" book.

In short, something strange is happening in the world of children's and YA literature. *That Book Is Dangerous! How Moral Panic, Social Media, and the Culture Wars are Remaking Publishing* illuminates where the left's moral panic came from, what it hopes to accomplish, and how it has already reshaped the practices of authors, editors, literary agents, teachers, librarians, and the biggest publishers acquiring books right now.

In chapter 1—"The Ideas of the Sensitivity Era"—I look at the origins of the current movement to rewrite, cancel, and otherwise censor what young people read. In the past decade and a half, scholars, social media users, reviewers, teachers, librarians, nonprofit organizations, and news outlets have helped to make children's and YA literature more inclusive. On the one hand, this movement addresses long-standing problems in the publishing industry. From a lack of LGBTQ+ and BIPOC characters to whitewashed covers and the segregation of characters into different genres, children's and YA literature still has plenty of progress to make. When books about characters from diverse backgrounds are hard to find, it can deter young people from reading. It can also undermine literature's potential to affirm the experiences of those who might otherwise feel like their experiences have no value. Moreover, a lack of diverse and sensitive books diminishes literature's power to help readers understand those who are different from them. This is a particular problem when authors perpetuate stereotypes in their work.

On the other hand, the movement for more diverse and sensitive books has created new problems. In the past decade and a half, the emergence of platforms as different as Twitter, Tumblr, TikTok, and Goodreads has allowed anyone with an internet connection to be a public literary critic. It has also allowed anyone with a "marginalized identity" to be a gatekeeper. When Jackson and others declare that "stories about the civil rights movement should be written by black people," that "stories of suffrage should be written by women," and that "stories about boys during life-changing times, like the AIDS epidemic, should be written by gay men," they are not alone.[12] Far from irrelevant, this movement uses social media and other platforms to pressure authors, agents, and editors to abandon the idea that people should be allowed to write and read what they want.

Sensitivity readers—individuals who, at bottom, share an identity with a fictional character—were not even mentioned on Twitter until 2016. Now they are hired by authors, agents, editors, and everyone else in the publishing industry to determine whether a book will offend readers who share their identity. As I argue, these self-described "cultural ambassadors" perpetuate the essentialist idea that people with shared identities think and act the same, and that there are "authentic" and "inauthentic" ways to be black, trans, gay, and so on.[13] These industry professionals have also eroded the idea that expertise is something a person attains, rather than something a person self-declares. As a result, authors are being told their stories are not "authentic" or "accurate" enough to be published. Ironically, many of these authors are authors of color who write stories about characters of color.

In chapter 2—"The Behavior of the Sensitivity Era"—I examine the punitive and cannibalistic nature of this movement. On social media, where self-righteous indignation earns more likes and retweets than measured criticism, children's and YA authors are accused of harming and corrupting the next generation. From an African American illustrator honored by the National Association for the Advancement of Colored People to an African American writer and editor who started the first major imprint for African American children's literature, most of the accused are part of the movement for diverse and sensitive books. Much like the Salem witch trials, where even the holiest people were accused of conspiring with the devil and corrupting the town's youth, progressives continue to shame, humiliate, and censor the people who are most sympathetic to their cause. In this chapter, I discuss the experiments I conducted with my colleagues at Cornell University's Social Dynamics Lab. As our controlled experiments with hundreds of readers show, it does not take much social pressure to start a literary bonfire. We were even able to pressure more than 40 percent of research participants to accuse Allen Ginsberg—a gay leftist—of homophobia; in the absence of social pressure, that number was close to zero. Our results suggest that the moral panic over literature may have less to do with the content of literature and more to do with the pressure to appear virtuous in public.

Drawing on the sociology of moral panics, social psychology, moral philosophy, and the historical record of comic book censorship in the 1950s—which included a US Senate hearing that investigated the relationship between comic books and juvenile delinquency—I argue that we are living through another moral panic over literature for young people. Moral panics tend to arise in response to real problems. Then they find scapegoats for those problems. Whereas the moral crusaders of the past believed they would defeat juvenile crime by turning comic books into didactic tools, moral crusaders in the present believe they will defeat racism, homophobia, and every other intolerance by turning children's and YA literature into an instrument for their moral lessons. In the process, they perpetuate the myth of childhood innocence. They also perpetuate the mythical idea that struggles over popular culture are equivalent to struggles over political legislation. Above all, the crusade for more diverse and sensitive books creates real problems for the National Coalition Against Censorship, PEN America, and other organizations that protect authors, illustrators, and their readers from censorship.

In chapter 3—"The Political Economy of the Sensitivity Era"—I discuss incentives. On the left, there is no shortage of sensitivity readers, diversity gurus, and other moral entrepreneurs selling consultations, seminars, webinars, weekend retreats, and so on. Other progressives are using the moral crusade over children's and YA literature to secure more book deals, speaking engagements, and other lucrative opportunities for themselves. Although many of these interventions are well intentioned, they fail to address the economic inequalities related to literary production. The solutions foregrounded by moral entrepreneurs are not public arts programs, better funding for public schools, and the abolition of unpaid internships and low wages in the publishing industry. The solutions are the kinds of interventions that fit neatly into the status quo. Notwithstanding its militant rhetoric, the moral crusade over children's and YA literature is not a radical alternative to business as usual. It is the latest version of business as usual.

On the right, politicians and pundits are exploiting this moral crusade to position themselves as the defenders of free speech, literary values, and young people. As some of Dr. Seuss's books got discontinued, Ted Cruz sold signed copies of *Green Eggs and Ham* to fund his next political campaign. He credited "lefties losing their minds" and the "cancel culture mob" for the $125,000 he raised in the first twenty-four hours.[14] For his part, House Minority Leader Kevin McCarthy accused Democrats of "outlawing Dr. Seuss" on the House floor.[15] In this respect, children's and YA literature is the new battlefield in America's culture war. While the crusade to cancel books distracts progressives from political work, it buttresses the political work of conservatives. When Donald Trump shouts "Let's get rid of PC!" or when Tucker Carlson, who hosted the most watched show in cable news, warns his followers about threats to literary freedom from the left, conservatives are not just connecting to people in their own echo chambers.[16] Research from sociologists, pollsters, and political strategists suggests they are building the broad constituencies needed to win elections. In early 2021, after progressives lost congressional seats, failed to flip even one state chamber, and barely defeated a president who left office with one of the lowest approval ratings in American history—despite winning the battle to cancel *Scrambled Eggs Super!* by Dr. Seuss—veteran Democratic strategist James Carville hit the nail on the head in an interview with *Vox*: "Wokeness is a problem and we all know it."[17] Without downplaying the genuine progress made by the movement for more diverse and sensitive books, this chapter argues that the biggest winners are left-wing entrepreneurs and right-wing politicians.

In chapter 4—"The Future of the Sensitivity Era"—I speculate about the future of this moral panic. In the midst of canceled picture books and YA novels, some publishers now require their authors to sign "morality clauses." These clauses allow publishers to terminate contracts for virtually any reason. To quote a clause from a recent HarperCollins contract, the publisher may terminate a contract if the author's "conduct evidences a lack of due regard for public conventions and morals."[18] Of note, the biggest defenders of these morality clauses are not free market conservatives but progressives committed to antiracism, feminism, and other forms of social justice. Other progressives, including a former US Poet Laureate, want the US government to intervene. Much like the 1950s, when concerned adults pressured American publishers and the US Senate to censor those who wrote and illustrated comic books, today's progressives appeal to the overreaching power of big business and the state. When literature is treated as an immoral disease that is spreading like the plague, censorship is the only answer.

As this moral crusade insulates itself from criticism by publicly shaming and discrediting its critics, it continues to enlarge the scope of its concerns. Racism, sexism, transphobia, and every other "-ism" and "-phobia" now mean whatever anyone with an internet connection wants them to mean. At the same time, sensitivity readers, morality clauses, and other Orwellian interventions, which have their origins in children's and YA literature, are now being imported into adult literary culture. Among other examples, journalists at the *New York Times* recently demanded sensitivity readers to ensure the newspaper of record does not offend its readers.[19] Condé Nast, which publishes the *New Yorker* and *Wired*, asked its journalists to sign a morality clause.[20] Likewise, adults are now trying to censor novels, poems, plays, and other literature in the name of protecting adults from "harm" and "danger." To put it simply, this moral panic treats all readers like children.

At a moment when people are focused on the right's moral panic over literature, it might seem strange that this book focuses on the left's moral panic over literature. After all, right-wing panic has had more influence at the legislative level. That is true. But left-wing panic has had significantly more influence inside publishers, agencies, and other corners of literary culture. This is the reason why many of the progressives I interviewed are more concerned about the left than the right. While the right is remaking the world in its image, the left is standing in a circular firing squad. As adrienne maree brown, a queer black feminist, reflects in an interview about her recent book *We Will Not Cancel Us*: "I have been doing movement work for 25 years. There was a real sense of, 'Why do I feel afraid to just observe something and speak about what I'm observing?' To me, that felt like it's its own proof of something being there. If there was no such thing as cancel culture or callout culture—in the sense that if you say the wrong thing, you can get disposed of—I don't think I would've felt that I was taking a big risk by speaking about it."[21]

That Book Is Dangerous! builds on her concerns and the concerns of my fellow progressives who are worried about a movement for more progressive books that is alienating the very people who want to write and read these books.

My interview subjects—who range from presidents and vice presidents at Big Five publishers, to senior literary agents at the most prestigious agencies, to executive directors of public library districts, to sensitivity readers, to award-winning writers, to individuals just starting their careers as editors, agents, librarians, and writers—reveal how much literary culture has changed in the past decade and a half, and how they are navigating the new terrain of Twitter, Goodreads, Bookstagram, BookTok, and other platforms. Many of these people are deeply concerned about literature in the era of social media, what I call the "Sensitivity Era."

As I think about these interviews, and the most frequent admission I heard—"I wouldn't have done this interview if it wasn't anonymous"—I am reminded of what Salman Rushdie said after religious crusaders burned *The Satanic Verses* and put a price on his head. "The hush of reverence is inappropriate for literature."[22] It is even less appropriate for a book about censorship in the name of progressive values.

1 The Ideas of the Sensitivity Era

Diversity

Each year, the Cooperative Children's Book Center (CCBC) at the University of Wisconsin–Madison publishes a report about the state of children's and YA literature. In their report, they look at the number of books by and about black and African people, Indigenous people, and people of color. Since 2018, their report has also documented other aspects of identity such as sexuality and disability. Predictably, the number of books written by or about people from historically underrepresented groups pales in comparison to the number of books written by or about people who are white, heterosexual, and able-bodied. For example, in 2019, the CCBC evaluated 4,035 children's and YA books. Of these books, just 232 were written by authors who are black/African, whereas 471 were about characters who are black/African. Similarly, just 46 books were written by Indigenous authors, whereas only 65 were about Indigenous characters.[1]

Similar disparities exist in other datasets. As a case in point, just 15 percent of books that made recent *New York Times* YA bestseller lists included main characters of color. Even fewer books included LGBTQ+ characters and characters with disabilities. Comparable disparities are apparent in *Publishers Weekly* YA bestseller lists as well as the Best Fiction for Young Adults lists, which are published annually by the Young Adult Library Services Association, a division of the American Library Association.[2] As an echo of the data on children's and YA literature accumulated by the CCBC, these data illuminate disparities that pertain to both authors and characters. Similar disparities exist in adult literature.[3]

To put this in perspective, one has to consider the fact that children's and YA books were even less diverse in the past. The number of books about characters of color, queer characters, trans characters, and so on has actually increased in recent years. Back in 1999, the CCBC documented just 151 children's and YA books about black/African characters published in an estimated market of 5,000 books. In 1985, just 18 books by black authors and illustrators were published in an estimated market of 2,500 books. Year after year, the disparities accumulate. In other words, when I talk about the relative lack of diverse books, I am not just talking about what was published last year. I am talking about hundreds of years of literary production that have privileged certain kinds of authors, illustrators, and characters at the expense of others. The same disparities pertain to literature written for adults. As one novelist told me during an interview, "There are people whose voices have been left out for a century or more. They've been effectively canceled for a good long time."

It would be hard to fully explain these disparities without acknowledging the overwhelmingly white workforce that makes up publishing. In their survey of the publishing industry, *Publishers Weekly* found that 84 percent of people who work in this industry are white.[4] Moreover, "nonwhite survey respondents were much more likely to be new to the industry than whites." According to other data, literary agents are anywhere from 71 percent to 80 percent white.[5] Many editors and agents gravitate toward books that connect to them on a personal level. As Clayton Childress observes in his ethnography of the industry, "white literary agents are significantly less likely to self-report an interest in representing 'ethnic' or 'multicultural' fiction than are nonwhite literary agents."[6] To be sure, there are white agents who favor ethnic and multicultural fiction. There are also white agents who favor authors of color over white authors. Yet the racial disparities at agencies and publishers are not irrelevant to the racial disparities that concern authors and fictional characters. As one agent explained to me, "Once you have people acquiring who have particular interests in more diverse issues around race, then you get different acquisitions." The same holds true for other aspects of identity.

In her 1990 article, "Mirrors, Windows, and Sliding Glass Doors"—an oft-cited article that is a prefigurative document of the Sensitivity Era—educator Rudine Sims Bishop explains why these disparities are a problem.[7] First, as mirrors, books are tools of self-affirmation. When a gay teenager reads a book about another gay teenager, it can help them recognize the value of their identity and their experiences. In the absence of these books, a gay reader might feel like their identity and their experiences have no value. That is, the absence of a literature of recognition can diminish a reader's self-esteem. In this respect, Bishop argues that it is important for readers to be able to see characters like themselves in the books they read.

Second, as windows and sliding glass doors, literature can introduce children and young adults to new identities and experiences. As Bishop puts it, "Books may be one of the few places where children who are socially isolated and insulated from the larger world may meet people unlike themselves." In other words, a book might be the first place a heterosexual teenager meets a gay teenager. Books are not just tools for self-affirmation; they are tools that can be used to build empathy and tolerance for those who are different. In Bishop's words, books (as windows) allow readers to see new worlds, and "these windows are also sliding glass doors" because "readers have only to walk through in imagination to become part of whatever world has been created."[8]

Bishop was not the first writer to express her concerns over literature for young people. Whereas W. E. B. Du Bois is widely recognized as a seminal theorist of race in the United States, he is less widely recognized as a progenitor of the movement for diverse literature. Yet, in the early twentieth century, he launched and edited *The Brownies' Book* serial. As Elizabeth Gettins, of the Library of Congress, explains, "It was the first magazine of its kind, written for African-American children and youths to instill in them a sense of racial pride and provide overall instruction on how to conduct oneself. Du Bois is credited with establishing the genre of African-American children's literature."[9] Decades later, Mississippi Freedom School teachers formed the Council on Interracial Books for Children to "to promote a literature for children that better reflects the realities of a multicultural society."[10] Although children's and YA literature has come a long way since Du Bois launched *The Brownies' Book* in 1920, since public librarian Nancy Larrick authored her influential "The All-White World of Children's Books" in 1965, and since Bishop introduced her concept of "Mirrors, Windows, and Sliding Glass Doors" in 1990, their concerns are still relevant today.[11]

As the data show, it is still hard to locate certain kinds of children's and YA books because comparatively few have been published. It also hard to locate these books because salespeople do not always know how to sell them. One Latina author, who has written more than a couple children's and YA books, described the situation to me: "It's one thing to buy the manuscript and produce it. It's another thing to know how to sell it in, let's say, a Latino community where you have English-dominant Latinos, Spanish-dominant Latinos, non-Spanish interacting Latinos. There's nuance. And there's how we reach those populations. You would be surprised how little publicity people necessarily know about those things. So that means you need marketing people who are really representative as well."

In his meticulous and insightful analysis of book covers, scholar Philip Nel implores his readers to never judge a book by its cover. As he explains, "Believing that books with a person of color on the cover will not sell, publishers put a White face (or a silhouette, or an ambiguously raced face) on the dust jacket of a book whose protagonist is not white."[12] Consequently, children and YA readers of color looking for protagonists like themselves, and white readers looking for protagonists unlike themselves, are left in a through-the-looking-glass landscape where things are never what they seem. "Nonwhite readers" in particular, reflects Bishop, "have too frequently found the search futile."[13] This problem is compounded by austere public budgets. Many public libraries and K–12 schools simply do not have the resources to make their collections more diverse.

These problems are not distinct to books about characters of color. Although "ten young adult titles with LGBTQ+ content were published in the 1970s, forty in the 1980s, eighty-two in the 1990s, 292 in 2000–2009, and 513 titles in 2010–2016,"[14] it is still less common for books to include LGBTQ+ characters. Furthermore, LGBTQ+ literature is a target of "gaywashing." In 2011, YA authors Rachel Manija Brown and Sherwood Smith explained to the public that literary agents had tried to "de-gay" their novel. Some gatekeepers believe a de-gayed novel is more marketable. As Brown reflects, "I think that when you cut certain types of people out of fiction . . . you're sending the message to teenagers saying that what they are inherently is so terrible that it can't be talked about and can't be portrayed, and I think that's really soul crushing."[15]

For some young readers, the dearth of books that connect to their lived experience will deter them from reading. To quote children's and YA author Walter Dean Myers at length:

> I read voraciously, spending days in Central Park reading when I should have been going to school. But there was something missing. I needed more than the characters in the Bible to identify with, or even the characters in Arthur Miller's plays or my beloved Balzac. As I discovered who I was, a black teenager in a white-dominated world, I saw that these characters, these lives, were not mine.

Books did not become my enemies. They were more like friends with whom I no longer felt comfortable. I stopped reading. I stopped going to school. . . . Then I read a story by James Baldwin: "Sonny's Blues." I didn't love the story, but I was lifted by it, for it took place in Harlem, and it was a story concerned with black people like those I knew. By humanizing the people who were like me, Baldwin's story also humanized me. . . . During my only meeting with Baldwin, at City College, I blurted out to him what his story had done for me. "I know exactly what you mean," he said. "I had to leave Harlem and the United States to search for who I was. Isn't that a shame?" When I left Baldwin that day I felt elated that I had met a writer I had so admired, and that we had had a shared experience. But later I realized how much more meaningful it would have been to have known Baldwin's story at 15, or at 14.[16]

During my conversations with writers, I heard similar stories. "When I grew up, there were two kinds of black people in literature," one Pulitzer Prize finalist explained to me. "You either came from the rural south or the urban north. And that's barring the antebellum stuff that one would end up reading. I was a middle-class kid. Where were my people? My grandfather was a doctor. My father was a doctor. There were no characters like this. But that wasn't because no one was writing this. It was because no one was publishing this."

When I interviewed people of color who work in publishing, their experiences echoed this writer's experiences as a young black reader. In fact, some of my interview subjects believe their personal experiences are central to the changes that have occurred, and continue to occur, in publishing. One editor of color reflects: "I feel like so much of what has helped the push along on the editorial side is because there are people like me. I would have loved to have seen more characters that looked like me when I was growing up. We're going out of our way to acquire more of those kinds of titles. I think as we have that trickle-down effect of a lot more people on the editorial, and sales, and marketing side also being people of color, also being queer, neurodiverse, looking for that kind of content, and going out of their way to support it, we're really behind a lot of that push on the bookshelves. But even if it wasn't for that, I think it's been swinging that way for a long time."

Although it has been swinging that way for a long time, the disparities still exist. They are especially visible in certain genres. In an analysis of close to two hundred African and African American children's books, Nel located just seven fantasy stories, seven science fiction stories, and thirteen adventure stories. In contrast, sixty-six stories were realist, and fifty-eight stories had a historical focus.[17] Despite the reality that readers from all backgrounds enjoy fantasy, science fiction, and adventure, stories about Africans and African Americans are often told through the lenses of slavery, civil rights, and other injustices. Of course, realistic literature with a historical focus is important. But imagination is important, too. As Ebony Elizabeth Thomas reflects in *The Dark Fantastic: Race and the Imagination from Harry Potter to the Hunger Games*, "When people of color seek passageways into the fantastic, we have often discovered that the doors are barred."[18] According to Nel, genre is the literary equivalent of Jim Crow.[19]

While Bishop, who is regarded as the "mother of multicultural literature,"[20] and her contemporaries, working in a tradition that dates back to Du Bois and *The Brownies' Book*, have struggled to resolve problems of underrepresentation, whitewashing, gaywashing, and literary segregation for decades, their efforts were supported by the emergence of Twitter in 2006. In less than a decade, niche conversations about diversity in children's and YA literature went mainstream. In part, this was due to movements such as #BlackLivesMatter and #YesAllWomen, which encouraged people to draw attention to other disparities in social life. In this context of hashtag activism, some of the Twitter interventions of those who read, write, edit, and publish children's and YA literature went viral.

For example, the hashtag #WeNeedDiverseBooks spread in 2014 after BookCon announced a superstar-author panel that had no women or people of color. By the end of the year, this hashtag evolved into the nonprofit organization, We Need Diverse Books (WNDB). Far from a fringe organization, WNDB's partners now include Penguin Random House and the Scholastic Corporation. Other projects, such as the Stories for All Project, have been established in the past decade to promote books that are mirrors, windows, and sliding glass doors for children and YA readers.

The senior decision-makers at the Big Five publishers now recognize the market for these books. According to one vice president I interviewed: "The truth is when books sell, we do more of the kinds of books that sell. It's that crass. When you look at the *New York Times* bestseller list, it tells you a lot about what is happening. In the last five years, you will notice more bestsellers by BIPOC authors in all age categories. So many BIPOC authors. We just had a census. We know what the population of this country is going to be in the next five years, the next ten years, the next twenty years. It's going to be heavily BIPOC, it's going to be heavily Latino, and Asian. We want to sell to everyone. We got to be ready. We need to be publishing these books." Another Big Five vice president, who has worked hard to acquire more diverse books, told me that they have "seen more changes in the past five years, than the previous twenty to twenty-five."

Publishers' efforts have been supported by news outlets. In the past few years, the *New York Times* ("The Apartheid of Children's Literature" and "Where Are the People of Color in Children's Books?"), the *Atlantic* ("The Ongoing Problem of Race in Y.A." and "Where is the Black *Blueberries for Sal*?"), the *Washington Post* ("Characters in Children's Books Are Almost Always White" and "Just How Racist is Children's Literature?"), *Vox* ("I Never Noticed How Racist So Many Children's Books Are Until I Started Reading to My Kids" and "Diversity in Children's Books Has Increased Exponentially Over the Past 10 Years"), *HuffPost* ("Children's Books With Characters of Diverse Body Types" and "Kids Books Still Have A Lack-Of-Diversity Problem"), *BuzzFeed* ("What's the Best Children's Book About Gender Identity and Gender Expression You've Ever Read?" and "26 YA Authors on Diverse Representation in Publishing"), and other newspapers and magazines have published a deluge of sympathetic articles. Today, "diversity" is a watchword in discussions of literature written for children and young adults.

Sensitivity

At its core, diversity is concerned with how many authors and illustrators belong to underrepresented groups. It is also concerned with how many characters belong to underrepresented groups. Thus, children's and YA literature will be more diverse if more books are written by African Americans and Asian Americans. It will also be more diverse if these books include more queer and Muslim characters. Some believe that the number of authors and characters should mirror the number of real Americans. If 2 percent of Americans are disabled Latinos, then 2 percent of books need to be written by and about disabled Latinos. The same logic extends to black women, Asian men, and so on.

Whereas diversity is concerned with a quantitative problem, sensitivity is concerned with a qualitative problem. To come back to Bishop, when children and YA readers encounter literature that includes "distorted, negative, or laughable" representations of themselves, "they learn a powerful lesson about how they are devalued in the society in which they are a part."[21] When I interviewed one children's author, who identifies as queer and trans, they spoke about their experience with distorted mirrors: "We've reached a point where it's no longer kosher to say, 'Oh, I think trans people are icky.' Ten years ago, you could say that. Twenty years ago, it was expected and standard in the culture. I don't know who I would be now if the first thousand times I had seen something queer or trans, it wasn't a joke or an insult. Who knows who I would be if I'd had that positive reflection of myself. So, if I can provide that for other people, heck yeah, I'm going to do that."

A sensitivity reader I spoke to, who identifies as disabled, has also seen their reflection in distorted mirrors. In children's and YA literature, and even in adult literature, identities are used as shortcuts to create characters who are laughed at by readers. They are used as shortcuts to create characters who are derided by readers. They are even used as shortcuts to create character arcs. For example: "I once read this romance novel where the hero was a very grumpy, Scrooge-like man who had a very negative attitude. And he used a cane. When he became a more positive and kind person, he didn't need to use the cane anymore, because he was better due to being a better person." When a disabled reader recurrently encounters these tropes in children's, YA, and adult literature, it can feel like they are stuck in a house of mirrors at a carnival.

The reflections can be frightening. Another sensitivity reader I spoke to described their experiences in the fun house of literature: "I work with publishing houses and, for the word choices, sometimes animalistic verbs or terms are used only for black characters. I've looked through the work. I've 'control find, command find' all of that. So I see, 'snarled,' 'growled,' 'bore his canines,' only for black characters, black males. It wasn't a fantasy work. It was contemporary. Again, it was only used for black characters.'" This was just one of the redundant tropes this black sensitivity reader talked about. As they explained, the problem is compounded by the fact that there are relatively few mirrors for black readers to see themselves in.

In a similar vein, when readers encounter distorted, negative, or laughable representations of people who are different from them, it can diminish their understanding and their tolerance. "The Negro enslaved by his inferiority, the white man enslaved by his superiority alike behave in accordance with a neurotic orientation," wrote philosopher Frantz Fanon almost seventy-five years ago.[22] The same is true for cis and trans people, queer and heterosexual people, disabled and able-bodied people, and other people enslaved by their inferiority, their superiority, or their ignorance of those who are different. At its best, literature supports the individual and interpersonal aims of multiculturalism. At its worst, it contributes to a neurotic orientation.

A year after #WeNeedDiverseBooks, another hashtag altered the landscape of children's and YA literature. First tweeted in 2015 by Corinne Duyvis, a YA author and cofounder of the website Disability in Kidlit, #OwnVoices aims to highlight "kidlit about diverse characters written by authors from that same diverse group."[23] In this respect, it harkens back to Du Bois's idea of double consciousness, "this sense of always looking at one's self through the eyes of others,"[24] and his decision to center black authors in *The Brownies' Book*. At any moment, one can see how popular the hashtag is on Twitter. It is used to promote books, authors, and events. On the most important websites for prospective authors—Manuscript Wish List, Agent-Query, Publisher's Marketplace, and Literary-Agents.com—agents declare their commitment to Own Voices books.

It is not just agents who want Own Voices books. As one editor at a Big Five publisher explained to me, "The hunger for it is coming from booksellers, and Amazon, and Costco. They're asking for it, and we're happy to publish it." Even in advertorials written to increase sales, Own Voices has left its mark. If people visit the Barnes & Noble website, they will find articles such as "25 of Our Most Anticipated #OwnVoices YA Books of 2019" and "14 of Our Most Anticipated OwnVoices YA Books of 2018: July to December." Bookshop.org, which supports local bookshops through online sales, has an "Own Voices Books" page to guide customers. For their part, publishers reinforce the sales drive with their own advertorials. On HarperCollins's website, "3 Reasons Why #OwnVoices Books Matter" might not read like another piece of advertising copy written to meet this publisher's bottom line, but it serves the same function. If #OwnVoices Books Matter, just like #BlackLives Matter, then readers have a moral responsibility to click their "Add to Cart" button.

At magazines, the Own Voices movement has reshaped review policies. In 2017, *Kirkus Reviews* announced: "Because there is no substitute for lived experience, as much as possible books with diverse subject matter and protagonists are assigned to 'own voices' reviewers, to identify both those books that resonate most with cultural insiders and those books that fall short."[25] In addition to these insiders, *Kirkus* now checks its reviews against websites such as Disability in Kidlit, Latinxs in Kid Lit, and American Indians in Children's Literature. Around the same time, *Kirkus* also started "identifying characters in children's and teen books by identity and/ or race—all the time."[26]

In the Sensitivity Era, people hire sensitivity readers. As author Marjorie Ingall explains, "Sensitivity readers (other, better terms include 'expert readers' and 'authenticity readers') are representatives of an oft-marginalized group who try to ensure that the portrayal of the group—be it Jews, people of color, LGBTQ people, or people with physical disabilities and mental-health issues—is not dimwitted."[27] To be authentic, a sensitivity reader must share an identity with an author's fictional character. For example, a heterosexual Chinese American author who plans to write a story about a gay Native American character should hire a gay Native American sensitivity reader.[28] If they do not hire this reader, their depiction might be "dimwitted."

In the words of one agent I spoke to, "Sensitivity reads are definitely something that have been happening more and more, especially if it's a white author. I use them mostly in the context of having publishers seek them out. I mean, they're helpful. Readers caught things I don't think I would have been aware of, that my authors certainly weren't aware of, that the editor wasn't aware of. It's helpful to get that kind of extra set of eyes, coming from a perspective you don't share or wouldn't have access to." Another adds: "I work with sensitivity readers. Sometimes the author will hire sensitivity readers before I submit their book to publishers. I have seen it happen before the book is sold, and then the publisher hires sensitivity readers once it's been acquired. The best sensitivity readers are of the identity you're getting a sensitivity read for, and they're very familiar with that area of the book market. For example, they're well read in middle-grade fiction about queer characters. Generally, I don't think they can hurt."

"We are calling on self-defined authenticity readers," explains one editor I interviewed, "whereas a couple of years ago we probably would have just relied on our good intentions and research. Now, we really do make every effort to be as sensitive as possible. If a person can be a good set of eyes for, say, Filipino American queer—sometimes they get very, very granular—that's amazing. Then you as an editor, an author, are not trying to find your way."

Sensitivity readers share this perspective. One sensitivity reader I spoke to, who has been doing these readings since 2016, recalled a particularly memorable moment with a publisher who asked for her help:

> The picture book wasn't deliberately bad. That was the worst thing. You could tell it was just someone who didn't quite understand. It's like, okay, but you'd still offend lots of people. So I had to be really honest and say, "I'm really sorry." I didn't quite say, "I can't give you a rubber stamp." But I said, "I can't pass it up." I thought they were going to go away and be angry, but a few months later, they came back and said, "We want to talk to you again." They had scrapped it. They came back with sketches. Because obviously they didn't want to do illustrations, again.
>
> The book was amazing. They had taken everything I said and revised it. They really had taken the text apart. They had taken the pictures apart. It was fantastic. It was the kind of moment where—because, again, it was meant for really young kids because it was a picture book—you just wouldn't have to worry. They wouldn't take anything negative away. It's that kind of reward of knowing that loads of little kids are going to have a great time and have a great book. It's knowing that even though it can be painful sometimes to do, you've helped an author and helped the people who read it, I guess.

#SensitivityReader does not appear on Twitter until 2016, the same year YA author Justina Ireland built a database of sensitivity readers.[29] Like #WeNeedDiverseBooks and #OwnVoices, it is now a hashtag that one finds all over Twitter. Most often, it is used by authors who need sensitivity readers or sensitivity readers who need work. Typical examples include the following: "Friendly reminder that I'm a sensitivity reader for the following things: trans (FtM) issues, ADHD, anxiety, depression, and fibromyalgia (chronic pain/fatigue)" and "Looking for a #SensitivityReader to read a spec fic short story (about 3500 words) featuring a trans side character. I want to make sure I'm not being a huge, ignorant jerk."[30] In the first tweet and the responses to the second, people who share identities with fictional characters are regarded as experts.

Just as #WeNeedDiverseBooks and #OwnVoices has influenced the acquisition practices of agents and editors in children's and YA literature, #SensitivityReader has had effects outside Twitter. On the supply side, there are a growing number of private companies that provide sensitivity readers. For example, Salt & Sage Books has a coalition of readers who consult authors on issues as different as African American culture, fatness, familial homophobia, conception via sperm donation, rural queer experience,

Chinese American culture, furry fandom, interracial relationships, contemporary Jewish culture, mental abuse by a parent, traveling while black, Hinduism, ableist physician experiences, Iroquois culture, men who survive rape, LGBTQIA2+ representation, and witchcraft.[31] These sensitivity readers exist alongside a mass of independent sensitivity readers who sell their services on Twitter.

On the demand side, some agents and publishers now require their children's and YA authors to consult sensitivity readers. As a case in point, Riptide Publishing "now requires authors writing outside their own identities to have their manuscripts reviewed by a sensitivity reader before it will accept them, submits all such manuscripts itself to a second sensitivity reader, and has promised to distribute a formal sensitivity guide amongst all of its staff and authors."[32] Likewise, "Kokila, a brand new children's imprint within Penguin Random House that focuses on 'stories for and from marginalized communities,' plans on sensitivity readers for all its books."[33] At other publishing houses, sensitivity readers are as close to required as one can get. Alexandra Alter, a *New York Times* journalist who covers publishing, explains that "in children's publishing, where there's a huge demand for diverse books, sensitivity readers have practically become a routine part of the editing process"[34]

In short, the Sensitivity Era is not just an era marked by the quantitative problem of too many white men on BookCon panels and not enough differently abled, plus size, and Indigenous characters in children's and YA books. The era is also marked by the qualitative problem of representation. As David Levithan, vice president and publisher of Scholastic, reflects, "There is a newfound fervor in children's publishing to be authentic and get the story right."[35] This fervor has generated a milieu of authors, agents, editors, publishers, reviewers, and readers who want to remove all material deemed insensitive from literature written for young people and, increasingly, literature written for adults.

Essentialism

Just as there is a conceptual difference between diversity and sensitivity, there is a conceptual difference between sensitivity and essentialism. For example, a sensitive reader can criticize a picture book that inaccurately portrays the civil rights movement. They can also criticize a YA novel that represents African Americans as buffoons with low IQs. At the same time, this sensitive reader might not believe that a book about African Americans needs to be written by an African American author. They also might not believe that a white author needs to hire an African American sensitivity reader before, during, or after they write their book. A reader can value diverse characters and sensitive descriptions without essentializing the relationship between identity and well-written literature.[36]

However, as the previous section argues, the Sensitivity Era treats identity as the precondition for well-written literature. In this respect, it is not just the editors at *Kirkus Reviews* who believe that there is "no substitute for lived experience." It is also the editors at Big Five and independent publishers, the agents at major and minor literary agencies, and the thousands of readers on social media who celebrate lived experience as the sine qua non of literature. For these people, who are active in the hashtag communities of #KidLit, #YATwitter, and #OwnVoices, sensitivity readers are indispensable. And, as author Jane C. Hu puts it, "In finding the right sensitivity readers for your project, identity is paramount."[37]

The essentialist link between identity and an "authentic" perspective is premised on the idea that hundreds, thousands, and, in some cases, millions of people are bound together by their identities. As political scientist Adolph Reed Jr. describes the situation in respect to African Americans, there is a "disposition to view Afro-American life as simultaneously opaque to those outside it (thus the need for black interpreters and line-bearers) and smoothly organic (with exceptions made for the odd, inauthentic 'sellout' leaders)."[38] When Dhonielle Clayton, a COO at WNDB and a black sensitivity reader, claims to offer a targeted editorial read for "the black American experience," she is performing the role of Reed Jr.'s black interpreter.[39]

Although Clayton, who is perhaps the most well-known sensitivity reader (everyone from the *New York Times* to the *Washington Post* has interviewed her), does not proclaim that the black American experience is opaque and organic, the ascendence of sensitivity readers like her depends on the idea that it is. Or, at least, it depends on the idea that black Americans share enough experiences to constitute what a black sensitivity reader for Tessera Editorial calls "the Black/African-American culture." Otherwise, sensitivity readers would not be celebrated as "cultural ambassadors."[40] They would be treated as individuals who could not possibly represent the divergent and often irreconcilable experiences, values, perspectives, and interests of millions of people whom they have never met. In the words of Brittany Talissa King, a black journalist, "There isn't a narrative, one black narrative—there's 40 million."[41]

Intersectional thinkers have long criticized the idea of racial homogeneity. For example, many feminists point out that "the black experience" misses the distinct experiences of gay black men, black women, black trans "folx," and other black people. But even an intersectional alternative to "the black experience"—for example, "the gay black experience"—is itself a reduction. Gay black men are not bound together by a culture. Neither are trans black women. The same is true for other combinations of identities. The belief that a writer can circumvent essentialism by talking to someone who has a few more identities in sync with their fictional character is not so much a departure from essentialism as it is a more layered version of essentialism.

Historically, the turn toward racial culture was accompanied by the turn away from racial science as the rationale for black incarceration, unemployment, and other social problems.[42] Throughout the twentieth century, more than a few black leaders emerged to translate "the black American experience" and "the black/African American culture" for white audiences. Their translations fueled attacks on the welfare state and its beneficiaries, infamously personified by caricatures like the "welfare queen." A similar game of cultural spokesmanship haunts the histories of other minority groups in the United States. Despite their differences, the reactionary interventions of the past and the diverse and sensitive interventions of the present coalesce around the self-described "cultural ambassador" who, unlike a real ambassador, no one appointed to speak on their behalf.

To be sure, "black American culture" is never defined by those who hinge their services on it. In the same vein, one does not find definitions of "Asian American culture," "half-Asian culture," "queer culture," and so on when one peruses the areas of expertise listed on Salt & Sage Books, Tessera Editorial, Quiethouse Editing, and other websites that advertise the services of sensitivity readers. As sociologist Karen E. Fields and historian Barbara J. Fields, two self-described Afro-Americans, reflect in *Racecraft: The Soul of Inequality in American Life*: "No matter how slipshod the definition of culture, no one can seriously assert that one culture unites those whom American usage identifies without hesitation as one race."[43] Though, as the era suggests, people do purport to be ambassadors for cultures bounded by race, sexuality, and other constructs.

Understandably, African American sociologists, historians, political scientists, psychologists, legal scholars, literary critics, and activists on the left have been some of the most passionate critics of essentialism. For African American literary critic Kenneth W. Warren, the assumption of a shared race-group interest, which was at least more plausible during the Jim Crow era, is even less plausible "at a time when the grounds for asserting black identity and black solidarity are even more tenuous."[44] Vis-à-vis decades of scholarship and activism, sensitivity readers give the impression that the grounds for asserting racial identity, solidarity, and a shared understanding of the world have never been stronger. The same holds true for other identities.

In the process, they perpetuate the idea that there are "authentic" and "inauthentic" ways to be black, gay, trans, and so on. In fact, their job is to distinguish "authentic" stories of identitarian experience from those that are "inauthentic." As Touré F. Reed, another African American historian on the left, reflects: "I've had nearly four decades of experience with the creepy essentialist language of 'racial authenticity.' . . . The sensibilities that fuel the quest for racial authenticity pose real threats not just to the mental health of black and brown people. They pose a threat to democracy itself. I suppose the damaging consequences associated with this kind of racial essentialism are most obvious, though, if you call the baseline problem what it is: an embrace of racist stereotyping, albeit by another name."[45]

When "racial authenticity" is not called by its real name, then stories that do not fit the mold of whatever "authentic" happens to be at any given moment have to be rewritten. Consider this author of color's confusion: "Whenever I write non-white characters, I get a lot of comments about how they're not 'accurate' representations. I'm not white and write people of my own race."[46] If this author wanted to follow the lead of Reed and other progressives, they might ask literary agents, editors, and publishers to abandon the idea of racial authenticity. In the words of novelist Junot Díaz, "Race is a monstrous fiction" and "racism is a monstrous crime."[47] The two are intertwined.

However, if this author wanted to take their lead from Scholastic's David Levithan, they could keep paying sensitivity readers per draft until they "get their story right." After all, the sensitivity reader is the self-declared expert who knows the difference between "right" and "wrong" representations of nonwhite characters. By way of example, Clayton knows the difference between an authentic and an inauthentic black character who likes to visit national parks: "I told the author that the first thing she needed to reconcile was, how did this black girl get into national parks? Historically, black people weren't allowed to visit national parks, so going to national parks is not a thing we do, as a group. I wrote to her that if this little girl loves to camp, you need to figure out how that happened, how that passion was stoked, how her parents and grandparents felt about it. Or you have to make her white. Because otherwise it's a paint by numbers diversity piece and it rings false."[48]

In the past, Jim Crow racists came up with rules for black people. In the present, sensitivity readers come up with rules for fictional black people. Here, a black character has to explain why they want to visit a national park. If the parallels between the past and the present are still not apparent, then consider what would happen if a white editor told a black memoirist, "You need to explain why you want to visit Yosemite National Park because visiting national parks is not a thing you people do." Or, "You're black, so you need to explain how your parents and grandparents felt that time you rented a canoe at Yellowstone." As Reed points out, the language of "so and so isn't *really* black" is not really antiracist language at all. It does not matter if this language comes out of the mouth of a Jim Crow racist or a black sensitivity reader.

To believe that a character can be black on the outside and white on the inside is to believe that "Oreos" actually exist. If "Oreos" exist, then "coconuts" must exist, too. As one sensitivity reader told me, they are able to identify a character that "reads like a white person, but the author's painted them brown." If "Oreos" and "coconuts" exist, then "Twinkies" must exist, too. This assumption is a perennial source of frustration for Asian American writers. As novelist Don Lee reflects, "Some Asian Americans have always assumed I'm a Twinkie: yellow on the outside, white on the inside, someone who would rather align himself with the East Coast white establishment intelligentsia than 'his people.' But really, who are my people?"[49] What does it mean to be yellow on the outside but white on the inside? What does it mean to be black or brown on the outside but white on the inside? Apparently, sensitivity readers know. In fact, their paychecks depend on their ability to shoehorn fictional characters into the fictional categories of race.

Literary agents also believe that they, too, have the expertise to distinguish "authentic" racial stories from "inauthentic" racial stories. When novelist Alisa Valdes-Rodriguez was looking for a literary agent, she eventually

heard back from Susan Bergholtz.[50] At the time, Bergholtz represented Sandra Cisneros and other Latina writers. Yet, in relation to *The House on Mango
Street*, Bergholtz did not think Valdes-Rodriguez's fiction was "authentic."
As Valdes-Rodriguez reflects, "Imagine my surprise when Bergholtz not
only rejected me, but called me to tell me why she was rejecting me and
my book. 'I only represent authentic Latina voices,' she whined. 'And from
what I've read here, you are not writing in an authentic Latina voice at all.'"
Valdes-Rodriguez and all six of her characters are Latina. "They're just not
Latina in a way that makes Bergholtz feel like she's on the beach in Cabo."

Valdes-Rodriguez's work satirizes "the notion of one single authentic and
monolithic Latino identity in the United States," which might be the reason it did not land with this gatekeeper in American publishing. To quote
Valdes-Rodriguez at length:

> I wanted people to come away from my book . . . realizing that to be used cor-
> rectly, the word "Latino" had to be synonymous with only one thing: *Human
> fucking being.* I used a *parody* of chick lit to address the complexity and diver-
> sity of the "Latino" universe, a social construct unique to the United States and
> informed in the public discourse primarily through stereotype and idiocy.
>
> This worldview of mine, in the simplistically exotic and profitable Bergholt-
> zian Cisnerian world of high Latina lettres, was deemed *inauthentic* by these jack-
> boots, presumably because it was not only confusing to Berghotlz [*sic*] personally
> for its refusal to be exotic, but also because the foundational premise of my book
> inadvertently threatened everything she and her minstrelized clients have been
> seeking to build for decades with their mediocre and sporadic prose, hackneyed
> magical realism, Guatemalan rebosos from Pier One, gallons of turquoise jewelry
> (drip, drip) and fancy paper flower headdresses.

To recap, the rules of authenticity will not permit a black character to enter
a national park unless they explain why they want to enter a national park.
In the absence of an explanation, their story is "inauthentic." Likewise,
the rules of authenticity do not leave room for a novel about six English-
speaking Latinas who met at Boston University. But, as Valdes-Rodriguez
reminds us, the rules do leave room for entrepreneurs whose "entire existence is predicated on not only the oversimplification of the 'exotic peoples'
they purport to represent . . . but also is dependent upon the continued
marginalization and exoticization of said peoples."

In a remark that looks like it was meant to illustrate this point, Clayton
describes sensitivity reading as "supplying the seeds and the gems and the
jewels from our culture" to writers who "don't understand it."[51] Ditto for

Indian sensitivity readers, Chinese sensitivity readers, disabled sensitivity readers, pansexual sensitivity readers, asexual sensitivity readers, and other sensitivity readers who see themselves as merchants selling exotic goods to writers who do not understand their "cultures." To borrow language from literary critic David Bromwich, these entrepreneurs "may have far more in common with one another than with the people they are supposed to represent."[52]

What is most disturbing about the "literary minstrel show" is that it only dictates what is "true" and "false" for certain people. "Imagine, for a moment, if this notion of white male authenticity were applied to all white male authors, or creatives in general," reflects Valdes-Rodriguez. "It becomes obviously absurd. And yet done to me and others 'like me,' it is considered to be an exercise in 'diversity.'" One agent of color hit the nail on the head when we spoke over the phone: "White people are allowed to be individuals. If you're white, you don't necessarily represent your community. It's not even thought of as a community."

A black novelist I interviewed, who won the Zora Neale Hurston/Richard Wright Foundation's Annual Legacy Award, shared this perspective: "The presumption that there is any board out there that that can weigh and measure authenticity is really depressing. Geography, religion, socioeconomic standing affect what you think, how you think, and how you live through this culture. The range of experience between black people and white people is probably exactly the same. No one expects that work of white Americans. Nobody reads a book by a white person and says, 'Well, this isn't authentic to white people.' That's crazy sounding. And it's crazy sounding when you say it about anyone. It's another kind of racism."

It is not just people of color who feel the pressure. It is anyone who has an identity that can be branded in the era of essentialism. In the words of one gay writer I spoke to, "One editor, in particular, he was like, 'Your stories aren't gay enough.' I said, 'I'll try and gay it up.'" When people who work in publishing expect gay writers to hold the seeds, and the gems, and jewels of an exotic culture that is indiscernible to outsiders, what else is a gay writer who wants to see their name in print supposed to do? This writer's admission—"Isn't there a beauty when people don't know if I'm gay or straight?"—could not be less fashionable in the Sensitivity Era.

If a writer wants to be free from agents, editors, and sensitivity readers obsessed with authenticity, they should fill their stories with cisgender, heterosexual white men. These characters are free to hike Yellowstone without an explanation. In her essay, "Fascinated to Presume: In Defense of Fiction," Zadie Smith, elaborates this point:

> What does it mean, after all, to say "A Bengali woman would never say that!" or "A gay man would never feel that!" or "A black woman would never do that!"? How can such things possibly be claimed absolutely, unless we already have some form of fixed caricature in our minds? (It is to be noted that the argument "A white man would never say that!" is rarely heard and is almost structurally unimaginable. Why? Because to be such a self is to be afforded all possible human potentialities, not only a circumscribed few.)[53]

The common thread from Smith's experience as a biracial writer, to Reed's experience as an African American writer, to Lee's experience as an Asian American writer, to Valdes-Rodriguez's experience as a Latina writer, is that literary culture "likes to conflate skin tone or last name with actual culture, asserting 'difference' where none often resides."[54]

Literary culture also likes to conflate sexuality and other aspects of identity with culture. Just look at bookstore sections. Although these sections help readers find books that are mirrors, windows, and sliding glass doors, they also irk authors. "When my first book came out, it was put in the gay section, and it's not where I wanted to be," reflects *New York Times* bestseller David Sedaris, "I just wanted to be in the bookstore."[55] But the literary marketplace *loves* identities. If a gay writer's work is not "gay enough" for this section, or gay enough to win a Lambda Literary Award, or gay enough to top a *Washington Post* article about "The Year's Best Gay Books," their publisher may ask them to "gay it up." Like BIPOC authors, LGBTQ+ authors are often pressured to assert difference where none often resides.

In cases where a cisgender, heterosexual author is writing about an LGBTQ+ character, or a white author is writing about a BIPOC character, sensitivity readers are hired to manufacture the difference. They are the architects of difference. Consider Clayton's own description of her expertise: "I'm giving those breadcrumbs and saying think about these things, that you didn't, that you might not have known because you don't walk around in my skin. You've, uh, written a scene and it's a black American family. And they're sitting around. Think about the food that's on table."[56] In this interview, journalist Katie Couric does not ask Clayton what a black American family is *supposed* to eat. Instead, her interview legitimizes the idea that Clayton has secret knowledge of an exotic culture that is indecipherable to outsiders. Accordingly, white authors must hire tour guides like Clayton to help them understand what happens when a black American walks into their kitchen. If one were to ask a black coworker, "What do blacks eat for dinner?" they might be reported to HR. If they pay a sensitivity reader for an answer, they will be lauded for trying to "get their story right."

If recent novels are an indication, one should assume that fictional black families are supposed to eat "authentic" foods like macaroni and cheese, fried chicken, and collard greens. After all, that is what characters eat in *The Hate U Give*, a number-one *New York Times* bestseller championed by Clayton's organization, WNDB. The commercial success of Angie Thomas's YA novel speaks to the issues raised by Reed and other black writers. On the one hand, Thomas recycles the worst stereotypes about black people. There is Daddy, a.k.a. Big Mav, who cheats on his wife and knocks up a prostitute. There is Starr Carter, the young black protagonist who obsesses over Air Jordan sneakers. There is Kenya, who loves to date "drug-dealing gangbangers." There is Fo'ty Ounce, who keeps all his belongings in a rusty shopping cart, and who always asks people for money to buy a "Fo'ty ounce from the licka sto' real quick." There is Mrs. Rooks, the woman with gold-plated front teeth looking to buy cigarettes and "Lotto tickets." Then there is King. Unlike Big Mav, who makes his kids recite the Black Panthers' Ten-Point Program like it is 1966, King beats women and sells drugs. At the end of the novel, he smokes a cigar and laughs—yes, laughs—like a minstrel villain as he and his violent gang of inner-city black men burn Big Mav's grocery store to the ground.[57]

What Black Lives Matter organizers Melina Abdullah and Patrisse Khan-Cullors said of the film adaptation is just as true of the novel: it is "replete with all kinds of stereotypical Black pathologies."[58] Notwithstanding the single plot point about a white police officer who kills an unarmed black teenager, most of Thomas's novel focuses on crime committed by black people. Moreover, her representation of anti–police violence protests is about as "authentic" and "accurate" as Mel Gibson's depiction of the First War of Scottish Independence in *Braveheart*. At one point, Starr is lifted into the air like a black Christ figure, during a protest involving what Abdullah and Khan-Cullors call "the strangely named social justice group" Just Us for Justice. Before the novel ends, Big Mav, the macho revolutionary, decides to become a landlord. He also decides to move his family to a more affluent neighborhood. Like Uncle Elroy in *Next Friday*, who flees "the hood" for

Rancho Cucamonga after he wins the lottery—"as soon as I got my check, I was gone!"—the Carters distance themselves from black characters who might as well have been created by a *Fox News* intern.[59]

On the other hand, Thomas has been celebrated as the new voice of YA literature. From *The Hate U Give* to *Concrete Rose*, she is revered as an expert on black culture. As one reviewer puts it, Thomas "expertly dissects black culture."[60] Another adds that Thomas "throws open the doors on black culture."[61] A third reviewer exclaims that Thomas "gives the world a glimpse into black culture," as if black Americans are natives on a newly discovered island.[62] This raises the question of what black culture is, how it differs from the worst stereotypes about black people, and what happens when a black author writes a novel about black people who are not dealing drugs, shooting one another, and spending their money on cigarettes, lottery tickets, Air Jordans, and gold-plated front teeth. If the experiences of Lee, Valdes-Rodriguez, and countless other novelists are an indication, they will be told to rewrite their work. Above all, the success of Thomas's novels evinces the reality that stereotypes are profitable. They are especially profitable when they are produced by an Own Voices author, whose black identity exempts her from the kind of criticism hurled like dynamite at white authors.

If readers are still unwilling to accept this argument, I invite them to read passages from *The Hate U Give* alongside passages from Percival Everett's *Erasure*. *Erasure* is told from the perspective of Thelonious "Monk" Ellison, a black writer disturbed by the literary marketplace. He is constantly told by agents and reviewers that he and his writing are not black enough. As Monk admits, he is not good at basketball. He cannot dance. He did not grow up in the inner city. His rejected novel is not about drug dealers and drive-by shootings. At the same time, Juanita Mae Jenkins's *We's Lives in Da Ghetto* is a runaway bestseller. Her novel, which captures the "exotic wonder" of "Black America," is hailed as "a masterpiece of African American literature."[63] Jenkins, who studied at Oberlin College, is compelled to write *We's Lives in Da Ghetto* after she asks herself: "Where are the books about our people? Where are our stories?" Frustrated by another rejection, Monk sells out. He writes *My Pafology*. Like *We's Lives in Da Ghetto* and *The Hate U Give*, it is a hit. He, too, joins the ranks of ethnic entrepreneurs.

What is interesting about *The Hate U Give* is that it recycles racist stereotypes about black Americans while delivering sermon-like indictments of America's racism. If one reads *Poets & Writers*, *Kirkus*, and the other magazines, one might get the impression that this formula—cliché racial exoticism mixed with antiracist finger-wagging—is the formula for *New York Times* bestsellers. Alex Perez, a Cuban American writer and graduate of the famed Iowa Writer's Workshop, describes the pressure:

> If you're a POC, you can't just submit any old story about the POC experience, but one in which the narrative framing is about victimization at the hands of America and "whiteness" and all the other predictable tropes that now dominate literary fiction. When you write into this framing, you're performing like a token good boy, hence, you've written a token good boy story. The trick to a token good boy story is situating the "brown" characters as victims while also providing the woke white editors palatably edgy scenes that never tip over into the problematic, so they feel like they're reading an "authentic" POC story. You slip in a word in Spanish or have a character cross the border and dodge a border patrol agent or two; you know, the stuff that makes woke whites salivate.[64]

This Iowa alumnus knows what he is talking about. Just read "Freedom," published in *The Adroit Journal*, a journal that prides itself for publishing "numerous United States Poets Laureates, MacArthur Fellows, and Pulitzer Prize winners."[65] Written in 2019, it is the last story Perez wrote before he gave up fiction.

Sensitivity readers, literary agents, and authors aside, other ethnic entrepreneurs are more interested in returning the United States to the nineteenth century. Whereas eugenicists were concerned with the size of people's skulls, the editors at *Kirkus Reviews* are concerned with a broader range of physical characteristics, which this magazine believes are evidence of "race." As noted, *Kirkus* has started "identifying characters in children's and teen books by identity and/or race—all the time."[66] Practically speaking, the point of this identification process is to help people find books about black characters, Native American characters, and other characters who are not white. As the data show, these books can be hard to find.

Yet, because race is a slippery, socially constructed concept with a scientifically and culturally dubious basis, problems arise when people shoehorn made-up characters into made-up categories. For example, in 2015, *Kirkus* published a review of *The Night Gardener* by Eric Fan and Terry Fan. Their picture book is about an old gardener who revitalizes a rundown neighborhood. In their review, *Kirkus* describes this old man as a white man. In response, the Fans wrote a letter to *Kirkus*. In their letter, they explain that the night gardener is based on their father. Their father is Chinese. The Fans included a photograph to prove it. In the Sensitivity Era, an editorial policy that compels authors and illustrators to prove the race of their fictional characters with photographic evidence is, apparently, what racial progress looks like.

For its part, *Kirkus* apologized. Vicky Smith, the children's and teenage editor, reflects: "Horrified, I looked at the book again and saw that although the Night Gardener is literally white—as in nonpigmented, since we see him only by the light of the moon—he is indubitably Asian."[67] Because people might have no idea what it means to be "literally white," but "indubitably Asian," Smith clarifies her position. "Instead of seeing a clearly Asian character," she explains, "I saw an avuncular old white man with his eyes peacefully closed." In plain English, this editor thinks Asians look like sleeping white people. Whereas *The American Phrenological Journal* examined skulls, *Kirkus Reviews* examines the amount of space between eyelids. Like those creepy essentialists, these editors believe that every person belongs to a "race." Their job is to figure out which one.

In the Sensitivity Era, whether a fictional character wants to go for a hike or garden under the moonlight, they have to look, speak, and act Asian, black, or whatever enough to receive the proper racial classification from the international magazine that awards the Kirkus Star, "one of the most coveted designations in the book industry." Above all, to receive a positive review, these characters must prove they are "authentic" members of a racial culture. These reviews influence the purchasing decisions of booksellers, librarians, and teachers. At the same time, they raise problems for writers and their publishers. In more than one conversation, my interviewees drew attention to the "damned if you, damned if you don't" reality of the Sensitivity Era. "You have places like *Kirkus Reviews*, and now *PW*—early trade magazines that are essential to getting the word out about a book—saying 'there's no black characters, there's no diverse characters,'" explained one agent. "Yet, if you're a white writer, and you try to write a diverse character, then you're slammed for doing that. I think we've backed a lot of writers and publishers into this corner where nobody really quite knows what to do or how to do it." Because it is "problematic" for a white author to write a book about a protagonist of color, they might include secondary characters of color instead. But this opens the door to accusations that all their secondary characters of color are not as developed as their white protagonist. Of course, if they have no characters of color, this, too, is a problem.

One woman of color I spoke to, who works in publishing, reiterated this agent's confusion:

> Last week, I finished an edit and sent it back to my author, who is a white woman. I remember thinking, as I was editing, this manuscript is just peopled with white people. That's all it is. I know this. But it's cool. Maybe this author just has white friends. But we're sensitive. We know what's going on right now. We know the conversation. Will people notice that there are only white characters? Probably. Can I ask her for someone of color? If we add a character, who is, say, Indian—is that okay? What makes it okay? Would it help if the author had a "sensitivity reader"? If they gave the manuscript to an Indian and said, "Can you read this and make sure the character feels authentic and real?" Is that okay? I just don't know what to do. On the other hand, books that we've wanted to acquire, we just think: "Oh, this is a white person writing a black character. We can't go there." I'm an editor, and I don't even know what to do.

If you lack the expertise of race taxonomists like Smith and Clayton, and you still do not understand the difference between "white culture" and other "cultures," or the difference between "authentic" characters of color and white characters who are "painted" other colors, the Smithsonian National Museum of African American History and Culture has created a helpful handout. According to this resource, aspects and assumptions of white culture include "objective, rational linear thinking," "cause and effect relationships," "quantitative emphasis," "work before play," "hard work is the key to success," "plan for future," "be polite," "rigid time schedules," and "delayed gratification."[68] Apparently, people of color do not share white people's interest in hard work, politeness, impulse control, and rational thought. Because the museum houses everything from James Baldwin's inkwell to a first edition copy of W. E. B. Du Bois's *Darkwater: Voices from Within the Veil*, it shapes how the public thinks about African American writers and their "culture." But one could be forgiven for thinking Richard Spencer wrote their handout.

Ironically, the idea that a book is first and foremost the artifact of an identity culture—"This is an important contribution to African American literature," "This should be on every Asian American literature syllabus," "Our agency just represented a Muslim novel," "We plan to publish two LGBTQ memoirs"—is one reason why diverse books are rejected by agents and publishers. As more than one agent told me, publishers profess their commitment to diverse authors and stories, but they will be quick to tell you they cannot accept a manuscript because, for example, they are already publishing two LGBTQ+ manuscripts in the fall. In the words of one *New York Times* bestselling author, widely recognized for their contributions to Latin/x literature: "Part of the challenge is helping people see that all these silos that they keep people in—black authors, Latino authors, Asian authors—are really the American story. We have to move it out into the mainstream, and not have people talk about the literature as separated by culture. For example, 'We're going to talk about adventure stories today, and we have them from all over the world.' It's how we frame the discussion."

For other writers, the problem is not so much categories like Latin/x literature or LGBTQ+ literature—among other benefits, the categories help readers find books—it is how omnipotent the categories have become. To come back to Percival Everett's *Erasure*, there is a scene where his protagonist walks into Borders's bookstore: "I went to Literature and did not see me. I went to Contemporary Fiction and did not find me, but when I fell back a couple of steps I found a section called African American Studies and there, arranged alphabetically and neatly, read *undisturbed*, were four of my books including *Persians* of which the only thing ostensibly African American was my jacket photograph."[69] The scene would be satirical if it were not so realistic.

At the level of form, the idea that people with different identities belong to different "cultures," which produce different literatures, is reshaping the way authors write. For example, the ascendence of what I call "the empathy chasm"—the belief that a writer will never be able to understand a person from a different "culture"—drives the decline of third-person narration. In the words of one novelist,

> I prioritize first-person over third-person. I have a narrator who is the same ethnic breakdown that I am, and if that person encounters people in the world who are from different walks of life, and reporting about those people, I'm not claiming to have interiority into those people. It's a little bit of a cheat-around. I'm a writer who works in first person a lot anyway, but it does feel like the bar is so impossibly high for third person, you have to have a lot of courage to even try.

When identities are conflated with cultures, a third-person narrative runs the risk of "harming" an entire culture. This is an obstacle for all the writers who do not want to write first-person stories about protagonists like themselves who, apparently, will never understand the interiority of characters unlike themselves. Stories with third-person omniscient narrators, who objectively present events, are especially "problematic." As the Smithsonian reminds us, white culture is objective. Nonwhite cultures are subjective. A writer whose work is recreating aspects and assumptions of white culture is, to use the epithet of the hour, "dangerous."

As the list of cultures continues to grow like segments of a capitalist market—queer culture, trans culture, dyslexic culture, fat culture, and so on—the number of self-declared experts grows, too. For example, like the fairy in *The Adventures of Pinocchio*, the editors at Standout Books claim to know the difference between real boys and fake boys. As editor Robert Wood explains, "A woman writing a man without considering how his life has been different due to his gender will usually write a woman in a man's body or, alternatively, write a woman with the more identifiably gendered attributes removed. . . . This is partly the case in J. K. Rowling's *Harry Potter* series, where male characters (especially the young boys) can ring untrue." Whereas Clayton and other sensitivity readers are concerned about characters from one race hiding in the bodies of characters from other races, this editor sees himself as a gender exorcist who knows when a young girl is hiding in the body of a young boy.[70]

According to Wood, "Ron and Harry are believable as children and young adults, states the female Rowling experienced personally, but they're less recognizable as boys and young men." In *Harry Potter and the Goblet of Fire*, Harry "expresses a generic sadness at being mistreated, but none of the specific worries about his place in the school hierarchy, or masculine identity, with which a real young boy might struggle." For this reason and others, "boys find less of themselves in reader-cipher Harry." As is typical of literary commentary published in the Sensitivity Era, not one boy is surveyed, interviewed, or even mentioned in an article that purports to know what boys think. Regardless, if writers want to create a character that is more relatable than one of the most popular characters in the history of the English language, they can hire Wood and editors like him. Unlike Rowling, these editors are not women. Therefore, they are experts.

Presentism

The Sensitivity Era assumes that young readers with underrepresented identities will most connect with fictional characters, written by Own Voices authors, who share their underrepresented identities. It also assumes that authors should promote progressive values in their work. That is, their fiction should be antiracist, antisexist, and so on. As Ibram X. Kendi, the author of the number-one *New York Times* bestselling children's book, *Antiracist Baby*, describes it: "One either allows racial inequities to persevere, as a racist, or confronts racial inequities, as an antiracist. There is no in-between safe space of 'not racist.'"[71] The same Manichean logic holds true for other intolerances. This is the idea that aspires to take over literature.

Importantly, ideas about racism, sexism, and other intolerances have changed over time. Yet the literature from the past remains the same. This incongruence between the past and the present is a source of anxiety for adults. This anxiety manifests in the urge to remove old literature from classrooms. Among other interventions, consider #DisruptTexts. As their website explains, "#DisruptTexts is a crowdsourced, grass roots effort *by* teachers *for* teachers to challenge the traditional canon in order to create a more inclusive, representative, and equitable language arts curriculum that our students deserve. It is part of our mission to aid and develop teachers committed to anti-racist/anti-bias teaching pedagogy and practices."[72] Founded in 2018, this organization, which partners with Penguin Random House, is part of the broader ecosystem of #Kidlit and #YATwitter.

Whereas essentialism reduces authors to their identities, presentism reduces authors to the time periods in which they wrote. Consider Lorena Germán's angst about books written before 1950. Germán, the author of *The Anti Racist Teacher: Reading Instruction Workbook* and cofounder of #DisruptTexts, explains: "Too many think that authors write disassociated from their cultural contexts. That is an illusion. Who we are shoes [*sic*] up in our writing. It's the skeleton."[73] If Germán is right and "context is everything," then readers should be alarmed by books written in older contexts. In a tweet to her thousands of followers, she elaborates: "Did y'all know that many of the 'classics' were written before the 50s? Think of US society before then and the values that shaped this nation afterwards. THAT is what is in those books. That is why we gotta switch it up. It ain't just about 'being old.' #DisruptTexts." The "THAT" is everything the Sensitivity Era rejects.

Professor David Bowles shares Germán's angst about old books. On November 30, 2020, the same day Germán sounded the alarm about every book written before 1950, Bowles had a public meltdown. In a series of tweets that earned him thousands of "likes," the award-winning YA author and professor of English at the University of Texas unleashed hell on the classics. For Bowles, it is obvious that young people do not want to read these old books. And he has little tolerance for people who think otherwise. "You disgusting worms, I can read in TWELVE DIFFERENT LANGUAGES. I have an MA in English and a doctorate in Education . . . and EVEN I think that the 'classics' are shit for modern kids. You're not on my level, trust me. So take a MOTHERFUCKING SEAT."[74] His Twitter rant, too long and incoherent to quote in its entirety, purports to know what kids think.

Apparently, kids share his view of old books. "So curl up with the books you love & let us help young people discover the ones THEY love," writes Bowles. "They won't be the same titles, I'm afraid." But Bowles is in no position to speak for any reader other than himself. Likewise, Germán is in no position to caricature every American author who wrote before 1950 (an arbitrary date given the de jure end of Jim Crow in 1964). Whereas their criticism of the canon speaks to the need to consider authors who have been overlooked and underread, it also speaks to the presentism that characterizes the Sensitivity Era. As historians Amna Khalid and Jeffrey Snyder describe the situation, there is "a cult of relevance that advances an extremely narrow vision of what kinds of texts will engage and inspire students."[75] This cult presents its own preferences as the preferences of young readers everywhere.

Much like Bowles, Ellen Oh sees herself as an ambassador for young people. The same day that Bowles had his meltdown, this YA author and CEO of WNDB started her own Twitter thread:

> We should do a WORST CLASSICS BOOKS EVER list and why they should not be taught in K-12 schools anymore because they legit cause kids to hate reading. Number one on the list: Moby Dick—it literally kills brain cells . . . NUMBER 2 WORST CLASSIC BOOK EVER Catcher in the Rye—AGHHHHHHHHHHHHHHHHHH and stop . . . But my NUMBER 3 is The Adventures of Huck Finn—Can we stop with the racist books already? . . . NUMBER 4 worst classics that shouldn't be taught in K-12 The Canterbury Tales—WHY?? WHYYYYYYY? . . . And anything by Hemingway—Because misogyny.[76]

Like Germán and Bowles, Oh does not include any surveys of young readers, any quotes from young readers, or any indication that she has ever talked to a young reader about what they like to read. Nonetheless, school districts should overhaul their curricula because this YA novelist screamed "AGHHHHHHHHHHHHHHHHHH" on Twitter.

Both presentism and essentialism reduce a text's relevance to the demographic characteristics of its author. In the case of essentialism, the focus is their identity. In the case of presentism, the focus is when they wrote. Together, these foci constitute the two sides of ad hominem criticism in the Sensitivity Era. Hence a TikTok user exclaims, "I am a bisexual woman with mental health issues, a book written by a straight white man decades or even centuries ago is going to miss my whole perspective on life. . . . So, fuck John Steinbeck."[77] According to this view of the past, Steinbeck is just another dead white man. He is no different from Henry David Thoreau, Ken Kesey, and Andrew Marvell. These writers are nothing but their identities and the time periods in which they wrote—both of which render them irrelevant to a modern audience.

They are especially irrelevant because, apparently, the purpose of all English classrooms is to center Own Voices stories, set in the present, about underrepresented characters who teach progressive moral lessons related to their identities. In the pages of *School Library Journal*, novelist Padma Venkatraman elaborates: "Even if we establish safe environments for discussion, classics privilege white readers. . . . *Uncle Tom's Cabin* broke out of the horrifically narrow confines of the era when it was written—but can it be considered progressive today?. . . . If we want to nurture readers of color, we must get rid of racist classics in homes, bookstores, and English classrooms."[78]

We must also get rid of them in public libraries. "I'm seeing this more and more," explained one of my interview subjects, the executive director of a large public library district in the United States. In our interview, he lamented a growing faction of librarians who are relocating and removing books. Typically, a librarian might relocate a book, such as Dr. Seuss's *If I Ran the Zoo*, from the children's section to the historical section if it is not circulating but it has historical value. However, some librarians are now relocating books that are circulating. This ensures that browsing readers will not find them.

Other librarians are not only relocating children's and YA books to the historical collection but also removing books from the historical collection. For some librarians, the historical import of a book like *Uncle Tom's Cabin* is less important than the purported harm it causes modern readers—whether their readers are children, teenagers, or adults. Librarians can also refuse to purchase books, even books that top the *New York Times* bestseller list, if they believe these books are bad for the public. Another library district director admits: "I have colleagues who say they won't buy Christian fiction."

Librarians do not have to be honest about why books are not on the shelves. When a child asks why his library does not have *A Fine Dessert*, or a teenager asks why her library does not have *The Continent*, or an adult asks why their library does not have *The Art of the Deal*, their librarian can blame the budget. This kind of censorship does not make the news because it is hard to discern, and it cannot compete with sensational stories about literal book burners. However, it does not mean that it is not a problem. "Access is a key component," explains one library system director, "of the freedom to read."

To be sure, most librarians are not extremists. Another librarian I spoke to told me that she is a democratic socialist who purchases books by conservative authors, even more controversial authors like Ann Coulter. This librarian sees herself as a public servant, rather than the arbiter of public morality. Most librarians share her view of the profession, which might be one reason libraries poll so favorably among the public.[79] In the words of another librarian, "If you poll public librarians, I would say nine times out of ten, if not ten times out of ten, they are really fighting for that freedom to read for everyone."

Yet the progressive extremists do exist—just read about Cameron Williams, a public library employee who removed Coulter's *How to Talk to a Liberal (If You Must)* before he burned it in an Instagram video[80]—and they do restrict the public's access to the literature of the present and the past. It is one thing to create a diverse collection via inclusion. It is quite another to create a uniform collection via exclusion. In the words of Zack de La Rocha, "They don't gotta burn the books they just remove 'em."[81] Historically, *remove* has been one of the many euphemisms for *censor*.

Notwithstanding the importance of "racist classics" like *Uncle Tom's Cabin*—two months before he signed the Emancipation Proclamation, Abraham Lincoln met Harriet Beecher Stowe and said, "This is the little lady who made this big war"[82]—Venkatraman, another Own Voices author of YA fiction, believes it is actually "more important to pay attention to books written by more recent Black authors" and "books vetted by resources such as We Need Diverse Books." Ironically, the movement for diverse books has a narrowly prescriptive view of books. "The best books," reflects the protagonist of George Orwell's *1984*, "are those that tell you what you know already."[83]

As a case in point, consider Amanda Gorman's "The Hill We Climb." #DisruptTexts wrote the Penguin Young Readers reading and teaching guide for this poem that Gorman recited at Joe Biden' inauguration.[84] If you think their guide brings the same critical spirit that their organization brings to Shakespeare and Twain, you have lost your mind. The directions include dictates like "Encourage students to perform their own renditions of 'The Hill We Climb'" and "Point out that many of the allusions are rooted in social justice and civil rights and why this is important." There is not one critical question—even something as pedagogically basic as, "Do you agree with Gorman's view of America?" or "What are the strengths and weaknesses of this poem?"

However, there are questions that ask students to make the sort of essentialist, telepathic moves that characterize the Sensitivity Era: "How might a person of color respond?" Unlike *Moby Dick* and *A Farewell to Arms*, which are considered so irredeemably flawed that teachers must remove them from their classrooms, Gorman's work is considered such an unblemished masterpiece of American literature that it must be widely taught with a step-by-step instructional guide that ensures no teacher or student asks the wrong questions. The boundaries between education, recitation, and indoctrination do not exist. Studying "The Hill We Climb" with Diverse Texts is like studying *The Little Red Book* with Chairman Mao.

Because many English teachers do not control their curricula, this poses a problem. In places where a school district did not purchase *They Call Me Güero* by David Bowles (a progressive Own Voices novel about a middle school boy who confronts racism in the twenty-first century), or *Finding Junie Kim* by Ellen Oh (a progressive Own Voices novel about a middle school girl who confronts racism in the twenty-first century), or *The Hate U Give* (a progressive Own Voices novel about a high school girl who confronts racism in the twenty-first century), teachers have to teach literature that does not fit the moral criteria of presentism. In districts where teachers still have to teach *The Grapes of Wrath*, *The Catcher in the Rye*, and *One Flew over the Cuckoo's Nest*, they are encouraged to "disrupt" the text. In other words, they are encouraged to teach these books in the exact opposite way they teach "The Hill We Climb." Christina Torres, an eighth-grade English teacher, explains what teaching *Romeo and Juliet* looks like in the Sensitivity Era: "I pause, give a thumbs-down and say 'Boo' when the play says something misogynistic."[85]

Here, there is little distinction between TikTok and the classroom. Teaching revolves around emotive noises and thumbs down. The only difference is that Torres cannot click a "thumbs down" button. I cannot imagine that this insultingly simplistic and didactic approach to Shakespeare will engender a new wave of feminists.[86] Though, I suspect it will provide more fodder for right-wing politicians who want to defund public education. Unlike #DisruptTexts, public education depends on bipartisan support from taxpayers. From California to Massachusetts and every state in between, the right presents teachers as liberal ideologues who do not know how to teach.

From a historical perspective, there is nothing new about removing a piece of old literature from the classroom. Nor is there anything new about "disrupting" it. "In the early days of the Russian Revolution," write Gary Saul Morson and Morton Schapiro, "many recommended that the new society reject entirely literature by those aristocrats Pushkin and Tolstoy and by all writers, Russian or foreign, compromised by prerevolutionary values." In the end, the Bolsheviks kept classical literature in their classrooms, "suitably reinterpreted in Marxist-Leninist terms, of course."[87] American teachers who want to see Shakespeare kicked off the curriculum are not so different from Maoist teachers. Under Mao's tenure, the Bard's plays were banned.

Notwithstanding the major difference—saying "Boo" to Shakespeare or choosing not to teach Shakespeare is not the same as state censorship of Shakespeare—it all exists on the spectrum of presentism, and state censorship is often the result of public pressure. Presentism is such a perennial feature of extremism that it even recurs in the fiction about extremism. In Fyodor Dostoevsky's *The Possessed*, revolutionary Pyotr Stepanovich promises to stone Shakespeare and cut out Cicero's tongue. He also promises a "system of spying" to "enforce equality."[88] Over a century later, Tyler Durden, the protagonist of Chuck Palahniuk's *Fight Club*, promises to replace the old with the new. "This is our world now," he exclaims, "and those ancient people are dead."[89] When the literature of the past remains, it is reinterpreted in terms of the present. From a feminist reading to an antiracist reading, there are a million and one ways to stone Shakespeare and cut out Cicero's tongue.

For Khalid and Snyder, presentism "turns reading literature into a whack-a-mole game of spot the 'problematic'-ism. It encourages students to take a self-righteous, judgmental stance toward fictional characters, scanning texts for any sign that they fail to live up to today's socially progressive standards." As the law of instrument says, "Give a small boy a hammer, and he'll find things to pound."[90] Aside from the preening nature of this approach to literature, which positions students as jury members in the high court of moral judgment—a court run by the teacher-judge who determines their grade—there is nothing particularly difficult about being a member of this court. Spoiler alert: Romeo does not talk like a twenty-first-century liberal at the Women's March. Neither does Mercutio, Benvolio, Tybalt, Juliet, nor her nurse. It is one thing to spot a "problematic"-ism; it is quite another to teach young people something about Shakespeare and his work. Of course, teachers can take a feminist, antiracist, or antiableist approach to the classics. But that approach should have some kind of intellectual substance.

In professional literary criticism, this, too, is a problem. John M. Ellis, a professor of literature at the University of California, gives an example of what it looks like:

> A race-gender-class critic looked at gender roles in *Grimm's Fairy Tales* and found that boys and girls reflect the sexual stereotypes of the time—which are of course bad. What has been achieved by doing this? Certainly, nothing very surprising; if the Grimm's *Tales* reflect the sexual stereotypes of their age, then presumably one could find those same stereotypes just about anywhere. That is what stereotypical means.
>
> What the critic has done here surely fails the test of significance because it amounts to saying nothing more than that the Grimms wrote in the early nineteenth century. Because the critic has said nothing that could not have been said about virtually everything else written at the time, nothing has been said specifically about the stories. It is as if we were asked to say something about Einstein and responded: "He has two legs."[91]

Because the prophets of presentism carve the world into simple moral categories—following Kendi's dictum, authors and their fictional characters are either racists or antiracists, sexists or feminists, and so on—both their lack of nuance and their disdain for classical literature are understandable. "In what is considered the first major literary theory in the history of Western ideas," writes Philippe Rochat, "Aristotle (*Poetics*, 335 BCE) proposes that the essence of tragedy as a major literary genre is the main character's *moral ambiguity*."[92] Moral ambiguity is not just a feature of *Dr. Faustus, Oedipus Rex*, and other tragedies. It is a feature of countless plays, poems, and novels that belong to the Western canon, what Harold Bloom calls "the school of the ages."[93] To use *Romeo and Juliet* or *Grimm's Fairy Tales* as cheap props in the modern theater of moral finger snaps is to avoid the discomfort of trying to understand the moral complexities of these complicated works.

Unlike much of what passes as progressive literature in the twenty-first century, the school of the ages is not as easily digestible as a bite-size cookie that says "Smash the Patriarchy."[94]

The problem of inane teaching is compounded by teachers who believe that old stories do not just contain misogynistic or otherwise insensitive content—but also that, in Bowles's words, they are "harmful" to students. As if classical literature was the Black Death, one #DisruptTexts teacher boasts of disrupting books that "plague" her school's curriculum.[95] With articles like "The Hidden Dangers of the Literary Canon,"[96] one would think teachers are saving lives every time they scream "Boo" during a reading of *The Taming of the Shrew*. The conception of classical literature as a threat distinguishes extremists from the innumerable number of people who simply prefer to read or teach something else. Indeed, one of the most interesting aspects of presentism is that it blames the Western canon for modern problems that, by any reasonable measure, have nothing to do with the Western canon. Take, for instance, incels. According to *Oxford Languages*:

> *Incel*, short for 'involuntary celibate', is used as a self-descriptor by members of an online subculture who deem themselves chronically unable to attract romantic or sexual partners. Brought together on internet forums such as Reddit, these men hold that it is women who are to blame for their forced celibacy by 'withholding' sex. The online spaces where *incels* communicate—such as the /r/Incels subreddit, which had reached 40,000 members when the forum banned it in November 2017—have consequently become hotbeds for the incitement of violent misogyny. . . . While such hate groups have existed online for years, it was in April 2018 that incel made front-page news worldwide; a man named Alek Minassian deliberately drove a van into pedestrians on a crowded Toronto street, killing 10 people and wounding 14 others. It was discovered that shortly before the horrific attack, Minassian had shared 'The Incel Rebellion has already begun!' in a now-deleted Facebook post.[97]

One might ask what any of this has to do with William Shakespeare, Charles Dickens, and Molière. Apparently, the answer is everything. In her *Guardian* article, "How Does the Literary Canon Reinforce the Logic of the Incel?," American English professor Erin Spampinato explains that because some characters in the canon are misogynistic, and because some members of the incel community are also misogynistic, there must be a connection.[98] She concludes: "I'm not naive enough to think that we will ever read or write misogyny out of existence, but. . . . If I am right that there are subtle but real connections between mainstream literary structural misogyny and violent subcultures like that of the incel, then perhaps our lives actually depend on it." As if this article was written to scare people, it is accompanied by a black-and-white photograph of an ominous young man holding an open book like a sniper rifle. Around the time "incel" was shortlisted as the word of the year so was "slacktivism."

One of the great ironies of these attacks on the Western canon is how decidedly Western they are.[99] If readers disagree, I invite them to visit Somalia, Sierra Leone, Egypt, and other countries where one is more likely to come across a woman scarred by female genital mutilation than a woman outraged over *Romeo and Juliet*. Other countries are politically incorrect, and intolerant, to a shocking degree. The problem with, say, what Holden Caulfield thinks about Sally Hayes in *The Catcher in the Rye* might seem like a pressing problem to American professors and a certain stratum of progressives who subscribe to the *Guardian*. But, if one were to show up in rural Sudan with a bag of Salinger books, ready to finger-wag local farmers for not understanding how "dangerous" this author is, they would be looked at like a Western missionary high on psilocybin mushrooms. Notwithstanding the Sensitivity Era's commitment to multiculturalism, the era is as American as Starbucks. It is hardly a coincidence that the writers I have met over the years who are most confused by the era's rules of decorum are those, like Amélie Wen Zhao, who were not born here.

Given the influence of K–12 teachers and English professors, it is understandable that their view of the classics is trickling down to students. Throughout the United States, the classics are now treated as a public safety problem. At Columbia University, undergraduate students "disrupted" *The Metamorphosis*: "Like so many texts in the Western canon . . . [it] contains triggering and offensive material that marginalizes student identities in the classroom. These texts, wrought with histories and narratives of exclusion and oppression, can be difficult to read and discuss as a survivor, a person of color, or a student from a low-income background . . . Students need to feel safe in the classroom."[100] Yet the criterion for acceptable content differs across time periods. As Laurent Dubreuil, a professor of comparative literature who grew up poor, puts it in his response to this disruption: "I particularly appreciate the absolutely condescending suggestion that a low-income student is going to be hurt by classical literature. . . . A little more intellectual humility might be useful for a small group of Ivy League students in the twenty-first century presuming to determine what is acceptable in an ancient Greek tragedy."[101] But presentism asserts that books should conform to what is acceptable in the present; if they deviate, they should be disrupted. Otherwise, readers are in real danger.

Whether we call the classroom an "interpretative community"[102] or an "optical community,"[103] it socializes students to read a certain way. One has to ask what happens when students are socialized to believe that old books will harm them. In *The Coddling of the American Mind: How Good Intentions and Bad Ideas Are Setting Up a Generation for Failure*, civil liberties attorney Greg Lukianoff and social psychologist Jonathan Haidt ask a question that all English teachers should ask: "Is safety versus danger a helpful framework for discussing reactions to literature? Or might that framework itself alter a student's reactions to ancient texts, creating a feeling of threat and a stress response to what otherwise would have been experienced merely as discomfort or dislike."[104] To be sure, affronts to dignity can feel like a slap in the face.[105] And when they occur in and through literature, they can be discussed in thoughtful ways. But educators who cultivate psychological fragility are not helping anyone—least of all their students.

As Lukianoff and Haidt observe, many educators and administrators are "teaching a generation of students to engage in the mental habits commonly seen in people who suffer from anxiety and depression." In the Sensitivity Era, students are running from old books because they have "been taught to exaggerate danger, use dichotomous (or binary) thinking, amplify their first emotional responses, and engage in a number of other cognitive distortions."[106] For Lukianoff and Haidt, who met to discuss their concerns back in 2014, the same year WNDB burst on to the scene, the current era of education is marked by three untruths: what does not kill you makes you weaker, always trust your feelings, and life is a battle between good people and evil people. These cognitive distortions are not only intertwined with rising rates of anxiety and depression, two serious problems among young Americans. They are also fundamentally at odds with critical thinking and civil disagreement, pillars of any serious English classroom. As young people become more fragile, teachers become more protective.[107] This cycle continues to produce increasingly eccentric notions of "safety" and "danger."

Notwithstanding the concerns of Lukianoff, Haidt, and Dubreuil, not all students mimic educators who teach them to be afraid of old literature. And not all educators support presentism and its ever-expanding notion of harm. In 2021, the board of trustees at Howard University, a historically black university, decided to cut its classics department. This department, which has existed since 1867, is as old as the university. Although some people supported the decision, other people did not. "At Howard, students are exposed to how themes within classics are interlaced and rooted into the works of political activists like Huey P. Newton and Angela Davis as well as Black literary thinkers such as the author Toni Morrison," reflects Anika Prather, an untenured teacher and former Howard student who lost her job because of the decision.[108] Tiye Williamson, a teenager and current student, explained that the classics department drew her to the university. Growing up, she was passionate about translating Latin. In addition to an online petition, other students mobilized the hashtag "#SaveHUClassics."

Some K–12 students are also sick of the attacks on the classics. In California, the Burbank Unified School District banned Harper Lee's *To Kill a Mockingbird*, Mark Twain's *The Adventures of Huckleberry Finn*, Mildred D. Taylor's *Roll of Thunder, Hear My Cry*, and other novels from its curriculum.[109] "Four parents, three of whom are Black, challenged the classic novels for alleged potential harm to the district's roughly 400 Black students." As one parent, who filed a complaint, put it: "the portrayal of Black people is mostly from a white perspective." Another parent, who also filed a complaint, noted that a student had used a slur he read in Taylor's novel to taunt her daughter. Bullying is reprehensible, but is it a reason to ban literature? Sungjoo Yoon, a sophomore at Burbank High, launched a Change.org petition to overturn the ban. "If you stand against censorship," he wrote, "and fight for virtue over comfort, we ask that you sign."[110] More than five thousand people signed.

Personally, I have taught everything from *The Great Gatsby* to *The Hunger Games*, *Laugh at My Pain*, and *The Killing Joke*. I have taught Emily Dickinson, Maya Angelou, and LL Cool J in the same semester. Different students love different texts. Young readers are not a monolith. Although no teacher should have to teach the classics, and people should continue to debate why these texts are considered classics in the first place, adults should not treat their own contempt for classical literature as a prescription for students. The connection between a reader and a text is more complicated than Oh, Bowles, Spampinato, and some of Burbank's parents would have it. It is a lot more complicated than the distinction between writers who have this or that identity or, in Germán's case, writers who published before or after this or that date.

Looking back, I have never heard anyone laud Melville more than Cornel West, an African American scholar on the left who sees more value in this author's work than those who believe he has nothing to offer young black readers in the twenty-first century. Likewise, Karen and Barbara Fields, two black scholars on the left, draw on William Faulkner's "brilliant" fiction to develop their own brilliant discussion of racial subordination in the Jim Crow south.[111] For his part, Martin Luther King Jr. references Socrates three times in his "Letter from Birmingham City Jail." Just as Socrates wanted to raise individuals "from the bondage of myths and half-truths," King Jr. wanted to raise individuals "from the dark depths of prejudice and racism."[112]

Dominican-born educator Roosevelt Montás titled his latest book *Rescuing Socrates: How the Great Books Changed My Life and Why They Matter for a New Generation.*[113] He also started a Great Books program for low-income high school students. Glenn Loury, an African American writer who grew up on Chicago's South Side, has said this more than once: "Tolstoy is mine. Dickens is mine."[114]

Ralph Ellison, an African American who won the National Book Award for Fiction, is another progressive writer inspired by the classics. Although literary critics place Ellison alongside Richard Wright, Langston Hughes, and other African American writers, Ellison placed himself on the shoulders of other giants. As he puts it, "In Macon County, Alabama, I read Marx, Freud, T. S. Eliot, Pound, Gertrude Stein, and Hemingway. Books which seldom, if ever, mentioned Negroes were to release me from whatever 'segregated' idea I might have had of my human possibilities."[115] As Ellison suggests, the relationship between a reader and an author is not reducible to census data, and it requires a "real poverty of the imagination" to believe otherwise. After all, Marx was a German writer born more than a century before Ellison published *Invisible Man.*

In *The Souls of Black Folk*, W. E. B. Du Bois imagines himself "arm in arm with Balzac and Dumas" and suffering neither "scorn nor condescension" from Aristotle and Aurelius. "I sit with Shakespeare and he winces not," wrote the cofounder of the National Association for the Advancement of Colored People.[116] For her part, a young Zadie Smith felt she *was* Jane Eyre and David Copperfield as she read Charlotte Brontë and Charles Dickens. In her "Defense of Fiction," this self-identified black novelist with brown skin and Afro-hair reflects: "Our autobiographical coordinates rarely matched. I'd never had a friend die of consumption or been raped by my father or lived in Trinidad or the Deep South or the nineteenth century. But I'd been sad and lost, sometimes desperate, often confused. It was on the basis of such flimsy emotional clues that I found myself feeling with these imaginary strangers: feeling with them, for them, alongside them and through them, extrapolating from my own emotions, which, though strikingly minor when compared to the high dramas of fiction, still bore some relation to them, as all human feelings do."[117]

The influence is reciprocal. "What the ideologues of authenticity cannot quite come to grips with," writes Henry Louis Gates Jr., "is that fact and fiction have always exerted a reciprocal effect on each other." As Gates Jr., the first African American scholar to receive the National Humanities Medal, reflects: "Many authentic slave narratives were influenced by Harriet Beecher Stowe; on the other hand, authentic slave narratives were among Stowe's primary sources for her own imaginative work, *Uncle Tom's Cabin*. . . . So it is not just a matter of the outsider boning up while the genuine article just writes what he or she knows."[118] Writers, like readers, do not exist in hermetically sealed bubbles—what the Sensitivity Era calls "cultures."

When Toni Morrison, the first African American woman to win the Nobel Prize in Literature, gave the Tanner Lectures at the University of Michigan in 1988, she placed William Shakespeare, Henry James, and Herman Melville on the list of authors she could never live without.[119] Despite the discomfort she experienced while reading *Huckleberry Finn* in junior high school, she placed Mark Twain on her list, too. In her introduction to Oxford University Press's edition of the novel, she laments the efforts to remove Twain's masterpiece from the required reading lists of public schools. "It [strikes] me as a purist yet elementary kind of censorship designed to appease adults rather than educate children." For Morrison, *Huckleberry Finn* cannot be dismissed. "It is classic literature," she explains, "which is to say it heaves, manifests and lasts."[120]

Even Barack Obama has waded into the debate. In an article that celebrates both Morrison and Twain, he reflects: "Not only is it important for young people to see themselves represented in the pages of books, but it's also important for all of us to engage with different ideas and points of view."[121] While the first black president of the United States defends Twain, other adults protect young black people from Twain. What Obama said about Twain's work—"it revealed something essential to me about our country's character and our history"—is a moot point. To use the boilerplate language: Twain's work was progressive in his time, but is it progressive in 2025? If you, too, care about the next generation, you should instead purchase a WNDB-approved book that came out last week. Although their books might not heave, manifest, or last, they have been declared safe for public consumption.

In *Nigger: The Strange Career of a Troublesome Word*, Harvard University's Randall Kennedy, an African American scholar of discrimination in the United States, offers an especially articulate defense of Twain, one that illuminates the incentives that circumscribe these debates over classical literature. In this book that was burned—setting *Nigger* on fire is, apparently, what antiracism looks like—Kennedy indicts those who "would cast a protectionist pall over popular culture that would likely benefit certain minority entrepreneurs only at the net expense of society overall."[122] Many of the adults trying to kick dead authors off the curriculum are the same adults competing for space on the curriculum. To use Orwell's language, "who controls the past, controls the future."[123] If the literature of the past is too dangerous to teach, school systems will have to turn to contemporary authors. First and foremost, books are commodities. One would have to be wildly naive to think that presentism has nothing to do with that.

In public, writers and their representatives can use all the moral language they want. They can talk about "correcting historical injustices," "centering the marginalized," and "social justice." But everyone who is making, or trying, to make money—from *New York Times* bestselling authors to industry professionals who market books to schools, libraries, and other customer facing institutions—knows what the stakes are. One agent, who represents both contemporary authors and the estates of dead authors, was brutally honest in our interview. "It's a zero-sum game," he explained to me. "For every new priority, somebody gets kicked off the list. They pretend that this isn't the case. 'Oh no, we're just expanding our list.' No. It was forty books last year. It's forty books this year."

The zero-sum game of literary culture helps to explain why so many contemporary writers publicly contend that their work is better than *Macbeth*, *Lord of the Flies*, "The Love Song of J. Alfred Prufrock," and other classics. One of my interview subjects describes it as "the Napoleon complex of literature":

> There is just no shame. There's these weird sort of ego battles. They'll never admit it. But it's not just about having a sustainable financial career. It's this fragile ego thing. Think of it as the Napoleon complex of literature. I think you do have to have some element of, I hate to call it, narcissism, to think your stories are important enough to even bother sitting down and writing them. But there is a lot built into the system that fosters this unhealthy competition, winner-takes-all, every-person-for-themselves type of mentality. It's so many people fighting for so few resources: fellowships, scholarships to grad school, foundation money, awards, contests, publications. All of it. Everything. It's all a competition. The system is trying pit me against other writers.

Whether it is the debut authors who land six-figure advances for their work, or the dead authors who continue to take up space on K–12 and college syllabi, the targets of criticism are typically writers who have accomplished what other writers can only dream of. This is particularly true of the select few who achieve canonical status. Whereas many writers celebrate those who came before them—think, for example, of T. S. Eliot's position in "Tradition and the Individual Talent"—the prophets of presentism celebrate themselves.

At publishing houses, presentism also manifests in editorial decisions after a manuscript has been acquired. When I spoke to an editor at a Big Five publisher, they described sending a contemporary novel set in the early nineteenth century to a black sensitivity reader—they rarely send a manuscript to more than one sensitivity reader—not to fact-check the history, but to determine what parts of the history are too incongruent with the present. In their words:

> I think the sensitivity reader was a university student, but I don't know if she had specific research accreditations. I can't speak to how certified you have to be to be a sensitivity reader. I don't think you take a course, and then are like, I am now accredited to do this. I think a lot of it is just you're finding people from that community to be like, I live that life. I know those terms. I know what would be derogatory. I would be the right person to look at that content critically and tell you whether or not other people from our community would probably find it offensive.
>
> I think for that particular novel, we weren't bringing them on to fact-check. We were just having them look at the language. And if as a reader they're like I know that this is historical, but seeing the N-word in print is just so jarring to me that you should just not do it, we just wouldn't. That's maybe a very harsh example. Nobody would print that, even if it was historically accurate, anymore. But the point remains, having that kind of gut reaction from a reader whose job it is to tell us what would be really upsetting is really what we're looking for.

We're going to trust that opinion. We'll cut those sections. Yeah, it is historically accurate. But I'm still trying to sell this to a reader. And if their experience
with the title is now greatly hindered by the language, then I have done a dis-
service to them and to the publisher in selling more copies. On the business side
and the moral side, it would just not be the right thing to do.

Perhaps this editor is right, and it is moral to whitewash the way planta-
tion owners, Reconstruction-era Klansmen, and Jim Crow segregationists
spoke. But if language is as powerful as this editor suggests, then its removal
will diminish literature's power to represent those aspects of history that
many people, especially on the right, would rather forget. As the market
demands more children's, YA, and adult books that do not discomfort their
readers—this editor works on adult literature—historical fiction might be
the place where readers learn that the past was not as bad as black people
remember it.

Just compare David Goggins's self-published memoir—"I was born broken, grew up with beat downs, was tormented in school, and was called *nigger* more times than I could count"[124]—with the demands that this editor,
and their sensitivity reader, place on literature. Goggins is not even writing
about the distant past. He was born in 1975. Having taught his memoir
more than once, I know it resonates with black teenagers who deal with
racism today. If publishers are so interested in "authentic" and "accurate"
stories, they might reconsider hiring people who care more about stories
that make readers feel comfortable.

To be sure, not everyone who works in publishing is on the same page.
For example, one vice president I interviewed, who did not want to be
recorded, lamented those who feel a book should not even include the
word "negro," even if the book is about a time period when people used the
word "negro." Although this insider empathizes with writers and industry
professionals who want to avoid the "the mess and the controversy," he
also believes "they're whitewashing history." Ironically, most progressives
associate whitewashing with the right. But if one agrees with the definition of "whitewashing"—"to try to hide unpleasant facts about somebody/
something; to try to make something seem better than it is"[125]—it is hard
to disagree with this vice president's use of the word.

One agent I spoke to was transparent about how utterly frustrating it
is to work with these progressives who want to whitewash history. She
explains: "A manuscript will be read by a dozen people at the publishing

house, and someone will say, 'Oh, I'm a little concerned about this. This character's misogynist.' And I say, 'He's misogynist. They exist. They existed at the time. They exist now.' You can represent them without damaging the women's movement. It was set in 1920. That's how they spoke. We're not going to give them the vocabulary of 2022. It's just not going to happen, and it shouldn't happen. I don't expect a deeply historical novel to be deeply feminist." But other agents, editors, reviewers, and even authors do have this expectation.

Presentism privileges the ideals of the present over the realities of the past and the present. Consider all the new books where adolescents of all races and classes attend school together, live within walking distance of one another, and so on. It is as if my current roster of Ivy League undergraduates —predictably, there are zero black students—does not exist. It is as if the median family income of these students, more than $150,000 in 2019, does not make Cornell look like a gated country club.[126] Although books about rich white kids who attend elite schools are as realistic as ever, they are not inclusive. For that reason, they are less attractive to publishers. As one agent admits, "a book like *Gossip Girl* wouldn't be published now." That is a win for readers who want diverse characters. It is not a win for realism.

To compound the problem, there is a market for bowdlerized editions of old books. Just consider the republished *James Bond* books. Ian Fleming Publications Ltd., which owns the rights to Ian Flemming's classics, brought in sensitivity readers for the seventieth anniversary of his debut novel, *Casino Royale*. A disclaimer will read: "A number of updates have been made in this edition, while keeping as close as possible to the original text and the period in which it is set." The updates range from the transformation of Bond describing African suspects as "pretty law-abiding chaps I should have thought, except when they've drunk too much" to "pretty law-abiding chaps I should have thought" to the complete omission of sentences like one where Bond describes the accents of a couple arguing in Harlem as "straight Harlem-Deep South with a lot of New York thrown in."[127] After news broke in 2023, people were upset that Ian Fleming Publications Ltd. did not make *more* changes.

These books are the products of people who, literally, rewrite the past in terms of the present. For those unfamiliar, the word "bowdlerize" dates back to the nineteenth century. Specifically, it dates back to the work of Dr. Thomas Bowdler. In 1818, two hundred years after Shakespeare's death,

Bowdler took it upon himself to edit Shakespeare's work. In the process, Bowdler omitted "those words . . . which cannot with propriety be read aloud in a family."[128] For example, Bowdler removed these lines from *Timon of Athens*:

> Obedience fail in children! Slaves and fools,
> Pluck the grave winkled senate from the bench,
> And minister in their steads! ~~To general filth~~
> ~~Covert, o' the instant, green virginity,~~
> ~~Do't in your parents' eyes!~~ Bankrupts, hold fast
> Rather than rend back, out with your knives,
> And cut your trusters' throats! Bound servants, steal!

In retrospect, censorship looks contingent. Bowdler did not have a problem with Shakespeare's gratuitous violence. He had a problem with his "profane" and "sexual" content. In a similar vein, nineteenth-century readers disdained the "vulgarity" and "rudeness" of *The Adventures of Huckleberry Finn*. It was Twain's popular vernacular that provoked them. After it was published, "the library in Concord, Massachusetts declared the book unworthy of its oh-so-respectable bourgeois readers and banned it from its shelves." Today, like Shakespeare's *Othello*, Twain's novel is "unworthy" because of reasons related to race.[129] The same Ovid who disturbed the moral liberalism of Columbia University students was exiled from Rome for disturbing the moral conservatism of Emperor Augustus. The list goes on.

Similar contingencies mark the history of children's literature. For example, an older edition of Hugh Lofting's *Doctor Dolittle* included references to skin color. The 1988 edition expurgated those references. A decade before, the African pygmies in Roald Dahl's *Charlie and the Chocolate Factory* were transformed into Oompa-Loompas. The current edition does not acknowledge the change.[130] More to the point, both books contain material that is now considered offensive for different reasons. In 2023, Penguin Random House announced it would be making hundreds *more* changes to Dahl's oeuvre (among other changes, Augustus Gloop will be "enormous" instead of "enormously fat"). The treadmill of presentism has no off-switch. It only has new historical moments that afford new reasons to rewrite an author's work.

Jacob and Wilhelm Grimm, in their own words, "carefully removed every expression inappropriate for children" from *Children's and Household Tales*, the published version of the folktales they collected.[131] Yet they kept other material that might be considered inappropriate today. As folklorist D. L. Ashliman reflects, "their story 'All-Kinds-of-Fur' (no. 65) has the threat of father-daughter incest as its central theme, while 'Old Hildebrand' (no. 95) is the tale of an adulterous adventure between a priest and a peasant woman. But still, in the main the Grimms avoided material that would have offended their nineteenth-century bourgeois public." The history of literature is the history of revision. The revisions are meant to align literature with the present.

If one purpose of literature is to help readers understand the past, then rewritten literature poses a problem. To stick with Twain, consider *The Adventures of Tom Sawyer* and *Adventures of Huckleberry Finn*. First published in 1876 and 1884, both novels take place in the antebellum South. As such, they include characters who use racial slurs. Around the time WNDB emerged, NewSouth Books published editions that replaced the word "nigger" with "slave." As editor Alan Gribben, a professor of English, explains: "The n-word possessed, then as now, demeaning implications more vile than almost any insult that can be applied to other racial groups."[132] But Twain's point was to depict the antebellum South as it was, not as he and other writers wanted it to be.

For Gribben, realistic stories are not as important as stories that comfort their readers. As he puts it, "We may applaud Twain's ability as a prominent American literary realist to record the speech of a particular region during a specific historical era, but abusive racial insults that bear distinct connotations of permanent inferiority nonetheless repulse modern-day readers."[133] So Gribben also transformed "Injun Joe" into "Indian Joe." Here, the verisimilitude of an old book is set in opposition to the feelings of modern readers. In the Sensitivity Era, feelings win. Much like Bowles and Oh, Gribben sees himself as a self-appointed ambassador for young people's feelings. He is no different from Ampleforth, the censor in *1984* who produces "garbled versions" of literature deemed offensive.[134]

Unlike many YA authors, Gribben is at least transparent about the market value of books that make their way on to the school curriculum. "Twain was probably our most commercially minded author ever. He employed an army of salespeople to knock on doors in cities and farmlands, his latest book in hand. . . . Who is to say that this chaser of fortunes and public attention might not smile upon a revision that would reinsert his boy books back into school classrooms and gain new readers?"[135] Aside from the

fact that Twain took unpopular positions that alienated him from potential readers—he was vice president of the Anti-Imperialist League during
the Philippine-American War[136]—Twain is not the one profiting from
NewSouth's garbled versions of his oeuvre. Given his penchant for irreverence, and his rejection of moral pieties, he is probably clawing at the lid
of his coffin.

Geoff Barton, the headteacher at King Edward VI School, described Gribben's censorship as "slightly crackpot."[137] "It seems depressing that we are
so squeamish that we can't credit youngsters with seeing the context for
texts. Are we going to teach a sanitized version of *The Merchant of Venice*?
What I would want to do is to explore issues of how language changes in
context and culture," he explained. Like other educators, Sarah Churchwell, a senior lecturer in US literature, regards Twain's novels as historical
documents that push readers to confront the past: "The point of the book
is that Huckleberry Finn starts out racist in a racist society, and stops being
racist and leaves that society. These changes mean the book ceases to show
the moral development of his character. They have no merit and are misleading to readers. The whole point of literature is to expose us to different
ideas and different eras, and they won't always be nice and benign. It's
dumbing down."

One can contest Churchwell's interpretation of Twain's novel. But, to do
that, one needs to read the novel that Twain actually wrote. Furthermore,
as Kennedy argues, if "eradicationists" like Gribben are consistent, then
they must want to "bowdlerize and censor poems such as Carl Sandburg's
'Nigger Lover,' stories such as Theodore Dreiser's 'Nigger Jeff,' Claude McK-
ay's 'Nigger Love,' or Henry Dumas' 'Double Nigger,' plays such as Ed Bul-
lins' 'The Electronic Nigger,' and novels such as Gil Scott-Heron's *The Nigger
Factory*."[138] Moreover, it is a small step from removing hurtful epithets to
removing hurtful scenes. One can imagine a future edition where Huck
never teases Jim. After all, if the justification for rewriting old literature is a
modern reader's feelings, then editors like Gribben still have a lot of work to
do. They might think about hiring sensitivity readers to help them.

Like Gribben, school officials also believe it is their moral duty to rewrite
other people's books. "To satisfy twenty-first-century 'sensitivity review
guidelines,' the New York State Education Department bowdlerized texts
for use in an exam, supposedly to prevent students feeling ill at ease," write
Keith Allan and Kate Burridge in *Forbidden Words: Taboo and the Censoring of*

Language.[139] In New York, books published as recently as a few decades ago were not up to par with the latest rules for how to write about race, body size, and other aspects of identity. For example, when the state censors turned their attention to *Barrio Boy*, Ernesto Galarza's 1971 memoir, they transformed "calling someone a wop, a chink, a dago, or a greaser" into "calling someone a bad name." Likewise, a "skinny" boy was transformed into a "thin" boy, and a "fat" boy was transformed into a "heavy" boy.[140] In an era of devastating budget cuts to public education, which have gutted everything from after-school sports to free lunch, this is what protecting students from harm looks like.

Expertise

In the Jim Crow era, there was a joke that any black man with a suit and a briefcase could claim to speak on behalf of "Black America." In the Sensitivity Era, anyone with an internet connection can claim to speak on behalf of black Americans, rural Americans, disabled Americans, and so on. In this context, every reader is also a literary critic with their own publishing platform. And, in the context of the era's central maxim—"No substitute for lived experience"—people with the right lived experience have more authority than historians, political scientists, sociologists, and professional literary critics with the wrong lived experience.

As a case in point, consider Metamorphosis Literary Agency's guidelines for authors: "Research is a first step, but keep in mind research is still not firsthand perspective. It is an important steppingstone, but is not equal to that of a person's firsthand experience."[141] One of the hallmark features of the era is that it elevates personal experience above professional expertise. Being is knowing. Here, what otherwise might be considered anti-intellectualism is regarded as the correct way to write literature.

It is also the correct way to translate literature. Victor Obiols, a translator of William Shakespeare and Oscar Wilde, was commissioned to translate Amanda Gorman's "The Hill We Climb" into Catalan. Marieke Lucas Rijneveld, a winner of the International Booker Prize, was commissioned to translate it into Dutch. Unlike Gorman, they are white men. Therefore, according to Sensitivity Era logic, they cannot understand the poem. So they were replaced. In addition to the point raised by Thomas Chatterton Williams—"one of the reasons it's so difficult to take seriously the idea that translators must or *should* be of the same 'racial' identity as authors is that the publishing industry banks on the fact that millions of 'white' and international readers can buy these books and grasp them!"[142]—the controversy raises the bigger question of how any reader can understand any piece of literature that is not their own memoir. "If I cannot translate a poet because she is a woman, young, Black, an American of the 21st century," reflects Obiols, "neither can I translate Homer because I am not a Greek of the eighth century BC."[143]

In the Sensitivity Era, the privileging of firsthand experience has no historical limits. When bestselling YA author Julie Berry decided to write about a member of the Harlem Hellfighters, an African American regiment in World War I, she consulted a black sensitivity reader named Kyle V. Hiller.[144] Hiller has no discernible interest, much less expertise, in World War I history. However, Berry consulted this sensitivity reader because she wanted the perspective of a person "who could directly identify." As Hiller explains, "What I want is to help you be sure that what you're writing is authentic and sensitive to cultures not your own."

One might ask how the culture of a black sensitivity reader in 2019 is the culture of a black soldier during World War I. Yet, when a "marginalized identity" is involved, obvious questions are rarely asked. Instead, culture is treated as transhistorical. By virtue of his racial identity, Hiller understands "how a black character would respond to a nasty comment by a white soldier to a group of black soldiers in the mess hall of an army training camp" more than one hundred years ago. Hiller's intuitive, almost mystical connection to Berry's fictional black character is enough to inform his comments: "I didn't grow up during that time period, but I trust that's not how black people interacted with racist white people." Here, real life looks like the "Ask a Black Dude" and "Negrodamus" sketches on *Chappelle's Show*, as historical evidence is replaced by the transhistorical instinct of one black person.

This racial mysticism can be traced back to the black nationalist movements of the twentieth century.[145] Although the Sensitivity Era conjures new expressions, the basic logic is the same.[146] "Thinking with one's blood"[147] takes precedence over thinking with historical evidence. Knowledge is the product of who one is, rather than what one knows. Accordingly, anyone with the right identity can lay claim to the past. They can also lay claim to the title of spokesperson for all the people—alive, dead, or fictional—who are bound to them by blood. "Beware the writer who sets himself or herself up as the voice of a nation," warns Salman Rushdie in his contribution to Toni's Morrison's anthology on literature and censorship, and "this includes nations of race, gender, sexual orientation," and so on.[148] In the Sensitivity Era, one must also beware of the "cultural ambassadors" hired by authors and their publishers.

When sensitivity readers are not treated as historians, they are treated as scientists of identitarian experience. For example, as YA novelist Heidi Heilig argues, "When you have science or math in your book, people understand that you'd call your scientist friend and say, 'Hey, does E=mc2?' But when it comes to depictions of race, it's HOW DARE! HOW DARE ANYONE!"[149] In the same vein, Madeline Pine reflects, "Gotta laugh at the peeps who say they'd 'never subject their books to a sensitivity reader!' Go ahead, get things wrong then. While you're at it, don't use a scientific accuracy reader. Have characters take their helmet off in outer space. What's accuracy worth at this point?"[150] As bestselling YA novelist Laura Lam more concisely puts it, hiring a sensitivity reader is "like hiring an astrophysicist to make sure a space opera isn't getting the science completely backwards."[151] In these examples and countless others, the sensitivity reader is treated as a scientist who can discern the laws of identity just like Albert Einstein discerned the laws of physics.

Unlike Einstein, whose research was scrutinized and debated by other scientists, many sensitivity readers require authors, their agents, and their publishers to sign nondisclosure contracts. This prevents public evaluation of a sensitivity reader's work. If public evaluation of one's work is central to fields of expertise, then it is unclear how sensitivity reading is a field of expertise. It is especially unclear how it is a field of expertise on par with physics. Yet the science analogy extends from physics all the way through medicine. As author Natalia Sylvester explains, "Much like one might ask a cardiologist to read their story about a cardiologist for accuracy, a sensitivity read helps ensure that the portrayal of characters and worlds unknown to the author ring true."[152] Other authors believe there is no difference between sensitivity readers and medical professionals at all. As a contributor to #WritingCommunity reflects, "If I were writing about a doctor, I'd get a doctor to beta [read] it to make sure I got it right. Same difference."[153]

Whereas progressives in the past tried to distance race, gender, and other socially constructed categories from science—among other high-profile battles, readers might recall the intellectual dynamite that paleontologist Stephen Jay Gould hurled at Richard Herrnstein and Charles Murray's *The Bell Curve* in his 1996 edition of *The Mismeasure of Man*[154]—progressives in the present use the language of science to describe the work of people who claim to diagnose what is authentic/inauthentic, accurate/inaccurate, and right/wrong about fictional black people, fictional gay people, and other kinds of people. This idea of a falsifiable identitarian experience extends to the dozens, if not hundreds, of other identities that sensitivity readers have commodified as their own areas of expertise.

To be sure, these are all analogies. But, as cognitive linguist George Lakoff and philosopher Mark Johnson argue, the analogies we use reflect and shape how we understand social life.[155] If racial experience, like gendered or sexual experience, is regarded as something that can be formulated like $E = mc^2$, it raises real problems for an era that aspires to celebrate people from diverse backgrounds in all their nuance. It also raises real problems for real experts—historians, political scientists, and so on—when sensitivity readers like Kosoko Jackson proclaim that "stories about the civil rights movement should be written by black people," "stories of suffrage should be written by women," and "stories about boys during life-changing times, like the AIDS epidemic, should be written by gay men."[156] To paraphrase Randall Kennedy, having an identity is not the same as having an area of expertise.[157]

In his recent book, *The Death of Expertise: The Campaign Against Established Knowledge and Why It Matters*, Tom Nichols argues that expertise is characterized by training, credentials, and peer evaluation. "Every professional group and expert community," he explains, "has watchdogs, boards, accreditors, and certification authorities whose job is to police its own members and ensure not only that they live up to the standards of their own specialty, but also that their arts are practiced only by people who actually know what they're doing."[158] This does not mean that experts are always right. Historians, sociologists, political scientists, and other professionals do get it wrong. But, as a whole, experts tend to be right more often than lay people. You can self-declare your expertise as a sensitivity reader. You cannot self-declare a PhD in American history from Harvard.

When identity replaces the requirement that people know what they are talking about, and there is money to be made regardless of whether anyone knows what they are talking about, it is understandable that people will lie about their identities to make themselves look like experts. In the past few years, academia has been rocked by progressives pretending to be other races. Jessica "La Bombera" Krug, a George Washington University professor who taught courses on African history and Caribbean immigration, faked a black, Afro-Latina identity her entire career.[159] Rachel Dolezal, a white woman from Montana, pretended to be African American when she taught African American studies at Eastern Washington University.[160] Beth-Ann McLaughlin, a former Vanderbilt University professor and founder of the #MeTooSTEM movement, created a fake Native American Twitter account. McLaughlin used this fake account to praise her own work.[161] H. G. "Hache" Carrillo, a novelist and creative writing professor, was celebrated for work that "plumbed the meaning of Cuban American identity." It turns out Carrillo is not from Cuba. He is from Detroit. His family's surname is not Carrillo. It is Carroll. There are no Latinos in his family.[162]

Given the demand for "own voices" who write about their "lived experience," it is hard to imagine that other novelists, poets, playwrights, and memoirists are above this.[163] Even if racial cosplay is just a campus activity—and, given the incentives, I doubt it is—the same intellectual problem remains. To put it in perspective, if I get diagnosed with cancer today, I will not turn into an oncologist tomorrow. Having cancer does not make me an expert on cancer. Likewise, if I self-identify as a dentist tonight, I will not know anything new about root canals in the morning. I am definitely not a legitimate cardiologist if I ask my patients to sign a nondisclosure contract that prevents them from publicly criticizing my surgeries. Just as I would never let a cab driver remove a tumor from my esophagus, I would never hire Ben Carson to evaluate a children's book about the civil rights movement, Sarah Huckabee Sanders to evaluate a YA novel about women's suffrage, or Dave Rubin to tell me if my adult novel about the AIDS epidemic "got it right." Expertise is not a game of self-revelation. Nor is consulting experts an *I Spy* game of spotting people with this or that identity.

Progressives already know this. Just as they would not want Carson running the African American children's imprint at Simon and Schuster, they did not want him to be the US Secretary of Housing and Urban Development. As they correctly pointed out, being black does not make one an expert on affordable housing and housing discrimination. Notwithstanding their rhetoric, the real problem was not Carson's lack of relevant expertise. The real problem was his conservative politics. Likewise, when Candace Owens, or Coleman Hughes, or any other black American argues against reparations, one does not find liberal Twitter celebrating them as "authentic" voices who illuminate what "Black America" thinks. They save that accolade for Don Lemon and Ta-Nehisi Coates.

In the words of Erec Smith, a black professor of rhetoric and communication at York College, "When we hear the demand to 'listen to black voices,' what is usually meant is 'listen to the right black voices.'"[164] At best, progressives ignore black conservatives. They ignore black moderates, too. At worst, they accuse them of *internalized racism*—another one of the Sensitivity Era's vague watchwords that can be deployed to win any argument. Simply put, progressives reject essentialism and racial spokesmanship in service of positions they dislike.

As a quotidian example, just look at the regularly inconsistent use of the "black friend" card. On the one hand, it is acceptable for critics to say, "Black readers think this novel is racist." On the other hand, it is unacceptable for a novelist to respond, "Other black readers don't think this novel is racist." They get accused of playing the "black friend" card, which is the same card the critics play. For critics, the card is a rhetorical advantage. For the accused, it is a rhetorical disadvantage. It is another sign that they, and any black reader who likes their novel, have internalized racism.

All this said, there is a kernel of truth in essentialism. If I wanted to write a realistic novel about black Bostonians who live in low-income housing, I would talk to black Bostonians who live in low-income housing. In addition, I would read relevant ethnographies, interviews, and the like. Although personal experience is not the sine qua non of knowledge, it is not irrelevant either. Some writers who write about the experiences of other people are ignorant. Some writers show no interest in becoming less ignorant. The historical record is testament to a lot of bad literature featuring characters, neighborhoods, and plots that are more inspired by racial caricature than reality. Importantly, the history of literature is also the history of minorities being denied the means of production to tell their own stories.

There is a difference between this recognition of personal experience and an author who now believes they understand "the female experience" during the Civil War because a female sensitivity reader gave them feedback on their YA novel. When people with no expertise are hired to opine about—fill in the blank: the Civil War, "the gay experience," what black people eat for dinner, and so on—one should expect to find a lot of bullshit. To quote Harry G. Frankfurt's tempest in a teapot: "Bullshit is unavoidable whenever circumstances require someone to talk without knowing what he is talking about. Thus, the production of bullshit is stimulated whenever a person's obligations or opportunities to speak about some topic exceed his knowledge of the facts that are relevant to that topic."[165] The unfortunate reality of bullshit is compounded by social media, which incentivizes bullshit artists.

Even agents and editors whom I spoke to, who had positive experiences with sensitivity readers, are ambiguous. "You have to find sensitivity readers who are valid sensitivity readers," explained one agent, "because there are a lot of bad ones out there." According to another industry insider I interviewed, you want a sensitivity reader who can say something besides, "this doesn't match how my family was, so therefore it's wrong." But if the only thing an editor knows about a sensitivity reader is their self-identification as a black person, they might end up with a black person who compares a dinner scene in a picture book to what their family eats for dinner. Even at the highest level, decisions about who to hire are an identity crapshoot. One editor at a Big Five publisher highlighted this mix of essentialism and luck: "When I think about sensitivity readers, I kind of spiral into this whole, how do I pick a sensitivity reader? Do I have to interview them on their life experiences? If there's a character who has some trauma in their life, can you trot your trauma out for me? If the author picks, they may send it to their friend Bill. Is that the right sensitivity reader? How do you even do this? I don't know what the right thing to do is. I don't know who to pick. I feel like I'm just sort of . . . I close my eyes and I just do it. Then I just brace myself for the mistake that I've made."

Just because a person identifies as a sensitivity reader for trauma, the rural gay experience, or whatever, does not mean they have anything helpful to add. On the same note, just because a person identifies as an Own Voices novelist does not mean their novel is ipso facto more accurate, more insightful, or more important than anyone else's novel. To be blunt, it does not even mean their novel is worth reading. Writing is a craft. Like other areas of expertise, it must be mastered.

Another problem arises when agents, editors, and other industry professionals compel their authors to become Own Voices authors. As the two of them prepared to query publishers, Alberto Gullaba Jr. recalls the moment his white agent asked him to write a biographical statement to include in their proposal. The novelist reflects:

He's like, "This is great, this is great, but since you're writing about race and identity can you make sure that you include your race." I was like, "Okay." So, I write that my parents are Filipino immigrants, and that's the moment where everything changed. The record screeched to a halt. I get on the phone with the agent, and he tells me, "Hey! You're, you're not black? You're Filipino? Oh my God, we gotta get ahead of this. We gotta get ahead of this. You're gonna face a shitstorm." I remember hearing that, "Gotta get ahead of this." I remember him over the phone; he had invested all this time in this book, and I truly believe that he was protective of it.

Well, basically, I get caught up in racial compliance. It had taken ten years to get to this point writing this book, but we're at the stage where the kinds of revisions and editing I have to make are about remaining in compliance with whatever racial rules there are in the industry. The agent is telling me, "Hey we gotta swap some races around. We need to get a Filipino in this book somehow because so far it's all black. I mean, there's some mixed-race people but, you know, they're black."

So we engage in some horse trading. I'm like, "Ok, how about this character? Can I make them half Filipino? He's half Korean. Just slide in the Filipino." And he's like, "Oh no, it has to be full, and it has to be, if not Filipino, it has to be . . . you gotta choose this column of other Asian races. And you can't choose Middle Eastern." It was very precise, and I was kind of shocked hearing him. He had it all kind of plotted out. He must have the secret crib sheet for all the oppression points or what have you.

A lot of the men I grew up around were in the military, and they talk about these near-death experiences, but talking to my agent I've never heard a grown man so scared.[166]

I experienced a similar conversation. One of my interview subjects, an award-winning author, declined to answer the first question I asked them, which was about right-wing censorship. They declined to answer the second question I asked them, which was about left-wing censorship. Then they ended the interview. After, they sent me an email asking me to delete the recording, followed by another email that asked me not to reference our interview at all. If you did not hear my questions, you would think I was on the phone with a Russian dissident who realized their phone was tapped by Vladimir Putin.

Notwithstanding the ascent of Own Voices—as one editor told me, "I've been seeing Own Voices in commercial women's fiction, upmarket book club books, and that sort of thing, which I never used to see"—there are industry professionals who refuse to use the term. Some of these people used to embrace it. One senior decision-maker I spoke to, who still had it in their professional bio at the time of our interview, laughed when I pointed this out. "People just wanted something fast and easy," they told me. "But Own Voices is problematic." In the words of another person of color who works in publishing,

> We don't use Own Voices really as a term anymore. It's a bit loaded. It's kind of a double-edged sword. It is really important what the movement was doing. When you looked around at, say, gay fiction ten years ago, and you're like all of the top gay titles with gay leads are written by straight, cis people. That was a problem. Own Voices really forced a lot of publishers and agents to look very critically at those opportunities, and give those opportunities to writers writing about their own experience.
>
> But it became this weird, like, "Well, if I'm only a quarter Korean, and my lead's Korean, and, you know, say Mexican, is it Own Voices when I am not also Korean and Mexican?" It introduced all these weird nuances. And I think it kind of took away from the creative work, especially when those stories might not specifically be about the race of the character. They might just be that race.

An agent of color echoed this perspective:

> The Own Voices movement was supposed to be a positive force. Now it's morphed into this identity purity test, which can actually harm BIPOC writers, or queer authors, especially when they feel like they have to prove their identity. Or, you know, if they're a queer author who hasn't come out, being forced to do something they don't want to do to prove that their book is truly "Own Voices." It's affecting authors who feel forced against their will to identify a certain way.

During my interviews, I spoke to people who believe these kinds of identity purity tests are not just anti-intellectual, not just random, not just inconsistent, not just perplexing and weird—but also condescending. One of my interview subjects, a neurodivergent gay writer with a disability, explains what it is like to realize that people only care about what you write insofar as you fit their conception of a "marginalized writer": "I remember speaking to an audience and people saw me as a white man. I remember telling this audience that I'm a gay man with a disability and, immediately, I sensed how different this audience became, even how they came up to me and talked to me afterwards. If I walk into an audience and say, 'I'm a gay man with a disability, who's neurodivergent,' why should that bring applause? I don't get it. Why wouldn't you respect me before?"

Other authors are glad they did not come of age in the Sensitivity Era. David Sedaris, a Generation X liberal who has penned more than one *New York Times* bestseller, reflects:

> When I was growing up, there weren't any books about gay people in libraries. You had to read *The Sun Also Rises* or *The Great Gatsby*, and I had to relate to those characters some way. And I would think, *Well, I'm a human, and so is this person.* I think people want to see a mirror; they want to see their reflection in a book, and I feel so fortunate in a way to have come up when I did because it taught me to relate to people simply because they were human, and I would read the book and I would say, "Gosh, I've felt lonely; I can relate to this," or "I've felt fortunate; I can relate to this," or "I've been left out; I can relate to this." I didn't need the person to be my age and be gay and twenty-two and to have dark brown hair and one eyebrow. I learned to relate simply because they were human beings.[167]

As the next chapter argues, the fetish for identity, the death of expertise, and the proliferation of bullshit undergirds a literary culture where every tweeter, Goodreads reviewer, and Tumblr blogger believes that they are a "cultural ambassador," an erudite book critic—even when they do not read the books they criticize—and a righteous guardian of children and young adults. In this landscape, literary criticism looks less like the criticism one finds in professional journals such as *PMLA* and *American Literature*. It looks more like the rituals of social degradation that fascinate sociologists, social psychologists, and moral philosophers. That is, it looks a lot like a moral panic.

2 The Behavior of the Sensitivity Era

Folk Devils in the Past

In *Moral Panics: The Social Construction of Deviance*, sociologists Erich Goode and Nachman Ben-Yehuda define their core concept: "The *moral panic* is a scare about a threat or supposed threat from deviants or 'folk devils,' a category of people who, presumably, engage in evil practices and are blamed for menacing society's culture, way of life, and central values. The word 'scare' implies that the concern over, fear of, or hostility toward the folk devil is out of proportion to the actual threat that is claimed."[1]

As a case in point, consider the moral panic over comics after World War II. In the first two decades of the twentieth century, comics were relatively benign.[2] In strips such as *Mickey Mouse* and *Mutt and Jeff*, characters took part in playful but harmless antics. By the time *Superman* burst on to the scene in 1938, comics depicted violence. Whereas some adults were concerned, a few adults had an outsize influence. In 1940, literary critic Sterling North unleashed the first national attack on comic books in the pages of *Chicago Daily News*.[3] Describing comic books as "a poison" and "a strain on young eyes and young nervous systems," North accused parents of "criminal negligence." According to *The Daily*, millions requested permission to reprint his article. It was a call to arms.

After the war, the concern over comic books escalated. The seminal moment came in 1948, when psychiatrist Frederic Wertham delivered a talk at a convention of psychiatrists. In his talk, he blamed comic books for juvenile delinquency. A few years later, he published *The Seduction of the Innocent*, which was lauded by sociologist C. Wright Mills and other scholars.[4] Newspapers and magazines, including *Time* and *Look*, added their voices to the burgeoning chorus. In the words of the *New Republic*, "Every hour spent in reading comics is an hour in which all inner growth is stopped." According to *Vogue* editor Marya Manness, comics were "the greatest intellectual narcotic on the market."[5] For *Saturday Review of Literature's* Mason Brown, they were "the marijuana of the nursery" and "the bane of the bassinet."[6] Articles like "Now Ban This Filth That Poisons Our Children," remind us that comic books were once considered a threat to public health.[7]

In 1953, the US Senate formed a subcommittee to investigate juvenile delinquency. A year later, Wertham and other experts were called on to explain the connection between comic books and crime. As a result of the hearing, publishers self-imposed a code of standards under the Comics Code Authority. The code "restricted sex and violence, forbade the criticism of religion, the use of slang words and a long list of unacceptable practices."[8] If a comic book had a seal of approval on the cover, it meant that it was "safe for young readers" (figure 2.1).[9] As Amy Kiste Nyberg, author of *Seal of Approval: The History of the Comics Code*, reflects: "There was never to be any disrespect for established authority and social institutions. Good always triumphed over evil, and if evil had to be shown, it was only in order to deliver a moral message."[10] At a press conference later that year, the head of the prepublication censorship office explained that they had already excised material from thousands of comic books.[11]

Interestingly, all five people brought in as censors were women. This was "tied in with notions of motherhood and the fact that in postwar America, caring for children was primarily a mother's responsibility."[12] In addition, women were deemed more emotionally sensitive and, therefore, more capable of identifying offensive material. To borrow the language of the US Senate, they were best suited to "prevent our nation's young from being harmed from crime and horror comics."[13] For its part, the Canadian government did not allow anyone to publish crime comics. In Britain, Parliament passed the Children and Young Person's Harmful Publication Act. According to this act, no one could distribute picture books or magazines that "would tend to corrupt a child or young person."[14] The British were especially concerned with "American-style" comic books like *Tales from the Crypt* and *Haunt of Fear*.

In addition to sex and violence, this moral crusade was concerned about how realistic these comic books were. For example, Wertham protested "that Superman's ability to fly and leap over tall buildings violated the law

Figure 2.1
Comics Code Authority Seal of Approval. Source: Comic Book Legal Defense Fund.

of physics, misleading children."[15] Similarly, the Comics Code Authority ensured that women were "drawn realistically without exaggeration of any physical qualities."[16] In the words of the *Hartford Courant*, comic books were an "intellectual opiate" that "violate[d] the tenets of good taste," and they were a "cancer which is eating at the vitals of young America."[17] In short, authors and illustrators were not just the progenitors of juvenile crime. They were not just liars who mislead children about physics, women, and everything else in the world. They were also the source of an immoral disease that had to be eradicated.

Like the government in Ray Bradbury's 1953 dystopian classic *Fahrenheit 451*, these governments acted in response to public pressure.[18] Everyone from women's organizations to the Communist Party and the Catholic

Church blamed comic books for juvenile delinquency. Other groups, like the National Organization for Decent Literature, were formed during this moral panic.[19] Just as this broad coalition enacted pressure at the legislative level, it also enacted pressure at the personal level. A number of authors and illustrators censored themselves to avoid what sociologist Harold Garfinkel calls "degradation ceremonies."[20] In plain English, they did not want to be stigmatized by the public. Even in the absence of state censorship, the reputational costs were real. As Nyberg describes it, "The decency crusades aroused little protest in specific cities where they were conducted. Since they were usually organized by civic and religious leaders in the community, few would speak out against their work. Also, most adults were not familiar with the content of comic books and were willing to accept the evaluations of the decency crusaders without question, or simply did not care. But perhaps most important, the issue was carefully constructed as one concerning the welfare of children, rather than being a censorship issue."[21]

During this period, many publishers went out of business.[22] "Between 1954 and 1956, more than half of the comic books on the newsstands disappeared."[23] According to sociologist Karen Sternheimer, this moral crusade "all but ended horror comics."[24] The authors and illustrators who remained in print were "forced into essentially infantile patterns" to avoid controversy, as the crusade "sanitized the literary creativity, artistic ingenuity, and social commentary that these publications contained."[25] Yet, like other moral crusades, it, too, came to an end. As the number of TV sets increased tenfold between 1950 and 1960, adults turned their attention to the latest perceived threat to young people.[26] The folk devils were no longer authors and illustrators but those who created images that moved.

Folk Devils in the Present

Alongside the emergence of Twitter in 2006 and Goodreads in 2007, a new moral crusade has taken shape. Like the moral crusade over comic books, this crusade accuses children's and YA literature of harming and corrupting its readers. It accuses literature of telling lies. Above all, it believes literature written for young people is responsible for racism, Islamophobia, and every other intolerance. Similar to the 1950s, the current crusade hopes to purify children's and YA literature.

As one of innumerable examples, consider the response to *Blood Heir*. Penguin Random House's blurb for Amélie Wen Zhao's debut YA novel reads: "In a world where the princess is the monster, oppression is blind to skin color, and good and evil exist in shades of gray . . . comes a dark Anastasia retelling that explores love, loss, fear, and divisiveness and how ultimately it is our choices that define who we are."[27] L. L. McKinney, another YA author, screenshotted this blurb for her 10,000-plus followers on Twitter. Above the screenshot, she exclaimed: "someone explain this to me. EXPLAIN IT RIGHT THE FUQ NOW."[28] Apparently, because the real world is not blind to skin color, it means Zhao's novel perpetuates "color-blind racism." Because Zhao is an author of color, it also means that she has "internalized racism." Like *Superman*, *Blood Heir* is not true. It is harmful to young people because it is not true.

Other people accused Zhao of other transgressions. For example, *Blood Heir* is set in the fantastical country of Cyrilia, where human trafficking and slave labor are common. In some respects, the country is inspired by Russia. From the perspective of some people, this, too, is a problem. "[R]acist ass writers, like Amélie Wen Zhao, who literally take Black narratives and force it into Russia when that shit NEVER happened in history," explains one crusader, "you're going to be held accountable."[29] Aside from the fact that Cyrilia is not Russia, and the other fact that Russia has its own history of slavery, it is unclear why fact should be a prerequisite for fiction.[30] It is even less clear why this debut author should be publicly branded as a racist. In response to the torrent of criticism, Zhao decided not to publish *Blood Heir*. In an apology posted to Twitter, she apologized for the "pain" and "harm" her unpublished novel had caused.[31]

One will have a hard time locating a teenager who participated in this degradation ceremony. For example, when one searches "teenager" in Goodreads's archive of 1,753 reviews of *Blood Heir* written in English, just one review is written by a user who identifies as a "teenager." In their review, they address the criticism that *Blood Heir* promotes human trafficking: "As a teenager in the precise target audience of *Blood Heir*, I cannot understand why *adults* do not realize that just because the author does not go out of her way to say that, 'Hey, human trafficking sucks and Ana [the protagonist] is a naive moron for not realizing it' does not mean the author supports the subject being represented." Below their dig at adults who panicked about

Blood Heir's representation of human trafficking, this teenager includes a *Spiderman* meme that says, "Kinda obvious."

Whereas *Blood Heir* was condemned for being racist, untrue, and on the side of human trafficking and other injustices, *A Place for Wolves* was condemned for being too true. As reported in *Slate*, the catalyst appears to be a viral review posted to Goodreads.[32] The review opens with the following sentences: "I have to be absolutely fucking honest here, everybody. I've never been so disgusted in my life."[33] The reviewer is disgusted that Jackson's villain in this story about the Kosovo War is an Albanian Muslim because Albanian Muslims were victims of Serbian war crimes. But Jackson did not want to write a simple moral tale. In his author's note, he explains: "All Albanians were not good. All Serbians were not bad, and as one can see, characters and people, can (and usually do) hold both alignments within them. Good people make bad choices. Bad people make good ones. And most people are somewhere in the middle."[34] However, according to this self-published Goodreads review, it is "too early" to look at the complexities. If published, Jackson's debut novel will "harm" the "real teens" whom this adult woman purports to represent.

Two months after Jackson went after *Blood Heir*, he canceled *A Place for Wolves*. In an apology letter posted to Twitter, he, too, apologizes to those he "hurt" with his unpublished work of fiction.[35] Jackson was not the only YA author who apologized. In another Goodreads review, Heidi Heilig praised *A Place for Wolves*. However, after the degradation ceremony erupted on Goodreads and Twitter, she hastily rewrote her review. In her new review, she apologizes to those she "hurt" with her first review.[36] This new review reads like other YA reviews that have been rewritten in the past few years. For example, *Kirkus Reviews* retracted and then rewrote a starred review of *American Heart*.[37] Although their reviewer loved Laura Moriarty's debut YA novel, some tweeters did not. *Kirkus* was bombarded with complaints.[38] Accordingly, the review was rewritten with their reviewer's help, and the star was removed. In the new review, it is "problematic" that one of Moriarty's Muslim characters is "seen only through the white protagonist's filter." Perhaps these editors and their reviewer had a moral revelation. Or perhaps they did not want to be publicly shamed, too.

In any case, finding a copy of the original review is as difficult as finding an unedited newspaper in *1984*. "Day by day and almost minute by minute," writes Orwell, "the past was brought up to date." No "expression of opinion, which conflicted with the needs of the moment, [was] ever allowed to remain on record."[39] After Moriarty posted both reviews to her Facebook page, illuminating the disjunction between them, *Kirkus* repeatedly called her publisher to demand that she take them down.[40] Yet, in doublespeak language straight out of Oceania, *Kirkus*'s public statement about the removal "celebrates[s] the free exchange of opinions and ideas."[41] The rewrite itself is not described as a decision that raises real problems for literary freedom in the era of social media outrage. It is described as an edit to provide "clarity" and "additional insights."[42]

Despite all their talk about celebrating minority voices, *Kirkus* decided that edits would be made before they contacted the Muslim woman of color who wrote the starred review.[43] Because *Kirkus* is worried about the "dangers" of literature, this was a real emergency.[44] Like Big Brother, they had to act fast to protect the public from harm. A few days after the starred review was published, it disappeared like crimethink in Orwell's novel. In the Sensitivity Era, the only Own Voices that matter are those that regurgitate goodthink.

There is nothing unique about the response to *Blood Heir*, *A Place for Wolves*, or *American Heart*. Before Keira Drake's *The Continent* was published, it, too, provoked a moral panic on Twitter. The panic spread to Tumblr where a blogger encouraged people to take action:

> There is an incredibly racist upcoming book that you guys need to be aware of. It's called The Continent and perpetuates extremely offensive stereotypes of people of color. Justina Ireland posted a summary and I screenshotted so you guys can see. . . . It's VERY important that we readers are vocal about our dislike and make sure that this doesn't happen again. The author received a HUGE marketing budget, a seven city tour if I recall correctly which hardly ever happens and means that they assume this book will sell like crazy. If it does, it will affect real lives. . . . SO please. Share and/or rate this book on Goodreads, don't buy it to "see for yourself." Don't support racism.[45]

If a reader wants to purchase Keira Drake's debut YA novel to form their own interpretation of it, like a thinking person, it means they support racism. If, however, they rate an unpublished novel based on a short Tumblr post and some screenshotted tweets, like an unthinking person, it means they are against racism. What one agent of color described to me as the "contingent of people taking issue—whether they read the book or not" is what antiracism looks like on Twitter, Tumblr, and Goodreads. When "real lives" are on the line, there is no time for reading. There is no time for thinking. Above all, there is no time for different interpretations. Like the moral crusade over comic books, there is only time to damage a writer's reputation.

This involves more than tweets, Tumblr posts, and Goodreads reviews. As Drake explains in the *New York Times*, "an organized campaign to find, attack and harass online anyone who had ever given my book a good review" took place.[46] In this context, the hastily rewritten reviews of *A Place for Wolves* and *American Heart* make sense. At the same time, Drake was sent messages filled with "hatred" and "disgust." One messenger even suggested that she kill herself. Like the firemen in *Fahrenheit 451*, other people burned advance reader copies of *The Continent*. As one Goodreads reviewer puts it, in language that reads like a verbatim statement from the fire department in Bradbury's novel, Drake's work "is really not fit for public consumption, not when it brings more harm than enjoyment."[47]

Another adds, "If THE CONTINENT is indeed published, it will only cause harm."[48] This white reviewer lambasts white readers who want to read the book themselves. "It is our responsibility to listen to people of color when they say representation is inaccurate, harmful, hurtful, racist, stereotypical, or all of the above," she goes on, "we have no right to question that." As John McWhorter argues in his latest book, *Woke Racism: How a New Religion Has Betrayed Black America*, this kind of anti-intellectualism is itself racist.[49] People of color are wrong just like any other group of people. To think that they should not be corrected, or even questioned, like any other group of people is to treat them as something not quite human. Because it matters to these crusaders, it should be noted that McWhorter is black. It should also be noted that he is not the only black person irritated by white liberals who can "no longer remain silent" and who see themselves as "allies" to people like himself. Above all, there were people of color who did not find this book inaccurate, harmful, hurtful, racist, stereotypical, or all of the above.

But this white woman does not just speak for readers of color, like McWhorter's daughters, who will only be harmed by *The Continent*. She also speaks for white readers, who will only be corrupted by *The Continent*. "And should their white peers also read this book, what harmful things will they come to believe?" If this woman actually wanted to answer her own question, she would spend less time self-publishing her opinion on Goodreads—currently, she has rated over 250 books—and more time asking young people what they think. That would be more of a contribution than yet another apocalyptic book review filled with empty calls to action—"we must listen" and "we must do better"—that serve no discernible purpose aside from signaling her own virtue to other moral crusaders on Goodreads.

Many crusaders acknowledge they never read the books they crusade against, nor do they intend to ever read these books, so it is important to recognize the distinction between "information cascades" and "conformity cascades." In an information cascade, "imperfectly or entirely uninformed people accept a rumor that they hear from others, and as more and more people accept that rumor, the informational signal becomes very strong, and it is hard for the rest of us to resist it, even it is false." This cascade is compounded by the "confidence heuristic," which predicts that people are more likely to follow those who are confident in their views; people assume that confident individuals are more reliable sources of information.[50] To wed both concepts together, one might hear a rumor about an incredibly racist book about to published, and that rumor might be delivered by someone who speaks without the shadow of a doubt. In a conformity cascade, "people appear to accept rumors, not because they actually believe them," but "because people do not want to face social sanctions."[51] On #Kidlit and #YATwitter, information cascades and conformity cascades overlap. Once they start, they can be difficult to stop.[52]

The response to the revised version of *The Continent* suggests a lot about the limits of revision in the Sensitivity Era. To be clear, Drake listened to her critics.[53] She removed the words "primitive," "native," and "savage" from her novel. She removed "almond-shaped eyes" and other descriptions that, according to her critics, made her characters read like stereotypes. She changed the race of her protagonist to avoid the "the trope of the dark-skinned aggressor or white savior narrative." She replaced a wall with towers to avoid triggering people who were reminded of Donald Trump's wall. In a move that would have satisfied the censors at the Comics Codes Authority, her revised novel even presents "a less militaristic approach to resolving conflict than in her previous version."

Yet, when one reads the criticism of her revised novel, one would think it was the same exact novel. For example, a one-star review on Goodreads explains:

> edit 2/19/18: (so apparently all those rewrites keira drake was supposed to be doing didn't fix a Damn Thing. yall. . . . . if this book was a person id fight it in

a Wal-Mart parking lot.) It's racist trash, and I'm getting really sick and tired of my genre being fucking corrupted by bullshit like this—A black groundskeeper, a pack of "savage" men obviously based on First Nations people, and a wise, calm ninja "with almond eyes." And, of course, the lily white MC. Look, as a white writer and critic, it is my moral obligation to tell the rest of y'all that this is not acceptable and, in fact, is just bad writing. So, you're being a terrible person and terrible at your job. . . . Listen better. Writer [sic] better. Be better.[54]

Aside from the fact that this reviewer ironically postures herself as a white savior who is morally obligated to talk shit on Goodreads, her barely literate review is not even true. To the contrary, it is a perfect example of "biased assimilation," which "refers to the fact that people process new information in a biased fashion," and they "may not easily give up their beliefs, especially when they have a strong emotional commitment to those beliefs."[55]

Other reviewers are less interested in parking lot brawls outside Wal-Mart and more interested in Drake's thought process behind her revisions. "Her decision to give Vaela that ancestry feels to me like a shield that gives Drake a way to say that this is not a White savior story," writes Debbie Reese, who founded American Indians in Children's Literature (the website *Kirkus Reviews* consults), in her own one-star review.[56] In this psychoanalytic trial, which is supposed to be a book review, Reese concludes that "Drake is trying to be a savior," and "her editor is enabling that motivation." More bizarrely, Reese wonders if Drake has ever performed genealogical research on herself, as if a subscription to Ancestry.com is the prerequisite for writing or, in this case, rewriting a fantasy novel. As one agent I interviewed laments, "A reader has the choice of reading or not reading, but not ruling over what gets written."

At the end of Nathaniel Hawthorne's *Scarlet Letter*, Hester Prynne learned that some stigmas disappear. At the end of *The Continent* controversy, Drake learned that other stigmas never disappear. In the world of YA literature, "racist trash" remains "racist trash." And "terrible" authors remain "terrible" authors. Even when an author confesses to their literary sins and repents, as Drake did—"Oh, my God. Oh, it's so true"[57]—there is no absolution. Attempts to appease the grand inquisitors of YA literature provoke new accusations, investigations, and verdicts of guilt. When Drake reflects on her response to the first wave of criticism, "I was embarrassed and ashamed,"[58] one is reminded of Prynne's predicament. "Shame, Despair, Solitude! These had been her teachers—stern and wild ones."[59] Unfortunately for Drake, her shame taught her nothing about writing because "all those rewrites [she] was supposed to be doing didn't fix a Damn Thing." In the Sensitivity Era, a scarlet "R" (for racist) never disappears.

In his classic book on the subject, *Stigma: Notes on the Management of Spoiled Identity*, sociologist Erving Goffman reminds readers of the etymology of "stigma": "The Greeks, who were apparently strong on visual aids, originated the term *stigma* to refer to bodily signs designed to expose something unusual and bad about the moral status of the signifier. The signs were cut or burnt into the body and advertised that the bearer was a slave, a criminal, or a traitor—a blemished person, ritually polluted, to be avoided, especially in public places." To be sure, no one burned Drake, Zhao, or these other authors. But, years later, the first page of Google will continue to advertise their polluted moral status to the world. With articles like "She Pulled Her Debut Book When Critics Found It Racist," who needs a physical scarlet letter? As Goffman notes, the term "stigma" is "still widely used in something like the original sense, but it is applied more to the disgrace itself than to the bodily evidence of it."[60]

In this context, it is worthwhile to consider the phenomena of "trumping up" and "piling on." According to moral philosophers Justin Tosi and Brandon Warmke, trumping up occurs when a person makes "spurious claims about a moral problem where in fact there is none," just as "a prosecutor might trump up false charges against a suspect." Piling on occurs "when someone contributes to public moral discourse to do nothing more than proclaim [their] agreement with something that has already been said."[61] In respect to spurious claims about a moral problem where in fact there is none, *The Continent* is still treated as "racist trash," even though its author removed the material that made it "racist trash." Likewise, a moral problem exists because Zhao reportedly wrote about Russian slavery in *Blood Heir* (she did not), when "that shit NEVER happened in history" (it did). In all these examples, the idea that there is a moral problem that needs to be addressed depends on the hundreds of likes and retweets that pile on to contribute nothing more than moral agreement. Deviance is a social construct.[62]

The field of children's and YA literature illustrates the kind of power discussed by Michel Foucault. In *Discipline and Punish: The Birth of the Prison*, Foucault examines Jeremy Bentham's panopticon. As a prison, the panopticon involves a watchtower surrounded by cells. The prisoners never know if they are watched or not. As Foucault puts it, "The surveillance is permanent in its effects, even if it discontinuous in its action." The panopticon is a model for power, applicable outside prisons, which appeals to those "who take pleasure in spying and punishing." In the case of Twitter, Tumblr, and Goodreads, authors and reviewers never know who is watching them. They never know where the next punishment will come from. However, they know that they could be next, and so they watch themselves, adapting their behavior to avoid punishment. "It is possible to intervene at any moment," reflects Foucault, and "the constant pressure acts even before the offences, mistakes or crimes have been committed."[63]

American crime fiction writer Patricia Cornwell, whose work has topped the New York Times bestseller list, describes what the pressure feels like at her desk: "I deal with this all the time, like you can't say a vehicle is 'manned.' It has to be 'crewed.' I spent about forty-five minutes yesterday trying to figure out the politically correct way to refer to people who fish for a living. Can't call them 'fishermen.' So I called them fisherfolks. Everybody's so worried about offending everybody. I mean, when are they going to say you can't call them black holes anymore? What will it be? A nonwhite hole?"

Cornwell, a lesbian who alienated many of her readers with her criticism of Donald Trump's political campaign in 2016—which exploited "fear of what happens if you had more same sex marriage and if women have rights over their own reproduction and their own bodies . . . it's craziness"—also alienated some of her readers with these comments.[64] In some cases, the political correctness panopticon ends a manuscript before it can even be criticized for using gender-exclusive language like "manned" or "fishermen."[65] E. E. Charlton-Trujillo's "When We Was Fierce" and Alexandra Duncan's "Ember Days," two more targets of prepublication panic, were never even published.

The political correctness panopticon is not limited to books, authors, and reviewers who "harm" people with their reviews. Trumping up and piling on circumscribe the most anodyne interactions. For example, when Katie Couric interviewed Dhonielle Clayton, she introduced Clayton as a sensitivity reader, because their interview was about sensitivity reading. The crime: she did not mention that Clayton is also a New York Times bestselling author. After, Couric was called out on Twitter. In the various threads, moral crusaders chimed in to express their moral disgust. Tweets in a thread started by New York Times bestselling YA author Angie Thomas include the following: "grrrrrr!," "ugh ugh ugh ugh UGH," "uggggggggh seriously?! not okay," and "haven't seen it yet but argh."[66] As utterly typical examples of public discourse in the era, the first tweet comes from a literary agent, the second comes from an author, the third comes from an author who is also a professor, and the fourth comes from another *New York Times* bestselling YA author who acknowledges that they did not even watch the interview.

Together, the tweets are reminiscent of the Two Minutes Hate in *1984*. During this ritual, the image of a social deviant is projected onto the screen. As Orwell describes it, "There were hisses here and there among the audience. The little sandy-haired woman gave a squeak of mingled fear and disgust. . . . The horrible thing about the Two Minutes Hate was not that one was obliged to act a part, but that it was impossible to avoid joining in. . . . And yet the rage that one felt was an abstract, undirected emotion which could be switched from one object to another like the flame of a blowlamp."[67]

On #YATwitter, the rituals of social degradation are also short in duration. One minute a crusader tweets about how disgusting and dangerous an author is. The next minute they tweet about a new recipe for kombucha. On Wednesday night, Katie Couric is the face on the screen. By Friday morning, it is someone else. Just as the characters in Orwell's novel are pressured to leap from their seats in outrage, no one wants to be accused of not participating in #YATwitter's Two Minutes Hate. To use one of the Sensitivity Era's most popular slogans, "Silence equals violence."

In the absence of silence, we get "duckspeak." As Orwell describes it, simple syntax and guttural sounds allow people "to spray forth the correct opinions as automatically as a machine gun spraying forth bullets."[68] This language of moral judgment, which linguist Roger Fowler and his colleagues describe as the language of "less thought and less effort,"[69] is the perfect language for Twitter. Grrrrrr, ugh, uggggggggh, and argh aside, more eloquent tweeters add that Couric's omission "feels nothing but intentional," and that even if it is unintentional, "intent is irrelevant when harm is done."[70] The degradation ceremony does not just render mistakes inconceivable; it renders them irrelevant, too.[71] As another example of the ad hominem moral criticism that pervades this community, and the psychological phenomenon known as "hostile attribution bias," Couric was transformed from an empathetic journalist—and her interview is nothing but empathetic—into a hostile journalist who secretly conspired to harm Clayton.[72] Like Zhao, Jackson, and Heilig, Couric hastily apologized.

Other YA and children's books have been subjected to different kinds of social degradation. After one blogger and bookseller declared that *The Black Witch* is "the most dangerous, offensive book I have ever read," crusaders emailed Harlequin Teen to cancel publication of Laurie Forest's debut YA novel.[73] They also organized a campaign to leave one-star reviews. Many of these reviewers acknowledge they never read the book. Nonetheless, their campaign tanked *The Black Witch*'s Goodreads rating to an embarrassing 1.71. Other crusaders demanded that *Kirkus* retract their starred review of this book, too. At the heart of the controversy were the prejudices of Forest's fictional characters. Yet, as other readers pointed out, just because a novel includes prejudiced characters does not mean the novel is prejudiced. To the contrary, Forest's novel is about a protagonist who questions the beliefs that permeate her stratified society. As one early review put it, the book is "an uncompromising condemnation of prejudice and injustice." In contrast to the moral crusaders, other reviewers claimed *The Black Witch* was too preachy.

For their part, adults who hated *A Birthday Cake for George Washington* signed a Change.org petition that asked Amazon to remove Ramin Ganeshram and Vanessa Brantley-Newton's picture book from their website.[74] In response, Scholastic pulled the book from distribution. After this success, the petitioners turned their attention to *A Fine Dessert*, another picture book about confections that, apparently, needed to be censored, too. During that crusade, author Emily Jenkins took to the *Reading While White* blog to confess, apologize, and publicly donate her author fee to WNDB as an act of "reparations."[75]

These "vile," "dangerous," and "absolutely disgusting" picture books were targeted for their "whitewashed" representations of slaves—specifically, they depict slaves who smile as they prepare food for their masters. Although the criticism of these books is more reasonable than the criticism of other books, it still relies on an inflated idea of harm and a condescending view of young people. This is the view that young readers are incapable of critical engagement with a flawed book; therefore, the book must be censored. It is also condescending to all the parents, K–12 teachers, and other adults who can read or teach a book while discussing its strengths and weaknesses.

As one Amazon reviewer puts it, "My daughter and I had a really interesting discussion as a result of this book that ended with her asking some really important questions about treating others fairly. It led to a great discussion that I don't think would have been brought up without the book."[76] This reviewer, like many others—*A Birthday Cake for George Washington* has 3.9 out of 5 stars on Amazon—thinks the material could have been handled better. But they do not think that this book about Washington's slave Hercules "glamorizes" slavery or that it needs to be pulled from distribution. If Amazon had removed this book from its website, this review would have disappeared down the Orwellian memory hole, too. Another reviewer adds:

> As an African American mother of 2 who has read a great deal about African American history, I found the book well-written, responsible, and culturally sensitive. . . . We need to ask ourselves why the image of a happy slave bothers us so much. Were slaves happy that they were not free? Of course not. Were slaves capable of experiencing joy at creating something that they were highly praised for such as a wonderful meal or a delicious birthday cake? Absolutely. Why not? To deny them the right to experience joy, is to deny them humanity in a similar way that the institution of slavery does. We should be teaching our children about the complexities of slavery and the intricate relationships between slaves and masters. We would like to think it was as simple as slaves hated their masters because they denied them freedom. But if you look at history and read the stories, the slave narratives, the literature and poetry from the time, you might find that it was not quite that simple.[77]

Yet simplicity is the grist of moral panic. A hashtag like #SlaveryWithASmile cannot convey the same level of nuance as this review. But it can go viral.

For her part, historian Ramin Ganeshram criticized the "over-joviality" of *A Birthday Cake for George Washington*'s illustrations, and she agreed that *A Fine Dessert* had been "rightly criticized for similar reasons."[78] But she took issue with other criticism: "I've spent hundreds of hours and pored through thousands of pages to understand Hercules and his world. . . . To say that Hercules couldn't have done certain things or lived a certain way because others who suffered under the criminal institution of slavery did not, is simply not historically true."[79] However, historical truth is irrelevant to presentism, which conjures essentialist ideas about the past and those who lived through it.

At the end of the day, this picture book provoked a mixed reaction from parents and teachers. If anything, that is a reason to read it. It is also a reason to read the criticism. As a case in point, one Amazon reviewer read both the book and the reviews to her seven-year-old.[80] If the petition against *A Birthday Cake for George Washington* had been a success, their review would have disappeared, too.

Like the 1950s, today's crusaders do not view their petitions as censorship. As they explain, people can buy books like *A Birthday Cake for George Washington* from other bookstores if Amazon removes them. The books are not banned by the government. But if book censorship is about rendering books inaccessible to interested readers, then the difference between Amazon censorship and government censorship is more semantical than practical. If Ganeshram's book had been published in 1994, the year Jeff Bezos founded Amazon, a petition targeting his website would be as relatively unimpactful as a petition targeting any small bookstore. However, in the Sensitivity Era, Amazon is *the* epicenter of the literary marketplace. As one editor at a Big Five publisher explains,

> Historically, so much of Amazon's rise in the book space is because they were very aggressively undercutting the book prices of all booksellers everywhere. Amazon has historically been taking a lot of losses on their books just to try and put a lot of other competitors out of business. People are like "Why would I buy this book in this independent bookstore for $22.99 when I can go on Amazon and get it for $11.99?" That is a problem.
>
> At the same time what Amazon has done that's great is they have really strong international infrastructure for delivery. So there are probably cities, countries where maybe they wouldn't have a bookstore, but they can get Amazon. That enables them to continue purchasing books, which I think is great. I will probably self-publish my first book on Amazon.

As this editor suggests, Amazon is not just the juggernaut controlling the market; it is the access point for readers who otherwise do not have access to the books they want. Against a background of shuttered bookstores and public libraries, Amazon is central. Even Borders could not compete. In 2011, the chain's last four hundred stores closed their doors, too.[81]

When Amazon removes a book in response to public pressure—as it did when crusaders accused Ryan T. Anderson's *When Harry Became Sally* of "dangerous" transphobia—it is not just a problem for the author. It is a problem for any reader who relies on Amazon for their books. This problem is especially salient during distribution crises, such as during the COVID-19 pandemic, which immobilized other booksellers. According to one of my interview subjects, a former Amazon higher-up, access to books is the company's biggest contribution to literary culture. Not everyone has access to in-person bookstores, public libraries, and the like. Amazon's reach is omnipotent. As one agent reflected at the end of our interview, "I would dream of doing a book that doesn't get sold on Amazon, but that's simply impossible now. It's a scary thing to think about. We sort of have to bow down to Amazon because that's where people buy their books." And Amazon, as the case of Anderson's book illustrates, will bow down to moral crusaders.[82]

Even public libraries, which depend on bipartisan support from taxpayers, have buckled at the knees. In March 2021, *The Adventures of Ook and Gluk* was pulled from bookstores and library shelves. With swiftness, Scholastic "removed the book from its websites, stopped processing orders for it and sought a return of all inventory,"[83] after a Change.org petition accused the book of literary crimes as different as the inclusion of a "'Kung Fu master' wearing what's purported to be a traditional-style Tang coat" and "a storyline that has the Kung Fu master rescued by the non-Asian protagonists using their Kung Fu skills (despite the fact that they were taught said skills from the supposed master)."[84] In a moral panic, institutions have to act fast. Even the author, Dav Pilkey, said he was "working to remove existing copies from retail and library shelves." "I hope that you, my readers, will forgive me," Pilkey went on, "I pledge to do better."[85]

In another textbook example of a single adult purporting to mind-read how every single child will interpret a book, the petition's author reflects: "While it is appreciated that they are pulling the book from retailers, this is not enough. The damage has been done. Every child who has read this book has been conditioned to accept this racist imagery as 'okay' or even funny."[86] Echoing the crusade over comic books, this crusade relies on adults with telepathic powers—we might call them "child whisperers"—to illuminate the "damage" that books do to children.

That same month, six Dr. Seuss books were pulled from publication and public libraries after they, too, were declared harmful. "In the 1950s, cars did not have seat belts. Now, we recognize that as dangerous—so, cars have seat belts. In the 1950s, lots of books recycled racist caricature. Now, Random House is recognizing this as dangerous," explains English professor Philip Nel in his interview with *Reuters*.[87] If *Reuters* had quoted Captain Beatty in *Fahrenheit 451*, who believes "a book is a loaded gun in the house next door,"[88] would anyone know the difference? According to moral crusaders, the problem is not offensive books. The problem is books that undermine public safety. In the Sensitivity Era, there is no distinction between the two.

Like the era of comic book censorship, there is no absence of a media circus to fuel this adult-driven panic over children's and YA literature. In the words of media studies scholar David Buckingham, "Journalists, media pundits, self-appointed guardians of public morality—and increasingly academics and politicians—are incessantly called on to pronounce on the dangers of the media for children."[89]

Authors and illustrators also deliver ominous proclamations. As a case in point, consider Christopher Myers's call to arms in the *Horn Book*. An industry veteran, Myers produced a finalist for the National Book Award, a Caldecott Honor Book, and a Coretta Scott King Book Award winner. In 2021, he delivered the prestigious Charlotte Zolotow Lecture, orchestrated by the Cooperative Children's Book Center at the University of Wisconsin–Madison. Before that, he was a featured speaker at the Children's Literature Association conference and an honored speaker at a WNDB event. Today, he runs his own imprint at Random House Children's Books. By any measure, he is one of the most influential voices in literature for young people.

In his *Horn Book* article, Myers suggests that Trayvon Martin might still be alive if George Zimmerman had read the right children's books. "If the man who killed Trayvon Martin had read *The Snowy Day* as a kid, would it have been as easy for him to see a seventeen-year-old in a hoodie, pockets full of rainbow candies and sweet tea, as a threat? What might have been different if images of round-headed Peter and his red hood and his snow angels were already dancing in his head?"[90] In the 1950s, Fredric Wertham and his moral crusade linked comic books to violent crime. In retrospect, their crusade looks idiotic. Yet, aside from the emphasis on race (*The Snowy Day* is about a black protagonist), who can distinguish Myers's take on violent crime from Wertham's take in *The Seduction of the Innocent*? Seventy years later, children's literature is once again the source of, and the solution to, violence.

In many ways, Myers's rhetoric resembles advertising rhetoric. In his classic essay, "Advertising: The Magic System," Raymond Williams argues: "We have a cultural pattern in which the objects are not enough but must be validated, if only in fantasy, by association with social and personal meanings. . . . The short description of the pattern we have is *magic*."[91] Axe Body Spray smells pleasant, and it can turn you into a guy who attracts beautiful women. Air Jordan sneakers look nice, and they can make you fly through the sky like Michael Jordan. *The Snowy Day* is an entertaining picture book, and it can prevent murder. If you, too, believe Trayvon Martin might still be alive if little Zimmerman had read the right books, then you should mail a check to Myers's "Make Me a World" imprint. Unlike books from other imprints, which publish books as dangerous as cars without seatbelts, his books prevent crime.

To reiterate, many books have problems. We should discuss them. We should debate them. We should also recognize their strengths. If someone tells you what a story is about, they might be right. "If they tell you that that is *all* the story is about," reflects novelist Neil Gaiman in his introduction to the sixtieth anniversary edition of *Fahrenheit 451*, "they are very definitely wrong."[92] As progressive author and grandmother Katha Pollitt puts it in her article on Dr. Seuss, *"And to Think That I Saw It on Mulberry Street* is a work of considerable genius, despite the offending cartoon of a Chinese man eating rice, and *McElligot's Pool* is pretty great too, despite its use of the outmoded word 'Eskimo,' complete with clichéd depiction of an Inuit in fur-lined parka."[93] The same is true of so many children's and YA books. Books are not like cars, which either have seat belts or not. Books are not like toys, which either have lead paint or not. Books are not the source of homicide. Nor are they the solution to it. Black-and-white thinking is a hallmark of fanaticism. It should not be a hallmark of literary culture in the twenty-first century.

The obsession with moral purity, what might be called "the one-drop rule of children's and YA literature," is a regrettable throwback to comic book censorship in the 1950s.[94] It is also the latest incarnation of a mindset that predates the 1950s. In *The Hatred of Literature*, literary historian William Marx reflects: "The condemnation of literature in the name of morality goes back at least as far as Xenophanes of Colophon and Heraclitus of Ephesus. Yet, it was Plato who would establish himself as the grand inquisitor and *The Republic* as the bible of anti-literature for centuries."[95] Plato was also the first person in the history of antiliterature to invoke children. In *The Republic*, he writes: "What they take into their opinions at that age has a tendency to become hard to eradicate and unchangeable. Perhaps it's for this reason that we must do everything to ensure that what they hear first, with respect to virtue, be the finest told tales for them to hear."[96] Like the inquisitors active today, the grand inquisitor of literature believed immoral authors must be censored.

To cut to the chase, one does not need to be a sociologist of moral crusades or a historian of literature to recognize the similarities between the past and the present. Moreover, one does not need to be a Ray Bradbury scholar to understand that, as he puts it in his coda to *Fahrenheit 451*, "There is more than one way to burn a book. And the world is full of people running about with lit matches."[97] Of note, Bradbury's 1953 masterpiece was itself silently rewritten by his publisher, without his knowledge, because it, too, offended some readers.[98] His publisher was "fearful of contaminating the young."[99] For six years, the censored edition was the only paperback edition in print. Fortunately, students alerted him to the rewrites. Despite what these moral crusades suggest, many young people do not want adults to censor what they read.

The Structure of Moral Panic

Like the authors and illustrators of comic books, the new generation of folk devils are accused of harming, corrupting, and otherwise putting young readers in danger. Whereas psychiatrist Frederic Wertham, author of *The Seduction of the Innocent*, believed that one of the best places to challenge youth violence was comic books, English professor and literary critic Philip Nel, author of *Was the Cat in the Hat Black? The Hidden Racism of Children's Literature, and the Need for Diverse Books*, believes that one of the best places to challenge racism is children's and YA literature.[100] Other crusaders believe that children's and YA literature is the best place to challenge every intolerance.

Understandably, the National Coalition Against Censorship (NCAC), PEN America, and the First Amendment Committee of the American Society of Journalists and Authors (ASJA) have raised concerns about this moral crusade.[101] For example, NCAC, which has historically defended authors, librarians, and readers from right-wing censorship, is developing a support network for YA authors pressured to cancel their own books.[102] Against this backdrop, it is worthwhile to consider the structure of moral panic and what it reveals about the present.

First, moral panics arise when people perceive a threat to their society. Between 1952 and 1956, the documented percentage of juvenile arrests grew.[103] Although this increase was a few percentage points, from just under 8 percent to 11 percent, and it occurred at a time when the FBI changed its data-collection procedures, the number of news stories about juvenile delinquents skyrocketed. In his 1955 book, *1,000,000 Delinquents*, Benjamin Fine, the Pulitzer Prize–winning journalist who edited the education section of the *New York Times*, warned his fellow Americans about the new threat. "Unless this cancer is checked early enough," he declared, "it can go on spreading and contaminate many good cells in our society."[104] *Cosmopolitan* asked, "Are You Afraid of Your Teenager?," and *Time* dedicated a special issue to "Teenagers on the Rampage."[105]

Like journalists, politicians warned the public in their widely publicized comments. "Not even the communist conspiracy," exclaimed Senator Robert C. Hendrickson in 1954, "could devise a more effective way to demoralize, disrupt, confuse, and destroy our future citizens than apathy on the part of Adult Americans to the scourge known as Juvenile Delinquency."[106] Adults who confronted these comments became concerned. Seventy years later, the threat has nothing to do with youth violence and everything to do with the lived experience of minorities. It is no coincidence that the concern over racist, homophobic, and otherwise intolerant books emerged around the time the right controlled the Oval Office, the Supreme Court, the Senate, the majority of state governorships, and the majority of state chambers and legislatures. For legitimate reasons, Americans are worried about threats to minorities.

In the case of books for young people, what literary critic Derritt Mason argues about queer YA literature is just as true of all children's and YA literature. He contends: "Queer YA and cultural texts that seek to address queer youth proliferate as both an anxiety management strategy (a potential antidote to the fact that queer youth are in crisis) and a producer of additional anxiety (what if this address fails in its mission?)."[107] From children interned on the US-Mexico border to African American teenagers shot dead by the police, there is no shortage of adult anxiety regarding young people. If progressive books function as one anxiety-reducing strategy—by reducing intolerance in books, adults feel less anxious about intolerance in the real world—it is understandable that this will also produce the additional anxiety regarding books that fail in their mission. Hence so much of #KidLit and #YATwitter is permeated by adults afraid that an author will, consciously or unconsciously, perpetuate this or that intolerance in their work.

Second, moral panics blame individuals who are not responsible for these threats. In the 1950s, the folk devils were comic book creators. Today, the folk devils are "racist ass writers" like Amélie Wen Zhao. Looking back, we know that teenagers did not assault and rob people because they read *Flash Gordon* and *Weird Fantasy*. However, we do know that poverty, domestic abuse, and other problems are related to juvenile delinquency.[108] These are difficult problems to solve. In contrast, it did not take much to cancel comic books. It also did not take much to get Scholastic to cancel *A Birthday Cake for George Washington*. Though, it is unclear that children will now grow up to be less racist because author Ramin Ganeshram, illustrator Vanessa Brantley-Newton, and editor Andrea Davis Pinkney—ironically, three women of color—were censored.

In this vein, consider Philip Nel's magnum opus, which was honored by the Children's Literature Association, the Association of American Publishers, and *Choice* around the time he was invited to lecture at Google. On the one hand, *Was the Cat in the Hat Black? The Hidden Racism of Children's Literature, and the Need for Diverse Books* is an insightful work of literary criticism that examines racist illustrations in children's books, whitewashed covers in YA novels, and other problems. On the other hand, this literary criticism is intertwined with grand, sweeping sociological arguments. The main thesis—one of the best places to oppose racism is literature for young people—is buttressed by no interviews with children, no interviews with teenagers, and no research from developmental psychologists.[109]

Nel is not the only scholar of literature for young people who makes these kinds of arguments. For this reason, one might contend that his widely praised book is indicative of a "disciplinary fallacy," in which "a discipline makes an enabling assumption to get started, and then its practitioners conclude that is has *proven* what it has in fact assumed." Literary critics assume that books for young people are one of the best places to oppose intolerance. The close readings that locate intolerance in books are then taken as proof of the assumption.[110] In this respect, the tendency in literary studies looks like other research on media for young people, which shows no interest in what they think.[111] It also follows the footsteps of literary critics in the 1950s, who, with the same disinterest in young people's voices, proclaimed that comic books were one of the best places to oppose juvenile crime.

Looking back, Sigmund Freud's concept of "the unconscious" is what binds the past to the present. Rhetorically, it stands in for empirical evidence. "Discrimination operates unconsciously," Nel reminds his readers, "sneaking into our thought processes and influencing us in ways of which we're not aware."[112] Nel is certain that everyone in American society has a contaminated mind because "messages seep in subtly, persistently, without your noticing."[113] Like cosplayers in Hogwarts robes pretending to practice legilimency (a kind of mind-reading in the *Harry Potter* universe), literary critics pretend to be psychologists who can diagnose what is lurking in the minds of authors, readers, and even fictional characters.[114] It is unclear what is less scientific: putting a person you have never met on the couch or putting Paddington Bear on the couch.

If one reads *Children's Literature* and *Children's Literature Association Quarterly*, the two flagship journals of the Children's Literature Association, hundreds of articles and reviews use the word "unconscious."[115] Of course, literary critics are not psychologists. They do not even use the language of most psychologists. Freud, and his infatuation with dark, hidden aspects of the human psyche, is more a relic of early twentieth-century psychology than a reference point for psychologists practicing in the twenty-first. Yet his theories live on in literary criticism—often without attribution. Like other critics, Nel never cites Freud, despite his Freudian flair for dramatic claims intertwined with pedantic Freudian lessons about how "it is very easy to be unconscious of what you have absorbed."[116] As Mark Edmunson, a professor of English at the University of Virginia, laments: "We quote Freud all the time without saying so, and often without knowing as much."[117]

The unconscious, as a rhetorical device, allows literary critics to have their cake and eat it, too. On the one hand, their interpretations are idiosyncratic to them (otherwise they would not be published by peer-reviewed journals and presses that, by their nature, are only interested in new interpretations). On the other hand, their interpretations are not idiosyncratic to them. They apply to all readers. By way of a hypothetical example, I can contend that *Curious George* promotes transphobia—a wildly creative interpretation idiosyncratic to me—while also contending, via the unconscious, that parents and their children share my interpretation. However, unlike me, they are unaware that they share it. If they were more aware and in touch with their unconscious, like me, they would recognize my interpretation as the correct one. If they knew how to "close read" a text to unearth its secret meanings, like me, they might even have reached this interpretation on their own. As a scholar of children's literature, one who professes to know what *Curious George* really means, it is both my intellectual and moral responsibility to educate the unenlightened masses.

Although relatively few literary critics write about capitalism, their pseudo-Freudian analyses of the unconscious have a familiarly Marxist ring to them. Just as working-class people do not understand their own material interests—unlike Marxist professors, these workers are imprisoned in "false consciousness"—so, too, with readers who see nothing "problematic" about *Curious George, The Cat in the Hat*, or whatever book provokes the latest cause célèbre. The literary critic, who sees their work as a moral vocation, is simultaneously a police detective searching for clues ("On the bottom of page three, George jokes about wearing a dress"), a judge offering the correct verdict ("HarperCollins must stop publishing *Curious George* because it is as dangerous as a car without seatbelts"), and a proselytizing missionary (I must deliver talks at Google, universities, etc. and promote my important work on Twitter with hashtags like #CancelThatMonkey). For parents who grew up reading these books with no adverse effects, and who now want to read these books with their children, the literary critic is also a killjoy.

Whereas literary critics deploy the unconscious as their deus ex machina—"You didn't prove that this book influenced anyone," says the social scientist. "That's because the influence is unconscious!" responds the literary critic—more serious researchers have tried to assess the effects of literature. Their conclusions are a lot different. For example, Princeton psychologist Elizabeth Levy Paluck and Columbia political scientist Donald P. Green evaluated close to a thousand studies of prejudice reduction.[118] Of these, just seventeen field experiments focused on literature read by children and YA readers. More than a third failed to produce positive results. Furthermore, the average length of these interventions was just five weeks, and they all took place in schools. That is, no intervention examined "the effect of literature on prejudice among general audiences."

Above all, no intervention measured behavior. As sociologists Colin Jerolmack and Shamus Khan explain in their article on the "attitudinal fallacy" in social science research, "self-reports of attitudes and behaviors are of limited value in explaining what people actually do."[119] By contrast, Nel asserts that "what we read in childhood" has a significant "influence on our adult responses to race and racism."[120] As is typical of scholarship written by moral crusaders, Paluck and Green's widely cited metareview of actually existing research appears nowhere in Nel's 290-page treatise on the subject.

Alongside basic problems of behavioral and longitudinal validity, some of these studies raise problems related to confounding variables, small sample sizes, and positive results that were never reproduced. Unlike Nel's conclusions, which assert that children's and YA literature is "one of the best places" to oppose racism and, with just as much rhetorical belligerence, that it is also a "key front" in the struggle against "Mr. Trump and his allies"[121]—exciting, attention-grabbing conclusions that earned him a feature interview in *Esquire*[122]—the conclusions of Paluck and Green are, for lack of a better word, sober: "Notwithstanding the enormous literature on prejudice, psychologists are a long way from demonstrating the most effective ways to reduce prejudice. Due to weaknesses in the internal and external validity of existing research, the literature does not reveal whether, when, and why interventions reduce prejudice in the world."[123]

Although Paluck and Green believe reading interventions are a promising avenue for prejudice rejection, they conclude that more research, especially better designed research, is needed. As an alternative to pie-in-the-sky theories about literature, a long-standing body of rigorous empirical research illuminates the most effective ways to frame antiracist political demands (increased funding for public schools in black neighborhoods, affirmative action, and even reparations) so that they actually win support from voters on different sides of the political spectrum.[124] Although it is less than clear how prejudice can be reduced, it is more than clear how we can use federal, state, and local legislatures to mitigate its effects. Given the widely accepted conclusion, reiterated time again in the research, that prejudice originates in "large-scale social forces such as intergroup competition for status and resources,"[125] we might also think about addressing the economic conditions that lead to prejudice.

As far back as John Milton's "Areopagitica,"[126] writers have also pointed out that eradicating bad ideas in books, of all places, leaves so many other places open to the same ideas and worse ideas.[127] In the era of Facebook, Twitter, YouTube, Reddit, TikTok, Netflix, Hulu, PlayStation, Xbox, Spotify, cable television, Hollywood films, YouPorn, and a billion-dollar advertising industry that ensures most Americans are exposed to thousands of advertisements every day, many of which use the worst stereotypes to sell products, Milton's point could not be truer.[128] In the Sensitivity Era, censoring this or that author is as effective as tilting at windmills. To reiterate, the targets are not the federal, state, and local legislators who shape the austere economic conditions of childhood, which are also the conditions of intergroup prejudice. They are the low hanging fruit of moral crusades. As sociologist Joel Best reflects in *Flavor of the Month: Why Smart People Fall for*

Fads, people love simple solutions to difficult problems.[129] More cynically, one might say many literary critics love solutions that make their literary criticism look politically important.

Looking at Nel's ascendence, one is reminded of Reverend Hale's ascendence in Arthur Miller's *The Crucible*. In the midst of a moral panic over witchcraft, Hale travels to Salem, Massachusetts. "This is a beloved errand for him; on being called here to ascertain witchcraft he felt the pride of the specialist whose unique knowledge has at last been publicly called for." Like Nel, and to a much greater extent more influential moral entrepreneurs like Robin DiAngelo and Ibram X. Kendi, Hale shows up with his "armory of symptoms, catchwords, and diagnostic procedures." As he puts it, "We shall need hard study if it comes to tracking own the Old Boy."[130] In Salem, the Old Boy was the Devil. In the Sensitivity Era, the Old Boy is intolerance and its increasingly furtive, borderline mystical forms. This intolerance possesses young readers in the Sensitivity Era—"sneaking into our thought processes and influencing us in ways of which we're not aware"—just like the Devil possessed young girls in Salem. Fortunately, we have our own versions of Reverand Hale.

As a counterfactual, imagine if Bayard Rustin, A. Philip Randolph, and Martin Luther King Jr. believed that literature written for young people was one of the best places to oppose racism in the United States. Their movement might have produced better books, but I doubt these books would have produced the March on Washington for Jobs and Freedom or the Civil Rights Act. Fortunately, civil rights leaders devoted their time, money, and other resources to a political movement, rather than a popular culture crusade. At the end of the day, these activists also put something on the line. By contrast, crusaders just think they are putting something on the line.

Unironically, Oxford University Press describes Nel as "fearless." This is a cartoonishly inappropriate description of almost any professor, let alone an English professor. Just look at the catalog of every academic press—*Harry Potter and the Other: Race, Justice, and Difference in the Wizarding World* by Sarah Park Dahlen and Ebony Elizabeth Thomas, *Racism in Contemporary African American Children's and Young Adult Literature* by Suriyan Panlay, and so on—and you will get a sense of how much courage it takes to write yet another treatise about racism in American literature. If you look at the number of Amazon ratings for these books, seven and zero, respectively, you will also get sense of how much dust these "fearless" books collect. In the Sensitivity Era, "scholar-activist" is the watchword.[131] It does not matter if the scholar's work has anything to do with activism, much less change.

The ascendance of the term "activist cultural criticism," what English professor Eric Cheyfitz calls an oxymoron, reflects this trend.[132] It is one of those terms that lends political import to business as usual. It is not as if English departments now give tenure to the literary critics who register the most voters. They give it to those who can publish their work with presses like Oxford University Press. To quote Stanley Fish, another English professor, "If you want to do political work, in the 'real world' sense, there are (or should be) better tools in your kit than readings of poems or cultural texts or even cultures."[133] There are tools. They are just not the tools of literary critics. They definitely are not the tools of tweeters and TikTokers offering their latest hot take on a YA novel.[134]

This does not mean that books are irrelevant. There are books—think, for example, of Harriet Beecher Stowe's *Uncle Tom's Cabin* or, more recently and regrettably, Robin DiAngelo's *White Fragility*—that have a considerable impact. On a personal note, a number of books have shaped how I think about the world. For better or worse, I can say the same for the high school and college students with whom I have worked. But there is a difference between contextualized truths—specific books have influenced me, an individual, in specific ways—and grand, sweeping assertions in which an individual claims to know how books will affect millions of other individuals they have never met. Given the borderline sexual fetish for *polysemy, irreducibility, multivocality, liminality, indeterminacy, resignification,* and *deconstruction* in English departments, it is remarkable that these totalizing claims about children's and YA literature come from tenured professors of literature.

Third, moral panics use the rhetoric of moral contagion. In plain English, crusaders believe the problem is spreading like a disease or a pollutant that must be contained.[135] After World War II, the dean of Fordham University's school of education was not alone when he called comic books a "cancerous growth." Nor was Wertham alone when he declared, "Just as we have ordinances against the pollution of water, so now we need ordinances against the pollution of children's minds."[136] It "is not a matter of suppression of ideas or of unconventional literature," wrote the *Sacramento Bee* in 1954, but "a matter of protecting youth and the community against sewage."[137]

When a reviewer of *A Place for Wolves* is "disgusted" by Jackson's "gross" novel, and alarmed because other reviewers do not experience "revulsion," too, she might as well be reviewing *Batman* in 1954.[138] Likewise, when Nel writes about books as "symptoms" of a "disease," books that are "dangerously wrong," the "wounds" produced by "harmful" books, and books that "infect developing young minds,"[139] it is unclear if he is writing literary criticism or a report for the Centers for Disease Control and Prevention.[140] It is equally unclear if he simply inserted today's watchwords—*racism, whiteness*, and so on—into *The Seduction of the Innocent*. In either case, the issue is, according to moral crusaders, never censorship.

Yet censorship is the pièce de résistance of the Sensitivity Era. Notwithstanding the bigger controversies, it manifests most in the closed-door decisions that never make the news. Even at small literary journals—where writers are not paid, subscriptions are free, and circulation is low—the fear of this crusade is real. Nobody wants to be associated with a writer who was accused of insensitivities. In the words of one editor I interviewed, "The writer I told you about earlier has submitted work to my journal. She's got chops. There is a chance I will want to accept her work on its merits (haven't read it yet). But if I did, I would run the risk of strangers influential in the corner of the internet I rely on for submissions throwing a bunch of loud tantrums about it. It could kill or cripple the project. So I'm probably not going to accept her work—not even on the basis of whether the work itself is inflammatory—because of fear of contamination by association. So, yeah, internet mob justice. I can't afford it."

In the era of contamination by association, agents are worried, too. They are reluctant to work with writers who have been, or who may become, targets of the internet mob. "I think I've been very wary of taking on white creators who are writing a main character from a person of color's point of view," one agent explained to me. "I think writers can be really careful in their research, if you've kind of gotten the blessing from, if you've had sensitivity reads done. But I think it's still going to be tricky. I think people are really gun-shy after a lot of the big Twitter blowups that have happened over the last five years."

This rhetoric of moral contagion is intertwined with an inflated rhetoric of harm.[141] A reader who thinks *A Place for Wolves, American Heart*, or *Blood Heir* are just poorly written does not understand how serious the situation is. They do not understand "the harm it can and will do to real people," especially the "real teens" whom every adult with an agenda purports to represent. Like the 1950s, these real children and teenagers are little more than abstractions. To quote media theorist Henry Jenkins at length: "The myth of 'childhood innocence' 'empties' children of any thoughts of their own, stripping them of their own political agency and social agendas so that they may become vehicles for adult needs, desires, and politics. . . . The myth of 'childhood innocence,' which sees children only as potential victims of the adult world or as beneficiaries of paternalistic protection, opposes pedagogies that empower children as active agents in the educational process. We cannot teach children how to engage in critical thought by denying them access to challenging information or provocative images."[142]

In other words, even if *A Birthday Cake for George Washington* is as bad as its critics believe it is, it does not mean that it needs to be removed from Amazon like firearms, ammunition, and related items. Even the worst books can be, and often are, valuable pedagogical resources. On a similar note, if you do not feel comfortable telling a community devastated by a drone strike that you, too, incurred "wounds" from a "harmful" experience—that time you read a YA novel at the beach—you should stop using the language of physical violence to describe an ephemeral emotional experience with a book. To use one of the Sensitivity Era's favorite words, you should stop "appropriating" the language of actual victims.

Fourth, moral panics reduce literature to a didactic tool. In 1954, the comic books code ensured that "stories dealing with evil shall be used or nor shall be published only where the intent is to illustrate a moral issue and in no case shall evil be presented alluringly nor so as to injure the sensibilities of the reader."[143] Today, moral crusaders have a similar view of children's and YA literature. When Becky Albertalli wrote her debut YA novel, *Simon vs. the Homo Sapiens Agenda*, she did not expect it to be offensive. However, one scene upset some readers. In this scene, a closeted gay teenager thinks to himself that it is easier to come out of the closet as a lesbian. He thinks that people find lesbians more alluring. As journalist Katy Waldman explains, "Albertalli hadn't originally given the passage a second thought: the character was obviously unworldly; elsewhere, he asserts that all Jews come from Israel. But in the latter exchange, readers pointed out, Simon's Jewish friend immediately corrects him."[144] Like the dystopian world of *1984*, there is no room for even one uncorrected thoughtcrime in contemporary literature written for young people.

Perhaps a didactic children's book like *Antiracist Baby*—a number one *New York Times* bestseller, written for babies aged three months to three years, that tells them to "confess when being racist" because "nothing disrupts racism more than when we confess the racist ideas that we sometimes express"—is an appropriate book for those who are still shitting themselves.[145] Perhaps *Not My Idea: A Book about Whiteness*—a *HuffPost* and *School Library Journal* honoree, in which the Devil gives children the opportunity to sign a "contract binding [them] to whiteness"—will turn the next generation into antiracist crusaders.[146] Perhaps *A is for Activist*, *Feminist Baby*, and *Woke Baby* are what the left needs now more than ever.

However, the deluge of atheists raised on the Bible, the Koran, or whatever other scripture was in the classroom or on the kitchen table should make adults skeptical of literature's power to place children on this or that path to moral salvation. Shoving an ideology down a young person's throat, as if one were a mother bird vomiting worms into a baby bird's mouth, might even produce a backfire effect. As political scientist Paul Kengor reflects, "I've met many conservative anti-communists who were born and raised Red Diaper Babies, only to flee their parents' politics like the plague."[147] For some young people today, rejecting the orthodoxies of their PC parents and teachers might be the equivalent of playing pinball in the 1940s, reading comic books in the 1950s, and listening to "Satanic" rock music in the 1980s.

Some of today's books are so didactic that one would think today's authors and illustrators are trying to outflank the comic book crusade by returning children's literature to the eighteenth century. As literary historian M. O. Grenby explains, "The pioneer children's writers of the 1740s and 1750s were already experimenting with short fictions designed to teach behavioral and ethical lessons: what would come to be known, towards the end of the century, as 'moral tales.'"[148] For example, *The History of Little Goody Two-Shoes*, one of the first full-length novels written for children, popularized the phrase "goody two-shoes," which is now used as a term to deride exceptionally virtuous people. This book, like so many others, was published by John Newbery, who is considered "the father of children's literature." Much like the influence of Plato, the grand inquisitor of literature, Newbery's influence cannot be overstated.

Like many children's books in the present, the didactic tales of the past provoked criticism from authors and readers. As Grenby reflects, "Romantic writers, in the early 19th century, found it expedient to make the moral tale the butt of their complaints about what they saw as the increasingly utilitarian direction society was taking. This kind of literature, they argued, suppressed imagination and true morality." Samuel Taylor Coleridge lectured against "moral tales where a good little boy comes in and says, Mama, I met a poor beggarman and gave him the sixpence you gave me yesterday. Did I do right?" Sir Walter Scott explained that when children read these moral tales, it is like having their minds "put into the stocks." E. Nesbit, who published *The Wouldbegoods* at the turn of the twentieth century, also mocked the moral tale. To be sure, there is nothing wrong with books that aspire to educate, but using books as blunt instruments to beat moral lessons into the heads of small children might not inspire them to love reading. Despite his flaws, Dr. Seuss at least knew the difference between a sermon and the irreverent silliness that so many children love.

Although it is unclear where the term "young adult" even came from, it "became primarily associated with the literary when the American Library Association formed a Young Adult Services Division, teenagers/youth/young adults became a desirable literary market, and YA was conceived as a saleable literary genre" in the 1950s.[149] To this day, the division, now called the Young Adult Library Services Association, continues to use the term to refer to young people aged twelve through eighteen. Similar to "teenagers," which was coined by advertisers after World War II to describe a new market segment, "young adults" have been a perennial source of anxiety for adults. This anxiety revolves around the reality that modern young people have cultures that exclude old people. Like children's literature, YA literature serves as an outlet for adults to deal with their anxiety. It is an outlet for them to try to control young people.

One agent I spoke to, who began her career in the 1970s, sees the current crusade as the latest incarnation of a sentiment she has dealt with before. Back in the day, adults were upset because she represented a popular book series that entertained young readers. Because these books were not written like textbooks, adults were worried. "I used to get so much criticism from people," she explained, "who said I was giving kids a diet of all candy." Because adult anxiety permeates the history of children's and YA literature—always in the background, bubbling like lava beneath the surface—moral panics might be considered the moments of volcanic eruption. These are the moments where the impetus to control literature for young people is most evident and, as the past decade and half illustrates, most influential.

From the past through the present, literary history is Darwinian. Different kinds of characters (dragons, soldiers, etc.), settings (space stations, jungles, etc.), and plot devices (clues, flashbacks, etc.) compete with one another in the aisles at Barnes & Noble, the pages of review journals, and the decision-making rooms at agencies and publishers. Whether it is *Twilight*-inspired vampires who piggyback on the success of Stephenie Meyer, or school mysteries that adopt the detective style popularized by J. K. Rowling, the literary marketplace ebbs and flows like the New York Stock Exchange. As any writer who has written a book proposal knows, one must situate their unpublished manuscript within existing trends. Some trends ascend. Others descend.

To use literary historian Franco Moretti's language, the "slaughterhouse of literature" is real.[150] The resurgence of Goody Two-Shoes characters, the rejection of minimalism (a writing style that refuses to pass judgment on "immoral" characters), and other hallmarks of the Sensitivity Era persist after this or that controversy ends. If the controversies continue, didactic books—unblemished in their commitment to progressive values iterated by Own Voices authors—will be best positioned to survive the social media slaughterhouse of literature.

The slaughterhouse extends from picture books to novels written for adults. The butchers on social media shape the reception of these novels. They also shape what happens behind closed doors before novels are published, marketed, and sent to reviewers. In the words of one Big Five president,

> There is a significantly increased amount of alertness on the part of not just my editorial teams, the people who have the very first contact with material, but also with marketing people, and publicity people, who have to create material around the material. I rely a great deal on these people to provide a filter that catches problematic things early on, and, if we're lucky and it's the right time, we can make the necessary corrections. Our primary challenge is to run a business, and make money, and sell books that are successful. We also have to protect our authors. We often have to protect our authors from themselves.
>
> We had a crime novel written by an author who's white, and male, and over fifty—super sophisticated and smart—which contained slightly objectionable anti-Asian sentiment put in the mouth of one of the character's who's clearly intended in this novel to be unsympathetic. We asked this writer to dial it back, this anti-Asian sentiment. He pushed back very, very hard and said "No, this is

what my character would say. That's what this character is like." We had to get tough. We said, "You have to make these changes." It was a standoff. The agent got involved. We reached a compromise. The author cut back some of it.

These conversations are very complicated. They are especially complicated between authors who've been publishing with a house, and working with a particular editor for a long time, and that editor is suddenly bringing in new levels of attention to a book. It created quite problematic tensions. But if that was the big event that happened after the publication of the novel—that there was a kind of squall on Twitter over that kind of thing—it would completely distract everyone from the fact that it's actually a really good book. That's a business problem.

Whereas this president was understandably concerned about how the novel would be received on social media, and the risk that readers might conflate a character "who's clearly intended in this novel to be unsympathetic" with the novelist, other people I spoke to echoed this novelist's frustration. One Pulitzer Prize finalist, who has been writing books for more than four decades, did not mince her words: "This is the silly season. It doesn't occur to people that you might portray racist people but not be a racist yourself." One agent I spoke to, with more than three decades of experience, was even blunter: "You can't say Cormac McCarthy is a butcher because his main character is a murderer." In the Sensitivity Era, you can. The biggest publishers in the world will listen.

They listen because they are scared, too. Even at the most senior levels, people are pressured to conceal how they feel. When I interviewed one vice president at a Big Five publisher—literally, one of the most powerful people in publishing—they also did not mince their words when they pondered people who want to restrict the kinds of characters who can be included in fiction. In their words: "It's a fucking novel." Yet this same vice president would not let me record our interview. Before we ended, they reconfirmed that their name would not be attached to one word they said. One might expect genuflection from the interns faxing memos, brewing coffee, and struggling to keep up with New York City rent, but it is a sign of the times that even the rich and powerful are afraid to express themselves. As this vice president told me, a lot has changed in the past ten to fifteen years.

Even in the most transgressive writing communities, writers are facing the pressure to not offend. Chuck Palahniuk, the author of *Fight Club*, has a reputation for discomforting people with his morally ambiguous characters. He had been workshopping his drafts with the same writers for decades. But at some point, he noticed a difference in how his work was received:

For several years, I was in a writer's workshop. And the core group of us had been meeting since 1990. So this is a workshop that was almost thirty years old. And gradually, people were asking each other not to use certain words. First, you know, nobody really used the n-word. But it was definitely a word you could not bring to workshop. And then in a story, I used the word "faggot." And a very good friend of mine said, "You're not bringing that word into workshop. You're not writing anything with the f-word." And it just became more and more tightly structured that way. And so eventually I realized, we were kind of writing to make each other happy, instead of to kind of confront each other.[151]

Palahniuk is a gay writer whose fiction has aroused controversy on the right for "promoting homosexuality."[152] He is also a minimalist writer, trained in the lineage of Gordon Lish through Tom Spanbauer, who refuses to pass judgment on his morally ambiguous characters. This is why, in recent years, his fiction has aroused controversy on the left. But, as Palahniuk puts it in his 2020 memoir, "There is enormous tension in unresolved social issues. . . . This is the reason I depict questionable behavior in my work but refuse to endorse or condemn it. Why preclude the wonderful energy of public debate?"[153] At a moment when literature is being blamed for problems as different as policy brutality and the rise of the alt-right, Palahniuk's minimalism might soon be extinct.

Bret Easton Ellis, a fellow gay writer in the minimalist tradition, has been quite clear about the fact that his own magnum opus, *American Psycho*, would never be published today. In the 1990s, it was one of the few books to lose a publisher after Simon and Schuster dropped it. But it was immediately picked up by another major publisher, Penguin Random House. To be sure, there was controversy. Ellis was accused of racism, sexism, and even homophobia after readers met his protagonist, the virulently racist, sexist, and homophobic Patrick Bateman. But as Ellis reflects in his recent nonfiction debut, *White*, "The difference between then (1990) and now is that there were loud arguments and protests on *both* sides of the divide. . . . The embrace of corporate censorship wasn't quite as acceptable in those days."[154]

Fifth, moral crusaders see themselves as the vanguard. In the past, they identified as members of the National Organization for Decent Literature, the Legion of Decency, and the Citizen's Committee for Better Juvenile Literature. In the present, they identify as Diversity Jedi. Summer Edward, the editor in chief of *Anansesem*, a magazine devoted to Caribbean children's and YA literature, explains that the Jedi are those "who speak up boldly against cultural misrepresentation, racism, bias, cultural appropriation, stereotyping and related issues in children's and YA books."[155] These adults have "emerged as the major representative voices of the children's book diversity movement," and "they often provide incisive 'take-downs' of problematic books on their well-read blogs and Twitter pages."[156]

The #DiversityJedi hashtag, coined by children's and YA author Cynthia Leitich Smith in 2015, was created after fellow children's and YA author Meg Rosoff referred to these clicktivists as "stormtroopers."[157] As Debbie Reese, who blogs for American Indians in Children's Literature, reflects: Rosoff "had NO IDEA who she was tangling with." Unlike *Blood Heir*, which was slammed for depicting a world where "good and evil exist in shades of gray," the real world is, according to Reese, a much simpler world. It is made up of "Jedi" and "not-Jedi."[158] The latter appears to be any person who disagrees with the Jedi. As Judge Danforth explains in Arthur Miller's *The Crucible*, "a person is either with this court or he must be counted against it, there be no road between."[159]

On #KidLit and #YATwitter, #DiversityJedi is a status symbol. Like the title of judge or minister, its grandeur depends on other people not having it. For example, the Association for Library Service to Children, a division of the American Library Association (ALA), made Diversity Jedi ribbons for ALA's 2018 conference. The president then apologized, after some tweeters contended that ALA appropriated the phrase. "This was a misstep on the long road—to which we are fully committed—to create a diverse and inclusive organization," wrote Nina Lindsay. "We will revisit the use of the ribbons and work to boost the history of the term, to prevent co-option."[160] Like Patrick Bateman, the Wall Street banker who obsesses over Ralph Lauren ties, Armani sunglasses, and other status symbols in *American Psycho*, Reese, the Diversity Jedi whose blog is consulted by *Kirkus Reviews*, wrote sixty-one tweets in a thread about these little black ribbons.[161]

Metaphors reflect and shape how we understand social life.[162] The Jedi metaphor helps to explain why so many adults have no reservation about publicly shaming and humiliating authors, reviewers, and readers. In some cases, the degradation ceremony continues until an author loses their literary agent, has their book pulled from distribution, or otherwise takes a hit that will diminish their ability to provide for themselves and their families. As an article in *Kirkus Reviews* explains, "The methods of the Diversity Jedi are often not gentle. I know this from personal experience. But (if you permit the extension of the metaphor) it takes concerted, violent effort to take out the Death Star."[163]

This approach is compounded by what psychologists know about social roles. Experiments, including the infamous Stanford Prison Experiment, show that role identification is intertwined with the dehumanization of those who do not share the role.[164] To quote one review of existing research on the neuroscience of intergroups relations, "Individuals tend to engage in more hostile behaviors toward opponents when acting as part of a group than when acting alone."[165] As the "minimal group paradigm" suggests, group-driven discrimination is a stable feature of social life.[166] When adults see themselves as crusaders in the Legion of Decency or Diversity Jedi, it becomes more acceptable to take "concerted, violent effort" against anyone who is considered a threat. Moreover, as the literature on social diffusion suggests, these influential "early movers,"[167] "super spreaders,"[168] and "opinion leaders"[169] shape the behavior of their followers. Some of these Jedi have thousands of followers.

This does not mean that opinion leaders and their followers are correct. It just means that social influence is real. For example, in their research, "Experimental Study of Inequality and Unpredictability in an Artificial Cultural Market," Matthew J. Salganik and his colleagues created "multiple worlds" with the same music.[170] In one treatment, participants saw how many times a song was downloaded. In another treatment, they did not. The same songs appeared in eight different worlds. Although their data showed that "songs of any given quality can experience a wide range of outcomes," they concluded that social influence in the real world "is far stronger than in our experiment."[171]

With their experiment, and other experiments in the "multiple words" paradigm as a reference point, it is reasonable to assume that the success of literature, like music, has a social component.[172] If a novel provokes early criticism online, just as a song generates early downloads online, it can produce a snowball effect. Who happens to review a book, and when they happen to review it, are not peripheral issues. As every publisher knows, early reviews from influential people are decisive. Today, reviews are written in 280 characters or less. The snowball effect is more relevant now than ever. The outcomes are just as random. In the words of one agent,

> To some extent, it depends on someone or some small group of people with the right platform hitting that note at a particular time and it spiraling. If that doesn't

happen to happen, the virtually identical book—there's so many published—might go unquestioned. It's so random. The right or wrong person decides to take this up and, two weeks from now, it's in the *New York Times*. It's a whole other level of anxiety for everyone.

In many ways, the book controversies on #Kidlit and #YATwitter are like the lottery depicted in "The Lottery." In Shirley Jackson's short story, a village randomly stones one of its own to death. Like *Fahrenheit 451* and other fictional works that illuminate the cannibalistic side of social life, Jackson's story was itself a target. In protest, hundreds of readers canceled their *New Yorker* subscriptions or wrote angry letters.[173] Published in 1948, the same year Wertham delivered his seminal lecture scapegoating comic books, one could not have asked for a more relevant piece of fiction. Seventy years later, "The Lottery" should be read by anyone trying to understand the social dynamics of literary culture today.

All of this ties into what sociologists know about public punishment. As Robb Willer, Ko Kuwabara, and Michael Macy show in their widely cited *American Journal of Sociology* (*AJS*) article, "people enforce unpopular norms to show that they have complied out of genuine conviction and not because of social pressure."[174] In their experiments, participants publicly enforced norms that they privately opposed. Importantly, it took little social pressure to get people to hypocritically punish other people. To quote another peer-reviewed article in *AJS*, which produced similar results through a different method, "Witches are created by anxious neighbors seeking to affirm their status in the community by accusing others of deviance, thereby perpetuating the fear that fuels the need for affirmation. . . . We need not assume this dynamic is some historical relic of superstition."[175] It is one thing to say you believe in the witch trials, even if you do not believe in them. But to show that you believe out of genuine conviction, rather than social pressure, you might help the true believers burn a witch.[176] A witch can be a woman in 1692, a comic book illustrator in 1952, or a YA novelist in 2022. A lit match, like the accusation of "harming" or "corrupting" a young reader, has many forms.

Alongside a library of conformity experiments, which show that people will conceal their true beliefs under minimal social pressure, this research raises the question of how many people on #YATwitter and #KidLit punished Amélie Wen Zhao, Ramin Ganeshram, and other authors to show they were not racist, even if they privately believed none of these authors are racist.[177] Decades of research in sociology and psychology, including results that have been replicated across multiple countries, suggests that it is a significant number of people. In the words of one agent I interviewed whose client was pilloried, "I had the strange experience of someone who had privately sent me very supportive notes. Then they 'liked' something. They actually 'liked' the attack. They 'liked' the accusation. I said, 'What was that about?' They said, 'I have to show support. Otherwise, I'll be on the other side.' I thought, 'Wow, that's really scary.' It's someone who I think of as quite a strong personality. But Twitter seems to be terrifying to people. They're all just trying to protect themselves. It's a sad thing to watch."

As literary critic Christopher Bigsby reflects in his introduction to *The Crucible*, "The witch finder is ever vigilant, and who would not rather direct his attention to others than stand, in the heat of the day, and challenge his authority?"[178] In a world where "groundless accusations are still granted credence, hysteria still claims its victims, persecution still masquerades as virtue and prejudice as piety," Miller's play about the Salem witch trials remains his most frequently produced work.[179]

My lab work echoes Miller's literary work. Along with my colleagues in Cornell University's Social Dynamic Lab, Michael Macy and Shiyu Ji, I conducted experiments with hundreds of American readers. We wanted to see if we could turn readers against an otherwise innocuous piece of litera-ture. In our first experiment, we had people read four poems: "How-To" by Anders Carlson-Wee, "Avenues" by Eugen Gomringer, "Sweeney among the Nightingales" by T. S. Eliot, and "A Supermarket in California" by Allen Ginsberg. We used pseudonyms instead of the poet's real names. We then asked readers to anonymously select three choices from a list of sixteen choices to describe each poem: well-written, awkward, antisemitic, sad, rac-ist, homophobic, insightful, poorly written, sexist, entertaining, unoriginal, progressive, sensitive, boring, silly, and none of the above. Out of the 161 readers who read "How-To," 9 selected racist (less than 6 percent of readers). Out of the 166 readers who read "Avenues," 9 selected sexist (less than 6 percent of readers). Out of the 140 readers who read "Sweeney among the Nightingales," 5 selected antisemitic (less than 4 percent of readers). Out of the 157 readers who read "A Supermarket in California," 12 selected homo-phobic (less than 8 percent of readers).

In our second experiment, we had another group of Americans read these poems alongside two sentences of criticism that I wrote. The criticism was attributed to a fictional critic. For example, "Blair Jackson" said this about "How-To": "I agree with all the readers who think this poem is racist. It causes real pain and harm to African Americans." Our participants were also told they might be asked to log in to their Facebook accounts after the experiment at which point their evaluations of the poems would be shared with other participants. Specifically, they were told that they might be part of a Facebook discussion, and other participants might screenshot this discussion to share on Facebook, Twitter, and other platforms. In this second experiment, every poem became problematic. Out of the 150 readers who read "How-To," 58 readers selected racist (over 38 percent of readers). Out of the 156 readers who read "Avenues," 81 selected sexist (over 51 percent of readers). Out of the 152 readers who read "Sweeney among the Nightingales," 51 selected antisemitic (over 33 percent of readers). Out of the 156 readers who read "A Supermarket in California," 67 selected homophobic (over 42 percent of readers).

In the real world, "How-To" was accused of racism, "Avenues" was accused of sexism, and "Sweeney among the Nightingales" was accused of antisemitism. But in the real world, my team and I are not familiar with anyone who accused "A Supermarket in California" of homophobia. It is a poem about walking through a supermarket written by a gay poet on the left. Among other places, the poem is anthologized in *The Columbia Anthology of Gay Literature*. But with just a little bit of social pressure, even Allen Ginsberg can be turned into a homophobe. If Ginsberg was still alive, and if this was not just a lab experiment, those accusations might have snowballed and damaged his career. Reading is a social experience, and today the experience is circumscribed by suspicion and groundless moral accusations. To come back to Bigsby's point, "the witch finder is ever vigilant, and who would not rather direct his attention to others than stand, in the heat of the day, and challenge his authority?" At a moment when #SilenceEquals-Violence, readers continue to join the herd as they drag authors and one another out to the social media stockade.

Of note, the artificial social pressure we created in our lab does not remotely approximate the real social pressure readers confront on Facebook, Twitter, and other platforms. Real opinion leaders like Debbie Reese and Dhonielle Clayton, and their herd of acolytes (a herd that includes authors, editors, agents, professors, etc. with thousands of followers) possess more social power than one made-up critic who expresses two sentences of criticism. If we repeated our social experiments with a sample of readers who are active on #YATwitter, Goodreads, and other platforms, and with a real opinion leader's name, the rate of conformity would be much, much higher. The people active in these spaces are the people who actually use hashtags like #SilenceEqualsViolence. These are the people who "have to show support," so they do not end up "on the other side," as the prominent literary agent I interviewed put it. These are the people who have the most to lose. These are the people who are most likely to conform.

While researching *That Book Is Dangerous!*, I came across social media accounts that looked like they were manufactured for the sole purpose of creating the social pressure needed to force people to conform. That is, the accounts looked like the fictional critic we created for our experiment. I was not the first person who noticed what appeared to be fake moral crusaders on social media. One editor I interviewed shared this story: "I heard it when I was in third or fourth grade. They were talking about the revolutionary war. There was this little island. The story is that someone was trying to hold a fort, and they only had like ten people. So, what they did is they marched their ten people that were guarding the fort along the tree line. They looped back and forth to make it look like they had tons of people. That's the kind of thing that happens. They have a whole bunch of sock puppet accounts. You think you're talking to three people. And you're talking to one with three different accounts."

As every moral crusader knows, there is power in numbers. If the numbers do not exist, just make them up. The research on social cascades shows that cascades full of manufactured opinions can initiate cascades full of real opinions. This is one reason why private companies purchase "likes," shares, retweets, and other forms of engagement. They know it will initiate real engagement.

In addition to the more overt status games—not every person deserves a Diversity Jedi ribbon, but some people deserve scarlet letters—the crusades themselves are symptomatic of the desire for social recognition. "One of the most common things I observed after studying extremists on social media," reflects Chris Bail, the director of Duke University's Polarization Lab, "is that they often lack status in their off-line lives."[180] One of the most common things I observed after studying the extremists on #Kidlit and #YATwitter is that most of these adults are not distinguished professors of literature like Philip Nel, *New York Times* bestselling authors like Dhonielle

Clayton, or award-winning reviewers like Debbie Reese. They are nobodies. But the woman who tweets at the Trump Campaign as she insults Hillary Clinton, and the man who tweets at WNDB as he insults Amélie Wen Zhao, are both part of something larger than themselves. If they are lucky, they might even get retweeted.[181]

One of my interview subjects, who publishes one of the most prestigious literary magazines in the United States, told me a story about observing this dynamic in real time. Specifically, they highlighted the relationship between lower-level crusaders who start fires and higher-level crusaders who fan the flames:

> For like six hours, I watched this person call it ableist. They got no traction. I saw the moment they switched tactics and called it racist. Then they got one of the higher-level, more influential people to start retweeting and talking about it.
>
> In California, there's people who walk around trying to start fires when there's wind and dry conditions. It's a serious problem. The same exact thing happens in this metaspace of Twitter. It's like watching someone walk around with a gas can trying to light a fire.
>
> If you go and find the people who have the original tweets, when nobody knew about whatever outrage you want to pick, it's always somebody who spends their entire day trying to provoke outrage.

If anyone disagrees, I encourage them to follow the Twitter accounts, hashtags, and websites mentioned in this book. Although no one knows what book will be burned next, the same people strike matches in the same places.

The Escalation of Moral Panic

Above all, moral crusades tend to become more extreme. As they become more extreme, they lose sympathizers. In the 1950s, the comic book crusade eventually alienated Americans who were concerned about what young people were reading. The current crusade over children's and YA literature is moving in a similar direction. People like Francina Simone, a black YA author who advocates for diverse and sensitive literature, have disengaged from this community. As she reflects: "It sucks to say, but the fear is valid in that you will get dragged if you say, 'Hey, maybe we shouldn't tell this author to kill herself because one of her characters said something offensive.'"[182]

Other people, who work at agencies and publishers, expressed similar sentiments when I interviewed them. One agent of color put it concisely:

"Our concern with cancel culture doesn't cancel out our concerns about the need for diverse and sensitive representation." Another one of my interview subjects, an editor of color, elaborated:

> I'm very left-leaning. I'm very liberal. I'm a feminist. I'm a woman of color. I'm an editor. I feel a responsibility in my position to give a voice to everyone and, certainly, to respond to things that are wrong. And really consider who we're giving a platform to—all of that. I've been in this business a long fucking time. I get it. Times change. We need to evolve. I benefit from that evolution myself. My daughter will benefit from that. But this just feels a bit insane to me now. It feels very frightening. I wish I could just use my voice and say what I feel and publish what I want to publish. I don't fit into this anymore. Isn't that what this is all about? Isn't that what we're talking about?

Although publishers strive to be more inclusive, what is the point if the people of color they hire are afraid to say what they feel and publish what they want to publish? According to this editor, and other people of color who work in publishing, there is a "noisy, vocal minority" who influence what goes on behind closed doors. They are not a minority in terms of their identities—many, if not the overwhelming majority, are cisgender, heterosexual white people—but how they conduct themselves. Like the crusaders on Twitter and Goodreads, their weapon of choice is shame. "Because there's shame attached to it—I could be called racist or terf or whatever—you panic right? Because you don't want those labels." If you are like this woman of color, you keep your mouth shut.

Some moral crusaders hold positions inside publishing houses—I heard horror stories about crusaders who publicly shame their colleagues in the office and on social media—but other crusaders are hired on an ad hoc basis. Their current role in publishing suggests a lot about the rapid institutionalization of this moral panic. To quote one Big Five president I spoke to at the end of 2022:

> There was a time earlier on, say a year ago, where all the major publishers were scrambling. We kind of realized we did need to do this more frequently. When we as publishers were being held accountable by the larger culture, it was one of those pledges that we made, that we would make sure that we were much more thorough in our reviews. Suddenly, we were all reaching out to the same three people who found themselves able to charge any fee they liked. The field has now opened up much more widely, and it's much easier to find sensitivity readers.
>
> My view in general is that we should skew toward the more vigilant, the more sensitive. We're now using sensitivity readers a great deal, as a kind of objective

point of view outside all of us that is a useful check. The sensitivity readers that we're employing are at the very, very, very farthest edges of the cultural police. They are overvigilant to a large degree. I've seen some editors push back hard against what they recommend. Nevertheless, it's great to have that. It's great to have the most extreme possible reaction to a book, which catches even the most apparently neutral points and casts a severe light on them.

Although this president is trying to gauge how his books will be received, and whether they will ignite the next social media bonfire, it is hard to imagine other professions where extremists on the fringes have this kind of influence. One would not expect the World Health Organization to consult QAnon activists before they publish a report about vaccines. Nor would one expect Miramax to consult the Westboro Baptist Church before it makes a film that depicts Christians. Yet, in the world of mainstream publishing, the most extreme people—"the very, very, very farthest edges of the cultural police"—have seats at the table.

When sensitive publishers hire extremely sensitive people to critique books that are already sensitively written, and written by sensitive authors who care deeply about sensitivity, one ends up with feedback that is, ironically, insensitive. The same president regaled me with this tale from Big Five publishing:

> We had a book, written by a gay man, for other gay men—very, very explicitly. The sensitivity reader went through it with a flying, fine-toothed comb, and sort of added all the other categories of queerness. Every time he said, "gay" or "gay men," she would add, you know, "LGBTQ," every other category of queerness and difference into it. In a way, it completely invalidated the book. It lost its point. It was absolutely specific to gender and a certain generation of gay men.
>
> In a sense, I could see exactly what her point was. The book in itself was exclusionary, and I understood her cultural resistance to, as she put it, "the primacy of white gay men at the top of the pyramid." But it was beside the point. And the author who is extremely sensitive to these things himself was absolutely, I could see him bristling at the idea of changing it. We had to reject that sensitivity report completely.

Although this publisher rejected this particular report, sensitive people accusing other sensitive people of not really being sensitive is what the Sensitivity Era is all about.

One of my more memorable interviews took place with a writer who was publicly shamed by their colleagues on an awards committee. To give some context, this writer is a progressive. They want more writers of color to win awards. They believe it is fair for award committees to give more attention to writers of color. They are a vocal critic of right-wing book censorship. Yet they, too, were accused of conspiring with the white supremacist devil. Just as the devil in Salem loved to possess church members, the white supremacist devil today loves to possess members of progressive award committees. In a statement that reads like a Twitter coda to *The Crucible*, this writer laments:

> That was a terrible time. The stuff that went on Twitter was abhorrent. There were lies. There were many lies posted about me. There were lies posted about another one of our board members who is Asian American. They were flat-out lies. She was very worried that she was going to lose her job over these tweets. It just got extremely fraught. I was in a position where I did not want to have to try to respond to every single accusation because that just becomes . . . it doesn't work. So I left Twitter for a couple of weeks, I think, because it was making me feel physically ill to go on Twitter and see these things that were being said. It was too much, so I did leave Twitter for a short time. But, apparently, that also looked bad. Like I was running away or something. It was a terrible time. People were accusing each other of all kinds of things. It was horrible. It was absolutely horrible. I thought I was going to lose my job. I didn't know what was going on. I didn't understand why it was happening. Because none of the things that were being said about me were true. No, I'm not a white supremacist.

In Salem, the accusations were prefigured by conflicts within the town that had nothing to do with witchcraft. In this awards committee, the accusations were prefigured by conflicts that had nothing to do with white supremacy. "All these things started building. Everyone was tired. Everyone was cranky. We hadn't met each other. It had been a really fraught time. People were on edge." Just as there are white supremacists, there are people who hurl false accusations of white supremacy with wanton indifference. Often, they hurl them at other people who hate white supremacy.

Even Philip Nel, who proselytizes about white supremacy with as much self-righteous indignation and technical fluency as Reverend Hale proselytizes about witchcraft, was dragged out to the public pillory. In an open letter, Debbie Reese accused him of being a "white savior" because he wrote a book about racism in children's and YA literature.[183] She suggested that he should have edited a collection of essays written by people "who aren't white males" instead.[184] For his part, Nel has accused other progressives of similarly dubious crimes. As less extreme people like Simone continue to flee online spaces like #YATwitter, and real spaces like publishers, agencies, and award committees, they will become even more extreme.[185] This problem is reinforced by the algorithmic "filter bubbles"[186] and "information cocoons"[187] that insulate extremists from an important antidote to their extremism: different viewpoints.[188] As Jonathan Haidt succinctly puts it in *The Righteous Mind*, "Morality binds and blinds."[189]

In this vein, consider what happened to YA novelist Jessica Cluess.[190] Recall that on November 30, 2020, Lorena Germán, the author of *The Anti Racist Teacher: Reading Instruction Workbook* and a cofounder of #Disrupt-Texts, tweeted: "Did y'all know that many of the 'classics' were written before the 50s? Think of US society before then and the values that shaped this nation afterwards. THAT is what is in those books. That is why we gotta switch it up. It ain't just about 'being old.' #DisruptTexts." For the thousands of people who follow Germán on Twitter, there was nothing provocative about her latest tweet. Grand, sweeping accusations about enormous periods of literature is the grist of presentism.

Yet YA novelist Jessica Cluess was provoked to respond. She tweeted:

> If you think Hawthorne was on the side of the judgmental Puritans in The Scarlet Letter then you are an absolute idiot and should not have the title of educator in your Twitter bio. This anti-intellectual, anti-curiosity bullshit is poison and I will stand here and scream that it is sheer goddamn evil until my hair falls out, I do not care. If you think Upton Sinclair was on the side of the meat-packing industry then you are a fool and should sit down and feel bad about yourself. Ah yes. That embodiment of brutal subjugation and toxic masculinity, Walden. Sit and spin on a tack. Remember how Louisa May Alcott wrote Little Women to uphold the patriarchy? If you do, stop taking drugs you hack. . . . Ah yes, remember Their Eyes Were Watching God, and other literature of the extraordinary Harlem Renaissance? I guess not. Dick.

Like much of what passes as communication on #YATwitter, Cluess's response was an emotive rant mixed with ad hominem attacks and accusations that "evil" was afoot. In this respect, it was utterly typical. Yet it was atypical to see a YA author criticize #DisruptTexts. Within the hour, Germán responded: "Sounds like I struck a confederate nerve. Any of my White T friends wanna jump in and get your girl? She's big mad." After the call for a pile-on was issued, a pile-on began.

The first reply came from Ken Lindblom, a white English professor whose Twitter name is a testament to virtue signaling: "Ken Lindblom is learning about White Supremacy."[191] In his tweet, which earned a public thank-you from Germán, Lindblom wrote, "I responded." Another white English teacher, barely able to contain her excitement, added, "I responded!"

A third white English teacher, of the Robin DiAngelo variety, tweeted at Cluess's publisher. "This thread screams #whitefragility instead of making a point," she exclaimed, "I'm sure @randomhousekids wouldn't want you talking to teachers like this." Other "allies" tattled on Cluess by tweeting at Random House Kids, too.

Another white English teacher tried to get Cluess in trouble with Twitter. "This middle-aged white teacher reported the account for targeted harassment and replied to her directly." Germán rewarded this white woman, who monologues in the third person, for her standout performance in allyship theater.[192] "Appreciate you," she tweeted, alongside the thumbs-up emoticon, as if she were Roger Ebert. In the theater of #YATwitter, white "allies" love to earn public brownie points from people of color. For the kind of liberal who spends hours a day on Twitter, prowling hashtag communities— #YATwitter, #Kidlit, #DisruptTexts, #DiversityJedi, #WhiteFragility, and so on—for the latest opportunity to "take a stand," this is what being an activist is all about.

These slacktivists genuinely believe their Twitter behavior is comparable to the great protest movements of the past. Laurie Halse Anderson, an award-winning children's and YA author, explains: "Are you in a lather cuz some of these critiques are harsh? Were they mean, angry, or used bad words? Asking nicely didn't make any changes in the Civil Rights movement. Being polite didn't desegregate schools. Tip-toeing didn't force voting rights for all."[193] For Anderson and other social media gadflies, there is no difference between activists who put a lot on the line and slacktivists who spend a lot of time online.

That said, the response to Cluess did not trump up a problem where none existed, unless one thinks that calling people idiots and accusing them of evil is not a problem. But the response did ramp up the nature of this problem. As Justin Tosi and Brandon Warmke explain, ramping up occurs when discourse "devolves into a moral arms race, where people make increasingly strong claims about the matter under discussion."[194] As the research shows, "members of a deliberating group usually end up at a more extreme position in the same general direction as their inclination before deliberation began." This social phenomenon, known as "group polarization," has been found in hundreds of studies, and it "provides a clue to extremism of many different kinds."[195]

In particular, it provides a clue to l'affaire Cluess. Although Germán acknowledged that she was not hurt by the tweets and, in fact, found them funny, other tweeters felt that "harm" had occurred. They denounced the tweets as "violence." They also condemned the tweets as "racist"—a particularly strange non sequitur, given that the tweets celebrated the Harlem Renaissance. For Glenn Loury, an African American economist in his seventies, the "self-righteous, smug tyranny" is familiar. "It used to be, 'You don't think like me, you must be Communist,'" he reflects, "Now remove 'Communist' and put in 'racist.'"[196] Before that, it was "You don't think like me, you must be a witch."

Predictably, accusations that a violent racist was running wild on #YATwitter—"The Devil's loose in Salem, Mr. Proctor!" and "We dare not quail to follower wherever the accusing finger points!"[197]—provoked a ritual of public shaming reminiscent of *The Crucible*, *The Scarlet Letter*, and other classics that these crusaders hate. Like Amélie Wen Zhao, Kosoko Jackson, and Nathaniel Hawthorne's Hester Prynne, Jessica Cluess learned what the scaffold of the pillory feels like. The next day, she, too, apologized:

> I am writing to apologize for a thread I tweeted yesterday.
>
> I take full responsibility for my unprovoked anger toward Lorena Germán and the impact of my words on her and all who read them. I neither expect nor will ask for anyone's forgiveness, or to engage with me further regarding this issue. I want to acknowledge the pain I caused, and to apologize sincerely for it. My words were misguided, wrong, and deeply hurtful. I must—and will—do better moving forward.
>
> I am committed to learning more about Ms. Germán's important work with #DisruptTexts. I agree that what counts as canon in literature changes over time, and that it can be and should be contested and expanded to other, more inclusive kinds of text.
>
> Again, I am deeply sorry. I will strive to do better.

The apology reads like it was written by a schoolgirl in Lois Lowry's *The Giver*, who just had her hands slapped with a "discipline wand."[198] All the emotion, sass, and originality in the initial tweets is replaced by language so dead and formulaic that one wonders if Cluess plagiarized the apologies of other writers who acknowledge the pain they caused, who had a moral revelation, who are still unworthy of forgiveness, who thank the congregation that publicly flagellated them, and who now promise to "do better." Like Lowry's dystopian classic, the "corrections and apologies are very prompt" on #KidLit and #YATwitter.[199] Like *1984*, the point is not just to punish the person who commits crimethink but to change them, too.[200]

The response to Cluess's apology makes the schoolgirl comparison look even more apt. Within a day, an English teacher marked up Cluess's apology with red ink and reposted it to Twitter.[201] In a textbook example of ramping up, she replaced "thread" with "threats," "unprovoked rage" with "white rage," and "misguided" with "racist." She also added a confession of "violent bullying," and a promise to "commit all profits from my upcoming book to #DisruptTexts initiatives." As Yale University English professor David Bromwich points out, "Rhetorically upping the ante" allows a person to charge "the atmosphere, morally, in a way as spectacular as it is unwarranted."[202]

This English teacher's tweet earned just under a thousand likes because treating adults like misbehaving children is what antiracist activism looks like on #KidLit and #YATwitter. "I am amazed you do not see what weighty work we do," proclaimed one of Abigail's followers in *The Crucible*.[203] "If they scream and howl and fall to the floor," wrote Arthur Miller, "the person's clapped in the jail for bewitchin' them."[204]

With the vitriol directed at dead authors like Miller and living authors like Cluess as the reference point, one is reminded of Mark Fisher's writings on the Vampires' Castle.[205] In 2013, this theorist tried to make sense of an emerging era of anti-intellectualism, punishment, and re-education on Left Twitter. In "Exiting the Vampire Castle," he reflects: "The Vampires' Castle specializes in propagating guilt. It is driven by a *priest's desire* to excommunicate and condemn, an *academic-pedant's desire* to be the first to be seen to spot a mistake, and a *hipster's desire* to be one of the in-crowd. The danger in attacking the Vampires' Castle is that it can look as if—and it will do everything it can to reinforce this thought—that one is also attacking the struggles against racism, sexism, heterosexism."

In the case of Cluess, people jumped in to condemn her tweets defending dead authors, to spot and correct the mistakes in her apology, and to show everyone else on #YATwitter that they, too, were part of Germán's righteous in-crowd. The pile-on evolved into an excommunication as Cluess's agent was dragged into the drama. The same day Cluess published her apology, Brooks Sherman published his own statement:

> I thank everyone who took it upon themselves to bring the recent tweets of my client, Jessica Cluess, to my attention. I also apologize for taking so long to

publicly respond; but I felt obligated to speak directly with my client and then gather my thoughts before making any sort of public statement.

Let me be clear: Jessica's behavior yesterday, in which she made a series of condescending and personal attacks on a Dominican American woman educator, was deeply problematic and inexcusable. It is another example of the white privilege and systemic power imbalance that pervades the publishing industry and this country. I care very much for Jessica, and I also hold her accountable for her actions.

I realize that my silence up to now may have given the impression that I am indifferent to what took place yesterday, or even that I am complicit. I promise this: I am listening, I am working to elevate the voices of those who have been historically marginalized in our industry, and I am committed to engaging in the hard conversations needed to move us all forward together.

The formation of an actual thought requires time. So it is unclear why waiting one day to respond is something that warrants a public apology. Yet, in the world of #YATwitter, where the lowest attention spans dominate and the present is all that matters, everything has to be as immediately consumable as a TV dinner. As one African American writer I interviewed described it to me, "It's so easy for us, these days, to bash someone and then get rid of them because we live in a microwave society where everything is instant."

It is also unclear why Cluess's agent and her publisher had to be alarmingly notified about a few tweets. Germán's "allies" are like helicopter parents who are incapable of letting young people work out disagreements on their own, so they badger school officials to intervene. It is even less clear why Germán's identity as a Dominican American woman has anything to do with Cluess's defense of Alcott, Hawthorne, and the Harlem Renaissance. It is just an unclear how one adult calling another adult a "dick" on Twitter exemplifies "white privilege" and a "systemic power imbalance" that pervades the United States. The whole point of concepts like "structural racism" is to redirect attention from personal behaviors toward actual structures.

Yet, as Columbia University English professor Jack Halberstam reflects, some people "seem to have equated social activism with descriptive statements about individual harm and psychic pain."[206] For Halberstam, this "finger snapping moralism," which makes people feel "erotically bonded through [their] self-righteousness," reflects "contemporary desires for immediately consumable messages of progress." It should be recognized as the internecine melodrama that it is. Moreover, people should "take a hard long look at the privileges that often prop up public performances of grief and outrage." The whole #DisruptTexts brouhaha demonstrates how much power Germán and her thousands of followers—not Cluess—have. To build on a point made by African American literary critic Kenneth W. Warren, crusaders adopt "the posture of speaking truth to the very power they themselves exercise."[207]

As expected, Sherman's statement was excoriated as insufficient. Two days later, he published a second statement. In another textbook example of conformity and ramping up, he replaced the adjective "problematic" with "racist." Because moral crusades revolve around guilt by association, what researchers call "moral contagion," Sherman also let the world know that he terminated his relationship with Cluess.[208] To return to the empirical research on the false enforcement of social norms, "enforcing a view is effective at increasing the apparent sincerity of that view, even if the enforcement occurs in a setting where suspicion of conformity and false enforcement would be very plausible."[209] In the Sensitivity Era, one communicates how moral they are by publicly punishing those who are declared immoral.

In this respect, the "You're fired!" atmosphere of Trump Tower looks a lot like the atmosphere of #YATwitter. One person even responded to Sherman's tweet with two clapping emoticons as if they were watching the latest episode of *The Apprentice*.[210] Like the wood-and-iron pillory in *The Scarlet Letter*, the digital pillory of #YATwitter is a constant source of entertainment. As Loretta Ross, a black feminist, teacher, and former program research director at the Center for Democratic Renewal/National Anti-Klan Network, reflects: "Why are [people] making choices to make the world crueler than it needs to be and calling that being 'woke?'"[211] The research suggests that a lot of people make the world crueler so no one will think they are on the side of witchcraft, communism, or, in more recent times, racism.

For the adults who participate in these degradation ceremonies, there is also a process of self-radicalization. Much like ramping up, this occurs when one's behavior gradually becomes more extreme. An adult might begin with a reasonable critique of *An American Tragedy* or *The House of Mirth*. This adult might move on to a less reasonable critique of every piece of literature written before 1950. In the end, this adult might demand that an author be stripped of their agent for disagreeing with their critique. As psychologist Hubert J. M. Hermans explains, "Self-radicalization takes place on a sliding scale of self-justification in which there is no particularly specific point where the participant recognizes 'this is not right.'" According to Hermans, "it all starts out innocently, but along a gradual scale the process creeps up to more radical levels without the participants coming to realize, 'Well, hmm, this is something different from what just happened earlier.'" This process is fueled by "models" who push people in the direction of more extreme behavior.[212] One minute, one is criticizing an old book. The next minute one is cheering as a woman loses her livelihood. "The exercise of power," wrote dystopian novelist Anthony Burgess in *1985*, "is the most intoxicating of narcotics."[213]

Self-radicalization is also a perennial feature of herd behavior. In *Moral Disengagement*, Stanford University psychologist Albert Bandura conceptualizes the ways in which people absolve themselves for immoral actions. For the herd, "cloaking detrimental activities in euphemisms" is a powerful resource.[214] Thus, ending a novelist's career over a handful of relatively innocuous tweets is not regarded as morally reprehensible behavior.[215] It is regarded as an act of "holding each other accountable" and "battling racism."[216] This euphemistic doublespeak is, to borrow a term from communications scholar J. Dan Rothwell's *Telling It Like It Isn't*, "linguistic Novocain."[217] It relieves moral crusaders of the shame they should feel.

What poet Charles Mackay calls "the madness of crowds"[218] is especially relevant to apologies. By way of example, imagine a situation in which one adult in a book club offends another adult. The second adult might talk to the first adult after the day's discussion ends. The two adults might exchange their perspectives. Perhaps the first adult apologizes. Perhaps the second adult realizes they overreacted. Perhaps they bring fresh eyes to the situation a week or two later. In any case, the exchange is dyadic. It relates to Ross's concept of "calling in," rather than "calling out."[219] There is no audience.

On social media, there is always an audience. "Third parties always introduce, represent, or develop a third set of interests once they enter into the proceedings," writes Nichols Tavuchis in his treatise on the sociology of apology and reconciliation. These interests involve a desire for retweets, "likes," and other forms of social recognition. "Apologies in such circumstances, if forthcoming, are likely in one way or another to become subject to standards the disputants themselves might otherwise not have applied."[220] In particular, the third parties inject a feeling of urgency. Like a commercial break during *The Apprentice*, the apology and the return to action must be instant.

These spectacles make apologies look inauthentic. An adult in a book club is not pressured by thousands of strangers and the threat of career loss to apologize. But the deviants on #Kidlit and #YATwitter are. Inevitably, this raises the meta-accusation, which might never be raised in a dyadic exchange, that the deviant is only apologizing to avoid public punishment. In other words, there will always be a specter of artificiality when apology and reconciliation are a third-party spectacle. Like the third parties described by Tavuchis, the third parties on #Kidlit and #YATwitter use apologies not to forgive and forget but to escalate the drama.

As was the case with the moral panic over comic books, many young people do not feel like they have a voice. In part, this is due to the amount of space these adults take up. According to Bowker Market Research, young adults are not the biggest market for YA literature: "55% of buyers of works that publishers designate for kids aged 12 to 17—known as YA books—are 18 or older, with the largest segment aged 30 to 44, a group that alone accounted for 28% of YA sales. And adults aren't just purchasing for others—when asked about the intended recipient, they report that 78% of the time they are purchasing books for their own reading."[221] Other sources estimate that "nearly 70 percent of all YA titles are purchased by adults."[222] In large part, what people call the field of YA literature is a field of adults writing books for other adults. Given the reality that children under 12 are even less likely to buy books for themselves, and the other reality that some of these children cannot read books by themselves, the percentage of adult consumers is likely much higher for children's literature. What I call the moral crusade over children's and YA literature is, in large part, actually a moral crusade over literature written for adults.

On #Kidlit and #YATwitter, adults have the loudest and most indignant voices. In the words of Sierra Elmore, a college student and queer book blogger of color, "I and other people I know (mostly teens) are terrified about speaking up in this community" because there is "no difference of opinion allowed, people reigning, etc."[223] To be sure, some teenagers do participate in the moral crusade over children's and YA literature. Mimi, the pseudonym of a teen book blogger, never read *The Black Witch* by Laurie Forest. But the handful of sentences she did read were "very hurtful, and very, like, just harmful and triggering."[224] She encouraged other people to avoid the book, too. Yet, like Elmore, Mimi expressed fear about talking to Kat Rosenfield, a journalist and YA author who, because of her criticism of #YATwitter, is considered a folk devil. "If anyone found out I was talking to you," Mimi told Rosenfield, "I would be blackballed." In other words, after she blackballed Forest, Mimi worried that she, too, would be blackballed. Guilt by association.

Mimi is one of the relatively few young people involved in the moral crusade over what young people read. When one looks at the most influential websites—American Indians in Children's Literature, Brown Bookshelf, Latinxs in Kid Lit, and so on—no teenagers or children are listed as contributors. Of all the websites recommended by the Cooperative Children's Book Center at the University of Wisconsin–Madison for their content reviews, only Indigo's Bookshelf is a website run by youth.[225] Specifically, it is run by youth between the ages of twelve and twenty. Unlike other websites, this website had just six posts in 2020. Most of these posts have zero comments. If someone believes the gatekeepers of children's and YA literature prioritize the perspectives of children and young adults, I encourage them to look around.[226] I also encourage them to try and spot someone without a college degree. As chapter 3 argues, there is a distinct class character to the moral panic over children's and YA literature.

Despite the progressive ideals of this crusade, conservative authors are rarely targeted. Amélie Wen Zhao is a Chinese immigrant who wrote *Blood Heir* as a "critique of the epidemic of indentured labor and human trafficking prevalent in many industries across Asia, including in my own home country."[227] Kosoko Jackson is a gay, African American sensitivity reader who works for Big Five publishers. His job is to make literature inoffensive. The month before he was transformed into a deviant, he participated in the witch hunt against Zhao. Vanessa Brantley-Newton, the illustrator of *A Birthday Cake for George Washington*, is an African American woman and a past finalist for the NAACP Image Award for Outstanding Literary Work for Children. The editor of her book, Andrea Davis Pinkney, is also an African American children's author and a past recipient of the Coretta Scott King Award. Pinkney also launched the first African American children's book imprint at Walt Disney.

Becky Albertalli worked as a clinical psychologist with LGBTQ+ teenagers. She wrote *Simon vs. the Homo Sapiens Agenda* as a progressive novel for them. Laura Moriarty, who consulted Muslim sensitivity readers as she worked on *American Heart*, wrote her novel as an artistic response to Islamophobia and xenophobia in the 2016 presidential election.[228] Before *Kirkus*'s retraction, this novel was starred in a review written by a Muslim woman of color who believed it was "a useful warning about the direction we're headed in."[229] Brought to tears by an *NPR* report about bombings in Iraq, Keira Drake "wanted to write about privilege, about the way that those who have it can so easily turn a blind eye to the suffering of those who don't" in *The Continent*.[230] Brooks Sherman, who was accused of racism via the guilt-by-association logic of moral crusades, is the same agent who shepherded *The Hate U Give* to publication. In the back of her novel, Angie Thomas describes him as a "friend" and "superhero."[231]

Like accusations of witchcraft in Salem, Massachusetts, which were hurled at church members, a minister, and a judge of the witchcraft court, accusations of intolerance are hurled at the authors, illustrators, editors, reviewers, and agents who are least likely to be intolerant.[232] To borrow Simone's language, "they're shouting at the people who already agree with them."[233] Indeed, all of these controversial books were celebrated by people who value diverse, sensitive, and progressive books. "While the world may indeed 'look' the same to people who happen to wear the same sociomental lenses," explains sociologist Eviatar Zerubavel, "it actually looks quite different to people who do not."[234] Books may look the same to the extremists on #Kidlit and #YATwitter—recall that "piling on" and "duckspeak" are pillars of these hashtag communities—but they actually look quite different to readers who are not extremists.

Hence the mainstream success of so many of these books. As a case in point, consider *Harry Potter*. On the one hand, J. K. Rowling is one of the most popular authors in the history of the English language. In the week of January 24, 2021, five of the ten most read works of fiction were *Harry Potter* books. These books have been on Amazon's list since 2017, when the first list was published, even though Rowling's series ended in 2007. Through her fiction, she has become one of the richest people in the world. On the other hand, she has become a punching bag for the moral crusade over literature. In the past few years, her novels have been accused of racism, sexism, ableism, transphobia, fatphobia, and antisemitism.

In the fall of 2020, *Newsweek* reported that videos of progressives burning her books were "spreading like wildfire across TikTok."[235] In one video, *Harry Potter and the Philosopher's Stone* is on fire atop a pile of other books, as the book burner condemns the "harmful fatphobia, racism, and valo-rization of supremacists and child abusers in her most famous work." For her part, moral crusader Anna María, a sensitivity reader and editor at the *Daily Dot*, demanded more extreme action from her Twitter followers: "I'm gonna need cis Brits to step it up. Why has this violent transphobe not got-ten jumped yet?" María hopes that Rowling's "nose breaks and it gushes all over her clothes (:" and "her teeth get knocked out and she can't find them (:"[236] When people make no distinction between words and violence—another sensitivity reader told me, during our interview, that "reading a story" can feel like "getting kicked in the teeth"—violence can feel like a proportionate response to words. According to María, jumping a female novelist who survived domestic violence is not what injustice looks like. It is what justice looks like.

This does not mean Rowling was "canceled." It also does not mean that Rowling or her work should be exempt from criticism. But there is a differ-ence between criticizing her novels, her comments about trans people, or whatever else one takes issue with, and acting like the firemen in *Fahrenheit 451*. Indeed, some progressives are as hysterical as the Christian fundamen-talists who burn *Harry Potter* books because they believe Rowling's oeuvre promotes witchcraft and the occult. "I have met thousands of children now, and not even one time has a child come up to me and said, 'Ms. Rowling, I'm so glad I've read these books because now I want to be a witch,'" Rowl-ing explained to the BBC.[237] Likewise, it is unclear that Rowling has trans-formed even one child into a racist and fatphobic anti-Semite. Regardless of whether one looks at the interpretations of the PC Left or the interpre-tations of the Christian Right, there is a glaring disjunction between their interpretations and how these books are interpreted by the general public.

This disjunction is what Meg Rosoff had in mind when she described Debbie Reese and the rest of these moral crusaders as "stormtroopers." Rosoff, the winner of the Guardian Children's Fiction Prize and the Printz Award for YA literature, reflects: "Isn't it interesting that the books targeted by the Debbie Reese Crimes Against Diversity stormtroopers keep appear-ing on the best books of the year lists?"[238] Rosoff and Rowling can ignore the book burners, but the debut authors who depend on these bloggers, Bookstagrammers, BookTokers, and tweeters for positive publicity cannot.

Given the progressive commitments of these authors, and the nature of the charges hurled against them, the old joke about progressives who form circular firing squads devoted to politically irrelevant issues does not sound like a joke. It sounds like someone is trying to describe the Sensitivity Era. Circular firing squads, which shoot faster and more viciously as their moral panic escalates in intensity and irrationality, is what adrienne maree brown had in mind when she titled her recent book *We Will Not Cancel Us* rather than *They Will Not Cancel Us*. An Octavia Butler scholar and a queer black feminist, brown reflects:

> Lately, as the attacks grow faster and more vicious, I wonder: is this what we're here for? To cultivate a fear-based adherence to reductive common values? What can this lead to in an imperfect world full of sloppy, complex humans? Is it possible we will call each other out until there's no one left beside us? I've had tons of conversations with people who, in these moments of public flaying, avoid stepping up on the side of complexity or curiosity because in the back of our minds is the shared unspoken question: when will y'all come for me?
>
> we've always known lynch mobs are a master's tool. meaning: moving as an angry mob, sparked by fear (often unfounded or misguided) with the power to issue instant judgment and instant punishment. these are master's tools. we in movements for justice didn't create lynch mobs. we didn't create witch trials. we didn't create this punitive system of justice. . . . the master's tools feel good to use, groove in the hand easily from repeated use and training. but they are often blunt and senseless.
>
> many of us seem to worry that if we don't immediately jump on whatever mob wagon has pulled up in our dms, that we will be next to be called out, or called a rape apologist or a white person whisperer or an internalized misogynist, or just disposed of for refusing to group think and then group act.
>
> I have been doing movement work for 25 years. There was a real sense of, "Why do I feel afraid to just observe something and speak about what I'm observing?" To me, that felt like it's its own proof of something being there. If there was no such thing as cancel culture or callout culture—in the sense that if you say the wrong thing, you can get disposed of—I don't think I would've felt that I was taking a big risk by speaking about it.[239]

To build on brown's point, can anyone guess the question that my interview subjects asked me the most? Some version of: "This interview is anonymous, right?" Even after my subjects read a recruitment message that guaranteed their anonymity, and even after they read a consent form that guaranteed their anonymity, and even after I asked them to confirm that they read this consent form that guaranteed anonymity, my subjects still wanted to reconfirm that they would not be named in *That Book Is Dangerous!* It did not matter if they were one of the most powerful people in the world of contemporary literature (for example, a Big Five vice president who would not let me record our interview) or a person with no power (for example, a recent graduate of an MFA program who has not even finished writing their first novel). Looking around, who can blame them? Likewise, who thinks adrienne maree brown is irrational? The answer: the moral crusaders who make these people afraid.

While progressives continue to point their fingers at other progressives, devouring their own side until no one is left, Big Five publishers continue to churn out books by conservative authors. At the time I was writing *That Book Is Dangerous!*, recent titles from Simon and Schuster included *Standing Up to Goliath: Battling State and National Teachers' Unions for the Heart and Soul of Our Kids and Country* by Rebecca Friedrichs and *Them before Us: Why We Need a Global Children's Rights Movement* by Katy Faust and Stacy Manning. The latter overturns "myths" like "love makes a family—biology is irrelevant," and there is "'no difference' in outcomes for kids with same-sex parents."[240]

Unlike Zhao, Jackson, and other progressive authors pilloried on Twitter, these conservative authors actually have the attention of politicians who make decisions that affect real children, real teenagers, and real parents. As Fred Deutsch, a Republican member of the South Dakota House of Representatives, puts it in his blurb for *Them before Us*: "Finally! A book that speaks to me as a parent and as a lawmaker about the need to protect children from much of the world's craziness, including the breakdown of the family." If progressives care about protecting young people from harm, there are bigger fish to fry than well-intentioned books written by other progressives. Above all, there are bigger fish to fry than books.

3 The Political Economy of the Sensitivity Era

You see, there were two Harlems. There were those who lived in Sugar Hill and there was the Hollow, where we lived. There was a great divide between the black people on the Hill and us. I was just a ragged, funky black shoeshine boy and was afraid of the people on the Hill, who, for their part, didn't want to have anything to do with me.

—James Baldwin, interviewed by Julius Lester, May 27, 1984

You got 1 percent of the population in America who owns 41 percent of the wealth . . . but within the black community, the top 1 percent of black folk have over 70 percent of the wealth. So that means you got a lot of precious Jamals and Letitias who are told to live vicariously . . . so that it's all about 'representation' rather than substantive transformation.

—Cornel West, interviewed by Joe Rogan, July 24, 2019[1]

The Haves and the Have Nots

One morning, Jason Allen arrived at a mansion in Bridgehampton, New York.[2] Like most writers, Allen punched cash register buttons, bartended at a restaurant, and threw on a hard hat to pay his bills. That morning, he arrived to clean a swimming pool. After he marched through the potentially tick-filled, waist-high grass he found the pool filter. As he opened the structure that contained the filter, he heard a hissing sound. Six or seven angry snakes blocked the handle that he needed to turn. Inside a studio detached from the mansion, the pool owner sipped her teacup and stared at the ceiling above her window. This person was a writer. She explained to Allen that she, too, was having a tough day. Writer's block.

Looking back on his time in Bridgehampton, Allen reflects: "There seems to be two camps most unpublished writers fall into: the Haves and the Have

Nots." If one reads Allen's article, it is apparent that the Haves are those who have the time, space, and other resources to do their work. The Have Nots are those who clean their swimming pools, bag their groceries, and deliver their Grubhub orders. Yet, if one reads the criticism produced in the Sensitivity Era, one would get a much different impression. In fact, one of the defining features of the era is its inattention to class differences. In the case of children's and YA literature, this inattention is a long-standing feature of literary criticism.

As a case in point, consider Ian Wojcik-Andrews's lament in a 1993 issue of the *Lion and the Unicorn*. Wojcik-Andrews, a scholar of children's literature, explains that because class is so important in the lives of children, "the absence of a sustained class analysis in children's literature criticism is surprising."[3] Over two decades later, Angela E. Hubler echoes Wojcik-Andrews's concerns. As she explains in *Little Red Readings: Historical Materialist Perspectives on Children's Literature*, the development of a literary tradition that "examines the way that gender and race are represented in children's literature" has not been matched by a similarly robust and critical tradition that examines the significance of class.[4]

In *Children's Literature* and *Children's Literature Association Quarterly*, the two flagship journals of the Children's Literature Association, just 176 articles even include the word "capitalism."[5] In contrast, more than seven hundred articles include "race," and more than one thousand articles include "gender."[6] Books that introduce readers to approaches to children's literature echo this trend. In *Children's Literature*, Pat Pinsent writes chapters on theoretical approaches such as "Gender Studies and Queer Theory," but no chapters on historical materialism or other class-based approaches.[7] Likewise, the recent edition of *Reading Children's Literature: A Critical Introduction* by Carrie Hintz and Eric L. Tribunella devotes chapters to "Race, Ethnicity, and Culture," "Genders and Sexualities," and even "Domesticity and Adventure," but no chapter to class.[8] An understanding of race, gender, and even domesticity and adventure in children's literature would be enhanced, not diminished, by a comparable attention to class.

In almost three decades of statistical work on black characters, disabled characters, LGBTQ+ characters, and characters with other identities, the Cooperative Children's Book Center at the University of Wisconsin–Madison has never looked at the representation of poor and working-class characters in children's and YA books. Nor have they ever documented the class backgrounds of the people who write these books. As they explain, "There is still a long way to go before publishing for children and teens reflects the rich diversity of perspectives and experiences."[9] In the Sensitivity Era, these diverse perspectives and experiences have nothing to do with the differences between those who live in mansions and those who clean their swimming pools.

The research on YA literature is similar. In a recent article in *Study and Scrutiny: Research in Young Adult Literature*, Crag Hill and Janine J. Darragh remind readers that "scholarship around the representations of poverty in YA literature is scant at best."[10] Furthermore, Todd Jennings's study of 142 university teacher preparation programs "discovered that only 3% of secondary programs foregrounding diversity in their courses emphasized social class, far fewer than those programs that emphasized race/ethnicity."[11] As the tenth anniversary edition of literary critic Walter Benn Michaels's *The Trouble with Diversity: How We Learned to Love Identity and Ignore Inequality* argues, talking about identities is still a lot more fashionable than talking about economic inequality.[12] "The effort to imagine a world organized by subject positions," writes Michaels, "and divided into identities instead of classes has of course, under general rubrics like postmodernism or postructuralism or posthistoricism, been widespread."[13]

It has been most widespread in English departments. Just read the job advertisements. When one searches "American literature" in the MLA Job List, seventy-two out of seventy-four positions in North America seek applicants who specialize in race, ethnicity, sexuality, disability, indigeneity, and other identities.[14] Typically, the identity is in the position title: "Assistant Professor of Latina/o/x Literatures and Cultures," "Assistant Professor of Latinx and/or Indigenous American Literature," "Assistant Professor in Black Rhetorics," "Assistant Professor of African and African American Literature and Culture," and "Assistant Professor of Race, Diaspora, and Indigeneity." In some English departments, it does not even matter what the identity is—as long as it is an identity and not a class. A typical job advertisement, this one for an "Assistant Professor of American Literatures at Illinois Wesleyan University," states: "We seek candidates who specialize in and can deliver engaging courses that focus on African American literature, Asian American literature, diasporic studies, disability studies, gender studies, queer studies, global literatures, Latinx literature, and/or Native American literature."[15] To be clear, there are scholars in these fields who do impressive work. But good luck locating a job advertisement that mentions class studies. Economic inequality tends to only be relevant, and typically never relevant enough to be mentioned in a job description, if it is understood within a silo of identity studies.

When one looks at the writing guides published in the Sensitivity Era, the literary festivals held in the era, the organizations that emerged in the era, the book review policies that structure the era, and who the era targets as its folk devils, economic inequality remains an inequality that few people talk about. For example, *Writing the Other: A Practical Approach* by Nisi Shawl and Cynthia Ward is structured by the ROAARS acronym: race, (sexual) orientation, age, ability, religion, and sex.[16] Likewise, the Festival of Literary Diversity centers "a diverse range of stories that are underrepresented in literary settings; that reflect variations in geography, ethnicity, race, culture, gender, ability, sexual orientation, and religion."[17] We Need Diverse Books recognizes "all diverse experiences, including (but not limited to) LGBTQIA, Native, people of color, gender diversity, people with disabilities, and ethnic, cultural, and religious minorities."[18] It is as if people are competing to see who can create the longest identity list that does not mention class.

Even pitching events are part of this competition. Consider Diverse Pitch: "#DVpit is a Twitter event created to showcase pitches from unagented, marginalized voices that have been historically underrepresented in publishing. This may include (but is not limited to): Black, Indigenous, People of Color (BIPOC); people living and/or born/raised in marginalized, underrepresented cultures and countries; disabled persons (includes neurodivergence and mental illness); people on marginalized ends of the cultural and/or religious spectrum; people identifying within LGBTQIA+; and more." In the end, people living and/or born/raised in poverty are not as interesting as "people living and/or born/raised in marginalized, underrepresented cultures."

Furthermore, book review policies are not designed to help poor and working-class readers find the books that do represent their experiences. Recall that *Kirkus Reviews* requires its reviewers to identify "characters in children's and teen books by identity and/or race—all the time."[19] Because race is still a scientifically and culturally dubious concept, it is not surprising that *Kirkus* cannot tell the difference between an Asian character and a sleeping white character. Though, their reviewers should be able to tell the difference between a character whose parents work on Wall Street and a character whose parents clean public restrooms for a living. But the editors at *Kirkus* are not interested in that kind of difference.

For example, their review of *The Hate U Give* never mentions that Starr's father is a small business owner and her mother is a nurse. The first sentence emphasizes Starr's identity as "a black girl."[20] Like the sensitivity readers who claim to represent this or that identity, the editors at *Kirkus* believe that what young readers want most are characters who share their race. According to this logic, a poor black child is more likely to identify with a story about the black child of a small business owner and nurse, than a story about a white child who also does not have school supplies, lunch money, or a stable roof over their head. If the matter were otherwise, the "duties of a reviewer"[21] might have something to do with the lived realities of people who are poor.

Furthermore, if these reviews were really as progressive as *Kirkus* suggests, they would distinguish the conservative literature of self-help—Starr's family moves to a richer neighborhood in the last chapter of *The Hate U Give*: the end—from stories where economic mobility is a shared project that occurs through strikes, sit-ins, and political legislation. The ascent of *The Hate U Give* as the social justice novel par excellence exemplifies how economically vacuous ideas about inequality and justice in children's and YA literary culture are.

These ideas also permeate bookstores. Politics and Prose, the celebrated independent bookstore in Washington, DC, reposts material from WNDB to its Tumblr website. On its home page, there is a section devoted to "Diverse Voices." Their in-store and online events have included the chance to hear Dhonielle Clayton, Ellen Oh, Justina Ireland, and other leaders in the moral crusade over children's and YA literature. Around the time this bookstore held their "Latinx" event featuring David Bowles, they also hired Jones Day, "a law firm known for its aggressive anti-union tactics," after they refused to recognize their employees' union.[22] Although Politics and Prose's owners love diverse books and #OwnVoices authors, they have far less tolerance for the voices of their own employees.

Like Politics and Prose, which prides itself as an independent bookstore, Amazon, which prides itself as the juggernaut of bookstores, paid Russell Brown, the head of RWP Labor, a whopping $3,200 per day to help them crush a union drive.[23] At the same time, their website reminds everyone to purchase the "must-read books by Black authors."[24] These authors matter. The employees who stock and ship their books do not.

In the Sensitivity Era, the problem is twofold. First, the era gives the impression that the inequalities that matter most are the inequalities not defined by money. Distinguished professors, *New York Times* bestselling authors, and other people love to talk about the differences between black people and white people, trans people and cis people, and queer people and heterosexual people, but many of these liberals have little or nothing to say about the differences between the overwhelming majority of Americans on the one hand and highly educated Americans with high incomes (themselves) on the other. In his award-winning book on children's and YA literature, it is easier for Distinguished Professor Philip Nel to confess his "white male, straight, cisgendered privilege,"[25] than to mention his $121,271.80 salary, his wife's $137,985.90 salary, and the egregious poverty that circumscribes their affluence.[26]

To be clear, class is not another difference to be recognized, celebrated, and treated as if it was just another identity.[27] One can have an equal world where there are men and women, gay people and heterosexual people, and people with different amounts of melanin in their skin. One cannot have an equal world where some authors have to work minimum wage jobs to support their writing and other authors have trust funds or partners with six-figure salaries. One cannot have an equal world where a pair of English professors rake in more than $200,000 per year, but the underclass who mows their university lawns, who caters their "distinguished" lectures, and who scrubs their office toilets lives paycheck to paycheck. In large part, the movement for diverse and sensitive books is appealing because it allows distinguished professors, bestselling authors, and other members of the chatterati to talk about social justice without talking to or about poor people. As Michaels might put it, it is the kind of movement that discomforts confessional liberals like Nel while "leaving intact the thing that makes them most comfortable of all: their wealth."[28]

Although it is unclear how these confessions benefit people of color, it is clear how they do not benefit poor white people. In a recent study published by the American Psychological Association, Erin Cooley and her colleagues assessed the benefits of reading about white privilege. Despite the au courant tendency for affluent white liberals to engage in public displays of maudlin introspection, this study found "when liberals read about white privilege . . . it didn't significantly change how they empathized with a poor black person—but it did significantly bump *down* their sympathy for a poor white person."[29] Yet, when one reads a scholarly book like *Was the Cat in the Hat Black?*, or a children's book like *Not My Idea: A Book about Whiteness*, one gets the impression that the biggest challenge confronting black people is white people's failure to talk about themselves.

This idea—the inequalities that matter most are the inequalities not defined by money—even manifests in submission guidelines. A few examples:

> We value the voices and stories of all marginalized writers. . . . There are no submission fees for Black writers for the month of February. . . . There are no submission fees for writers living with both visible and invisible disabilities for the month of March. . . . There are no submission fees for all API [Asian American and Pacific Islander] writers for the month of May. . . . There are no submission fees for LGBTQIA2+ writers in June. . . . There are no submission fees for Latinx writers from September 15th to October 15th. . . . There are no submission fees during the month of November for all Indigenous writers.
>
> —*New Orleans Review*, Loyola University[30]

> We aim to support work by those often marginalized in the artistic conversation, including (though certainly not limited to) people of color, women, disabled people, LGBTQIA people, and people with intersectional identities.
>
> —*Portland Review*, Portland State University[31]

> "Black and Indigenous submitters may email their submissions, for no fee. . . . We especially strive to magnify voices that are traditionally and systemically silenced. Writers of color, queer and trans writers, disabled writers, immigrant writers, fat writers and femmes: you are all welcome and wanted here."
>
> —*Black Warrior Review*, University of Alabama[32]

If you are a poor white writer who cannot afford these submission fees, you are out of luck. If you are a writer of color, you are "welcome and wanted here." (I particularly appreciate how even fat writers are considered more "systemically silenced" than poor writers). The same is true at *Southern Humanities Review*, *Hayden's Ferry Review*, and other magazines that wave fees for writers who have enough melanin in their skin.[33] "The U.S. already struggles with a social imagination that conflates race and class, equating economic struggle or poverty with dark skin and economic stability or wealth with light skin," reflects scholar Stephanie Jones.[34] Literary magazines reinforce that conflation.

When one looks at Manuscript Wish List, AgentQuery, Publisher's Marketplace, and Literary-Agents.com, the story is similar. Throughout, one finds statements like this: "I am an editor of picture books and graphic novels, and am only accepting unagented submissions from POC at this time."[35] This is not a statement from a fringe figure in literary production. It is a statement from Kait Feldmann, an editor at Scholastic, who has since been promoted to senior editor at HarperCollins.

To put it differently, if you are an African American writer like Colson Whitehead, the Harvard-educated child of wealthy Manhattanites who own a house in the Hamptons, Feldmann believes your birthright entitles you to the additional privilege of her attention.[36] If you are Jason Allen, a white writer who cleans pools for a living, you are not allowed to send Feldmann your manuscript. In one of the most economically unequal countries in the world, this is what literary culture—and literary justice—looks like.

Unlike Whitehead, Allen must also pay submission fees. According to the gospel of white privilege, he is the living, breathing personification of privilege. If he contends otherwise, it is just one more symptom of his "white fragility." In more ways than one, the Sensitivity Era exacerbates the differences between authors who have wealth and authors who do not. Identity politics is the insult added to "the hidden injuries of class."[37]

During one of my interviews, I asked a vice president at a Big Five publisher what they thought about white authors who feel like they might be at a disadvantage. "Well, isn't it curious?" this VP asked me, "Because back in the day, BIPOC authors and illustrators were not given chances. It was not a level playing field. So the harsh assessment is now you know what it feels like." Yet the writer who "knows what if feels like" now is not the same writer who benefited "back in the day." White writers are not a transhistorical monolith. They are individuals who might reasonably not feel privileged when they are, literally, barred from submitting their work to editors.

My favorite subgenre of the white privilege discourse stars white VPs, editors, agents, and other industry professionals who regularly lament the overrepresentation of white people in their own professions. However, I never once encountered an industry professional who talked about giving up *their* position to a person of color; indeed, some of their lucrative salaries could sustain multiple entry-level jobs. To borrow a concept from Rob Henderson, a moral psychologist at Cambridge University, these are "luxury beliefs."[38] These are beliefs that publicly endow VPs, editors, agents, and other gatekeepers with moral capital while not requiring them to sacrifice anything in return.

In other words, it is great to tweet, "Publishers need to stop hiring white people," alongside the hashtag #PublishingSoWhite, when you are an affluent white person who already has a job in publishing. It is not so great if you are the white intern, with $70,000 of student debt, who has to pick up this person's latte from Starbucks. Likewise, it is great to tweet "agents should trash manuscripts from white writers," alongside the hashtag #DVPit, if you are a white writer who already has an agent. When the world is seen through the lens of identities—rather than identities and classes—luxury beliefs dominate. They allow the privileged to buttress their class power with moral power, further exacerbating the difference between the Haves and the Have Nots.

As another case in point, consider the use of sensitivity readers. Many sensitivity readers earn more per hour than public school teachers, daycare workers, bus drivers, firefighters, dentists, and doctors. According to one university: "As of March 2019 the average pay for a sensitivity reader was $0.005—$0.01 per word. For a work of 60,000 words, you can expect to receive between $300 to $600."[39] At an average reading speed of 250 words/minute, a 60,000-word manuscript will take four hours to read. This means sensitivity readers make an average of $75 to $150 per hour. If they work 40 hours/week, they can make between $156,000 and $312,000 per year.

For unpublished writers, it is easier to be a sensitivity reader than a published writer. As one sensitivity reader explained to me: "I had written my first novel, but I wasn't getting any kind of interest from the agents or publishers at the time. I was part of a writing group, and I would sometimes say, you know, 'This isn't great.' Or they'd tell me from their experiences, 'This isn't great.' And I realized I've kind of been doing it anyways. I thought I can do this." Many people have an aspect of their identity they can rely on to say, "This isn't great," so the barriers to entry are virtually nonexistent. Moreover, because no writer wants to be accused of insensitivities—even this sensitivity reader uses a sensitivity reader—the demand is bottomless. "I have my own book sensitivity read, despite it being from my own experience, because you worry. You know, you never know." As *Vulture* reports, the business of sensitivity reading is booming.[40]

More than a few agents now require writers to hire sensitivity readers before they submit their manuscripts for review. Some authors consult a

number of sensitivity readers for each manuscript, and they exhort everyone who is against racism, sexism, and other "-isms" to do the same. Dhonielle Clayton, the COO of We Need Diverse Books, is one author who does
not stop at ten or eleven readers.[41] For *The Belles*, this *New York Times* bestselling author, sensitivity reader, and small business owner with three college degrees stopped at twelve. In a culture where authors are compelled
to hire these self-appointed experts, it raises obvious problems for authors
who cannot afford them. As one agent told me, "I feel uncomfortable
sometimes asking the author to go out of pocket so much. It can become
a money thing for a lot of authors who don't always have the resources to
hire someone."

Because paying sensitivity readers is regarded as a proxy for how antiracist, feminist, or otherwise moral an author is, we now live in culture where
authors who have the resources to hire sensitivity readers are seen, invariably, as more committed to social justice than authors who do not have
these resources. As a case in point, consider the disjunction between the
self-aggrandizing advice James Tilton offers in his *Publishers Weekly* article
and some of the responses to his article. Tilton writes: "As a straight white
male who's spent the past four years writing a queer love story, I've used
nearly a dozen sensitivity readers so far, and I will no doubt use several
more once my agent and I go on submission. . . . If you're an author writing a character outside of your lived experience, don't lament the existence
of sensitivity readers. Appreciate them; listen to them; and, of course, pay
them. They deserve it."[42]

In typical fashion, Tilton first confesses his heterosexual and white privilege. Then he encourages his readers to give their money to sensitivity
readers and WNDB. In contrast to other people, Tilton does not "cry censorship." Nor does he talk "nonsense" about sensitivity readers. The content
and tone of his public performance in allyship theater might be the reason
that one reader asks: "What was this written for? If anything, the way you
display yourself as a massive stereotype just reinforces the hate towards
sensitivity readers." Another reader responds: "Yeah, so if I have to write a
character that isn't a 'male, white, black haired, Italian, heterosexual, nerdy
guy, who is graduated and worked at a convenience store' (which is me,
if it wasn't already clear XD) I should pay 12 people who sort of resemble
the characters out of my sphere of experience in order to write them right.

Yeah, sure boy, everyone of us authors has that much money to throw out the window and all that time to wait for [their] precious responses."

This person explains that there is a difference between consulting experts and consulting people who think they are experts because their identity sort of resembles the identity of a fictional character. This person also explains that the turn toward sensitivity readers is intertwined with a literary culture that punishes authors. The white author who publicly confesses that he hired a dozen sensitivity readers, that he pays a monthly tithe to WNDB, and that he just returned from a weekend retreat where he learned how to write an "authentic" gay character is not the same author who is struggling to survive on a minimum wage convenience store job with no health insurance, vacation time, and other benefits.

Looking around, one might be reminded of sociologist Pierre's Bourdieu's famous essay "The Forms of Capital." For Bourdieu, cultural capital exists in three forms: the embodied state, the objectified state, and the institutionalized state. The first includes knowledge, skills, and the like. The second deals with books, instruments, and so on. The third pertains to forms of institutional recognition such as certificates and degrees. Social capital concerns social relationships. As Bourdieu argues, cultural and social capital are "disguised forms of economic capital."[43] To proclaim that one uses twelve sensitivity readers is to also proclaim that one pays twelve sensitivity readers. In the Sensitivity Era, cultural and social capital are not free.

One might think about linguistic capital as another disguised form of economic capital. In *Forbidden Words: Taboo and the Censoring of Language*, linguists Keith Allan and Kate Burridge draw attention to the middle-class politeness criterion (MCPC). As they explain, "It is surely relevant that behavior which offends against the MCPC is often referred to as *coarse behavior*; and language which offends the MCPC is *coarse language*. . . . Thus, *coarse language* is, by association, that of the vulgar classes, untrammeled by the middle-class politeness criterion."[44]

This is not to suggest that poor and working-class people would not be offended by a person's malicious use of racial slurs. It is to suggest that the more esoteric forms of linguistic correctness, which define the Sensitivity Era, are forms of linguistic capital. To put it bluntly, the new linguistic rules are not coming from the local homeless shelter. (As I recently learned from an Ivy League student who is not homeless, "homeless" is an offensive term. "Housing insecure" is a more polite term. To steal a quip from stand-up comic Jon Laster, perhaps "doorknob deficient" is even better.) From Dhonielle Clayton to Debbie Reese, the grand inquisitors of literature are people with MAs, MFAs, and PhDs.

As one of my interview subjects explained to me, it is a certain kind of person who "can afford to have these complicated, impossible to follow belief systems as a way of showing—kind of as a way of relieving their guilt for being so privileged." For this editor, who runs one of the more prestigious literary journals in the United States, the class dynamic of the MCPC should be self-evident to anyone who still has one foot in the real world. According to them: "It's only people who can afford to be thinking and studying and keeping up with this who can follow along. It's impossible for people like my friend Mark, who trims trees for a living. What hope would he ever have of following all the rules when he's out in a tree with his crew every day? But if you're a student, or a postdoc, or a professor at Harvard, you have all the time in the world to worry about the ways you're using language. As we get more concerned about other kinds of privilege, it's a way of hiding privilege."

It is not just students, postdocs, and professors at Harvard who have the time to conjure new linguistic rules out of thin air. It is anyone on campus who wants to pick up a mallet to play linguistic whack-a-mole. Whether you are a professor at Oberlin College or a student at Middle Tennessee State University, your tenure case or your course grade depends on finding new moles to whack. For the writers at *Vox, BuzzFeed, HuffPost,* and other places churning out a never-ending stream of articles—"The Stand and the Ableism of Stephen King," authored by a writer with three college degrees, gives you a sense of the landscape[45]—paychecks depend on new content. Fortunately, these writers are enlightened. They are here to re-educate the Marks of the world.

In *Virtue Hoarders,* Catherine Lieu argues that this class of people finds in its "particular tastes and cultural proclivities the justification for its unshakable sense of superiority." For Lieu, "virtue hoarding is the insult added to injury," when those with wealth, advanced degrees, enormous platforms, and others forms of power look down on the reading habits of, say, the person who picks up *The Stand* as they push their shopping cart through their local grocery store. Whereas the snobs of the past told you why Shakespeare's plays are the pinnacle of "sweetness" and "light"—to use the language of Matthew Arnold—the snobs of the present tell you why Shakespeare is too "problematic" to read. They also tell you why "Stephen King is a problematic author," too. Problematic-splaining is their livelihood.

Just look at the article titles. You might get a flashback to elementary school when your teacher wagged a finger at you and said, "We need to talk about what happened at recess." Whether one visits websites that no one has heard of—like *Villainesse* where you can read "We Need to Talk about Women in Classical Literature" by Ben Mack (a writer with a graduate degree from the University of Canterbury)—or websites that people have heard of—like *Book Riot* where you can read "There's a Weird, Sexist Problem in Fantasy That We Need to Talk About" by Mya Nunnally (a writer with degrees from Rutgers University and Barnard College at Columbia University)—one will find no dearth of literary problems related to identity that we, apparently, need to talk about. One will even find, verbatim, the same finger-wagging: "Publishers, do better. Readers, let's do better too."[46]

At a moment when virtually everyone has access to the Great Books as well as paperback thrillers, not everyone has access to the linguistic capital of the virtuous.[47] Not everyone understands why Dr. Seuss had to be pulled from circulation, why *Blood Heir* had to be canceled before publication, and why *Harry Potter* is so racist and fatphobic it has to be burned. In the same vein, not everyone understands dactylic hexameters, iambic trimeters, and caesuras. That is how linguistic capital works. Its value depends on other people not having it. It does not matter if a person dresses their capital, and sense of superiority, in moral clothing. It is still capital. As Lieu argues, "We have to reject making a virtue out of taste and consumption habits."[48]

Yet the virtue of taste and consumption habits inundates the Sensitivity Era. It is even apparent before publication. As a case in point, consider the submission guidelines for *Folio*, a prestigious literary journal published by American University. For an upcoming horror issue, their editors write:

> Please do not send work which upholds the "typical" horror tropes. We are looking for high-literary taste and atmosphere. We prefer no fantasy or hard sci-fi. Don't take us to another planet or gore us to death. As a rule, no gratuitous blood and guts, no profanity, and no pornography. We want a "full-bodied" experience when reading your work.
>
> If your jam is recreating Grimms' fairytales with a badass feminist spin, we want to hear from you. If your love language is recommending stories by Carmen Maria Machado, your taste is up our alley. If you correspond to how Jordan Peele

corners the intersection between horror and racial-social commentary, send us your stuff!

FOLIO does NOT tolerate racism, bigotry, misogyny, homophobia, transphobia, Islamophobia, xenophobia, anti-Semitism, ableism, or any work that promotes harmful stereotypes and viewpoints.[49]

Unlike my friend Lauren, a barista with a high school education who loves to read novels about aliens who blow shit up on other planets, *Folio*'s editors have "high-literary taste." They want work with a "feminist spin" and "racial-social commentary." When they are not looking down on readers like Lauren for liking literature with—*gasp*—profanity, they are publicly showcasing how tolerant they are (as if *Folio* is getting such a flood of racist, antisemitic, and otherwise intolerant submissions they now have to use ALL CAPS to get the attention of Klansmen, Nazi, and other bigots who are considering submitting their sonnets and short stories to this hyperprogressive corner of literary culture). Whereas Lauren loves to read science fiction books, the snooty tastemaker loves to proclaim how tolerant they are.

One of my interview subjects, a trans author who has seen their book about a trans character banned from K–12 public schools, spoke to the virtue-signaling aspect of literary culture: "The people who end up reading, or finding about, or buying my book after a ban are adults in liberal towns who want to feel cool about themselves. But there's still a kid in Kentucky who needs that book who can't get it. But, you know, whatever, Randy with his beard in Portland has a copy of a book on the shelf now, good for him." Although this author and I laughed, and they acknowledged that their comment was reductionist and flippant, the kernel of truth is there. There is a certain cachet that exists in literary culture. That cachet is not independent from issues of region, politics, and class. In cities like Portland, there is no shortage of liberal yuppies who will gentrify a black neighborhood on Tuesday and stick a Black Lives Matter sign in their front lawn on Wednesday. Those liberals buy books. As this banned author reflects, they love books banned by the right.

It is not just about the books themselves. It is also about the bookish culture that surrounds books. Whether it is Bookstagram photographs of one's bookshelves, or BookTok videos spotlighting the curtains, couch pillows, and candles stamped with quotes from one's favorite books, the internet is the public square where people flaunt their bookish identities. In *Bookishness*, Jessica Pressman elaborates: "Much like the Great Books of the

Western World series or the hardbound encyclopedia sets that filled the bookshelves of mid-twentieth-century bourgeois American living rooms, bookishness is about class and consumerism. It is about constructing and projecting identity through the possession and presentation of books."[50] While one connoisseur places a first edition print of *Pride and Prejudice* on their fireplace mantel—centered for all their dinner guests to see—another connoisseur posts a picture of their signed edition of *White Fragility* to Twitter. And look! There's an inscription from the author: "Keep up the antiracist work Karen!" If you think this is about books, you are half right. It is also about the presentation of self.[51]

Moral Entrepreneurs on the Left

The Sensitivity Era incentivizes moral entrepreneurs. Sociologist Howard Becker defines moral entrepreneurs as people "who may also experience a rise in status due to their leadership role" in a moral crusade.[52] For example, consider Dhonielle Clayton, a COO at WNDB. When one visits WNDB's website, Clayton's own books are front and center. Whether one clicks on "programs" or "resources," *The Belles* and *Tiny Pretty Things* are at the top of the page. In an interview with *Vulture*, she criticizes white authors who include characters of color in their stories. As she explains, "The problem is that they're showing up and they're taking a seat. And they're not realizing that them writing a story about a black kid prevents me from writing one, because when I show up with my manuscript, the publisher tells me that the position is filled."[53] For this *New York Times* bestselling author with a Netflix adaptation deal and her own business, "that's what real censorship looks like." There is no distinction between Clayton's personal financial interests and the moral crusade over literature.

Once again, identity politics looks like the multicultural version of trickle-down economics. Whereas conservatives proclaim that what is good for Charles Koch is good for America, liberals proclaim that what is good for Dhonielle Clayton is good for "Black America." Regardless of which nationalism one subscribes to, the success of a handful of elites is supposed to trickle down and benefit everyone else. Yet it remains entirely unclear how more "black faces in high places," to borrow language from poet Amiri Baraka, will benefit the millions of poor and working-class black people who are not up late fretting about who got the latest $500,000 book deal from HarperCollins.[54] "And what we got here in this town?" asked Baraka in 1972, "black faces in high places, but the same rats and roaches, the same slums and garbage." Five decades later, there are even more black faces in high places, but the income gap between black Americans at the top and black Americans at the bottom has only widened.[55]

As one indication of how much elite representation matters to black Americans, "in a year when a black woman was on a major party ticket for the first time in US history, the margin between Democrats and Republicans among black women shifted 9 percentage points in the other direction—towards Trump. Trump saw comparable gains with Black and Hispanic *men* as well."[56] Recalling Joe Biden's call to arms—"Well I tell you what, if you have a problem figuring out whether you're for me or Trump, then you ain't black."[57]—which sounds like a bestselling novelist posturing themselves as the "authentic" voice of "Black America," the relationship between elite spokespeople and the people they purport to represent often looks cartoonishly stupid. It does not look any less cartoonishly stupid when the self-appointed spokesperson is black.

Like Uncle Joe, Clayton and other moral entrepreneurs give the impression that a win for them is actually a win for all the people they have never met. To quote black historian Paul Gilroy at length:

> At its worst, the lazy, casual invocation of cultural insiderism which frequently characterizes the ontological essentialist view is nothing more than a symptom of the growing cleavages *within* the black communities. There, uneasy spokesman of the black elite—some of them professional cultural commentators, artists, writers, painters, and film makers as well as political leaders—have fabricated a volkish outlook as an expression of their own contradictory position. . . . It incorporates commentary on the special needs and desires of the relatively privileged castes within black communities, but its most consistent trademark is the persistent mystification of that group's increasingly problematic relationships with the black poor, who, after all, supply the elite with a dubious entitlement to speak on behalf of the phantom constituency of black people in general. . . . The idea of blacks as a national or pro-national group with its own hermetically enclosed culture plays a key role in this mystification.[58]

When Clayton and others demand more book contracts, writing fellowships, and prestigious awards for themselves, it does not speak to the material interests of poor and working-class black people. It speaks to the "special needs and desires" of a privileged class of black people. The growing cleavage between black elites and the majority of black people—Gilroy writes of "that stubborn order of class differences"[59]—undermines the already dubious notion that black elites, by virtue of their blackness, represent anyone other than themselves. Whereas some black writers use their platforms to push for universal healthcare, higher wages, and other forms of progress—just read *Jacobin* or *Nonsite*—moral entrepreneurs see their personal progress as the progress. Here, the biggest problem is not any of the actually existing problems that confront millions of black parents and their children on a daily basis. The problem is who has a "seat at the table" where lucrative book contracts are signed.

One of the most striking aspects of the "seat at the table" rhetoric is how much it has increased since George Floyd's death. In his article "Who Actually Gets to Create Black Pop Culture?" Bertrand Cooper reflects:

> I was born into Black poverty, and I will not forget that George Floyd was born into the same. For Floyd, the particulars of poverty were this: to be raised in the Cuney Homes projects, to endure years of deprivation, and to die violently in a manner common to our caste. Were Floyd still alive, or somehow reborn, he would not be hired to work within any of the institutions which now produce popular culture in his honor because he never obtained a bachelor's degree. . . . I accept that Floyd's final suffering becomes a political currency for the many, but I struggle with the fact that it purchases opportunities for the Black middle- and upper-classes, without securing a pen or a publisher for the children of Cuney Homes, without an expectation that it should, and without condemnation that it doesn't.[60]

Few writers have profited more than Ibram X. Kendi. His book *Four Hundred Souls: A Community History of African America, 1619–2019*, edited with Keisha N. Blain, was a number-one *New York Times* bestseller. According to his publisher: "This collection of diverse pieces from ninety different minds, reflecting ninety different perspectives, fundamentally deconstructs the idea that Africans in America are a monolith—instead it unlocks the startling range of experiences and ideas that have always existed within the community of Blackness." Yet, as Cooper points out: "Out of 92 different Black writers (counting Kendi and Blain), 91 have bachelor's degrees, 49 attended elite colleges, and 62 are college faculty. You might not be able to sell a community history of Black America without the continued suffering of the Black poor, but you can apparently write the history of the 'Black community' without more than one or two of them."

The best thing to happen to Ibram X. Kendi's career was George Floyd's death. A glance at the *New York Times* bestseller list a few weeks after his death—"every one of the 10 books on the *New York Times*'s combined e-book and print nonfiction best-seller list this week is about anti-racism"[61]—illuminates the alchemy project that converts police violence against poor black people like Floyd into soaring mountains of literary profit for black writers like Kendi. When black people from the projects get killed, black elites get book deals, speaking engagements, and Macarthur Genius Grants. As Cooper observes, there is no expectation that these opportunities should trickle down.

When one looks at the Big Five publishers responsible for bestsellers like *Four Hundred Souls*, their CEOs act more like Gordon Gekko than Martin Luther King Jr. Kendi's publisher, Penguin Random House, actually sued the Internet Archive, forcing it to shut down the National Emergency Library, which provided free ebooks to teachers and students who needed them during the pandemic—students like those who live in Cuney Homes. They were joined by HarperCollins, Hachette, and Wiley, which together represent over $10 billion in annual revenue. The only thing that matches Penguin's commitment to "ripping off public schools," as one journalistic investigation describes it, is its commitment to antiracism.[62]

Whether it is Penguin's partnership with WNDB, or its proclamation to "hire an outside organization for anti-racism training," or its declaration to "set targets for increasing our diversity," or its use of sensitivity readers, there is no reason to believe this is empty PR.[63] CEOs can care about removing "hurtful" language from a novel, just like they care about stock prices. There is no contradiction between antiracism and business as usual. In fact, antiracism is now business as usual.

Kendi, whom Cooper describes as "the prevailing Black consciousness of white liberals," has a particular knack for profiting off every single corner of the literary marketplace. Since 2019, Kendi has churned out *How to Be an Antiracist* (a number one *New York Times* bestseller), *How to Raise an Antiracist*, *How to Be a (Young) Antiracist*, *The (Young) Antiracist's Workbook*, *Goodnight Racism* (a picture book that alludes to Margaret Wise Brown's *Goodnight Moon*), *Antiracist Baby* (a picture book that was a number one *New York Times* bestseller), *Stamped: Racism, Antiracism, and You* (a YA book that was a number one *New York Times* bestseller), and *The Antiracist Deck*, a card game—one might consider it the reverse *Cards against Humanity*—that forces partygoers to answer questions like "Why is talking about race important?" Penguin Random House assures customers that this deck of cards is not a total waste of $22.00. Because "meaningful change can start at the micro-level," the cards enable you to "uncover your antiracist power within to transform your community." Who knew progress was this easy? At Burger King, one can buy the Whopper, the Whopper Jr., the Ghost Whopper, and so on. At Penguin, one can buy different versions of *The Gospel of Kendi*.

In all seriousness, Kendi should title his next book *How to Be a Capitalist*. After all, it takes a Gordon Gekko level of cognitive dissonance to charge a public university $32,500 (about $541 per minute) for a Zoom talk about "equity,"[64] at a moment when public universities are struggling to survive. In Boston, where Kendi holds an endowed professorship, the median net worth for nonimmigrant African American households is $8.00.[65] Tickets to Kendi's most recent Boston event, part of the *How to Raise an Antiracist* global tour, started at $61.00.[66] Put differently, the African Americans who Kendi purports to represent cannot afford to hear Kendi speak. The affluent whites who shop at Brookline Booksmith, the posh bookstore that sponsored this event, can.

To be sure, if Kendi ever wrote *How to Be a Capitalist* it would end his brand. His brand is built around being a representative of "the black experience" (rather than an elite whose experience in America could not be less representative) and a perennial victim of American society (rather than one of its biggest benefactors). Just as Kendi asks people to ritualistically confess their racism—according to him, "the heartbeat of antiracism is confession"[67]—people should ask Kendi to ritualistically confess how much money he makes off antiracism, where all this money goes, and how his Gekko-like commitment to profit is aligned with "equity."

Kendi's moral entrepreneurship is so in your face and over the top that even *The Onion* would have a difficult time satirizing it. Though, I assume the real reason "Ibram X. Kendi" returns zero results on their website has less to do with writer's block and more to do with the fact that affluent white liberals love *The Onion*. In this vein, the *Babylon Bee*, which satirizes televangelists, might have an easier time with Kendi. Yet even they might be perplexed about how to parody real articles written about him. In a feature article, "Preacher of the New Antiracist Gospel," *GQ* unironically describes Kendi as a "kind, dignified, preternaturally wise, and soft-spoken teacher, indefatigable in his quest to set you on the path toward true knowledge."[68] You would not have found nicer words about Jim Jones in Jonestown.

Though, unlike Kendi, Jones was not invited to speak at the Aspen Ideas Festival—"a social event," according to black community organizer Bruce A. Dixon, "where one percenters showcase their current crop of 'thought leaders.'"[69] You will not find Dixon there either. Vis-à-vis Kendi, who was awarded a $625,000 MacArthur "Genius" Grant, most community organizers do not posture themselves as Preachers of the New Antiracist Gospel. In this respect, John McWhorter's description of Kendi as a "prophet-priest" is accurate, given his obsession with confessions, Manichean binaries (one is either a racist or an antiracist), and other hallmarks of religious fundamentalism.[70] But unlike *GQ*'s 4,500-word testament to Kendi's beatitude, McWhorter's description is not meant to be a compliment.

When the Sensitivity Era regards moral entrepreneurs as the prophet-priests of "the Black community," it recreates a belief in what, according to Paul Gilroy, "can no longer be credibly called a single racial community."[71] The era also perpetuates a belief in all sorts of other communities that could never be called single communities. As a case in point, when Kosoko Jackson proclaims that only gay authors should write about young boys during the AIDS epidemic, it suggests that sexuality is also a hermetically sealed community that is only accessible through prophet-priests like Jackson. But when no moral entrepreneur demands the exclusive right to write about poor and working-class characters, presumably because so few of these moral entrepreneurs have ever been poor or working class, it suggests that class does not constitute a shared aspect of social life like "the black experience," "the gay experience," and other commodities in the literary marketplace.

In reality, many writers point out that their class makes them feel distant from those who share their race, sexuality, and other identities. For example, bell hooks, a queer black feminist, reflects: "When I left the segregated world of my poor and working-class home environment to attend privilege-class schools, I found I often had more in common with white students who shared a similar class background than with privileged class black students who had no experience of what it might mean to lack the funds to do anything they wanted to do."[72] Put otherwise, the idea that only black adults like Kendi should write about black children, or that only gay adults like Jackson should write about gay children, are ideas that do not comprehend the lived experience of children. As hooks suggests, lived experience is complicated. It is intersectional. More to the point, it is made up of glaring disparities in wealth that explode reductive ideas about "the black experience," "the gay experience," and so on. Yet, as novelist Upton Sinclair puts it, "It is difficult to get a man to understand something when his salary depends upon his not understanding it."[73]

The commitment to race reductionism is a perennial feature of American literature. As one of innumerable examples, consider Flannery O'Connor. Asked in 1960 why "Negroes [don't] figure more prominently" in her stories, she responded, "I don't understand them the way I do white people. I don't feel capable of entering the mind of a Negro." As literary historian Mark McGurl reflects: "Hardly a passionate critic of racial segregation, O'Connor sees that fact of Southern life as being doubled, internally, by a segregated cognition. Thus while she, even burdened by a graduate degree, can 'enter the mind' of abjectly ignorant poor whites like Nelson and Mr. Head with little trouble, racial difference produces an impenetrable barrier to 'understanding' which in turn conditions the form of her fiction."[74] Sixty years later, O'Connor is now celebrated for her belief in segregated cognition. In a recent *New Yorker* article, Paul Elie endorses O'Connor's idea of "the mind of a Negro." For Elie, a finalist for the National Book Critics Circle Award, O'Connor's remark reveals that she "was admirably leery of cultural appropriation."[75]

In his book on literature and cultural authenticity, Christopher L. Miller describes this as "the ethics of ethnicity: the unwritten code that says each group should represent itself, perhaps exclusively, perhaps only with permission." In the Sensitivity Era, it is not an unwritten code. Nor is it a code limited to ethnicity. As Miller explains in his discussion of authors who impersonate identities that are not their own, "The stronger the quality of the work—the more it is convincing—the more harm it may do to *the ethics of ethnicity* and its requirement for *self*-presentation."[76] To push the argument further, any work of strong quality written by an "outsider," regardless of whether that "outsider" is pretending to be an "insider," undermines the ethics of identity and its requirement for self-presentation. Policing the boundaries of what can be written by whom is one way to ensure strong work written by "outsiders" is never written. The ethics of identity is like a no-bid contract for writers trying to build their careers as the voice of "the black experience," "the gay experience," or whatever other experience is in vogue this season at Penguin Random House, HarperCollins, and other publishers.

When I spoke to a past recipient of the Zora Neale Hurston/Richard Wright Foundation's Annual Legacy Award, they lamented the idea that writers should only write about people who share their identities. They also lamented the "authenticity police." As we discussed a recent work about Emmett Till, which was created by a white woman, this black writer told me: "That history is as much her history as it is my history." But a shared history creates problems for writers who have built their careers as ethnic entrepreneurs. "It's a weird kind of proprietary thinking employed by these people on social media who want to correct other people," this writer continued. "It's fascist behavior. It's leftist fascist behavior. We have fascists on both sides now. You can't say anything. There's as much exploitation of this notion of authenticity by people in their own 'races,' and I use that term with quotation marks because 'race' is a ridiculous and bogus category, one that we've constructed to do whatever it is we do with this idea." For ethnic entrepreneurs, "race" is the bogus category that turns their lived experience into proprietary ownership over Emmett Till's lived experience.

But even if one subscribed to the Sensitivity Era's first commandment—"No substitute for lived experience"—it is still unclear why the most important lived experiences are those that are not defined by class. hooks offers one hypothesis: "A thriving, corrupt 'talented tenth' have not only emerged as the power brokers preaching individual liberalism and black capitalism to everyone (especially the black masses), their biggest commodity is 'selling blackness.' They make sure they mask their agenda so black capitalism looks like black self-determination."[77] Black self-determination could look like a universal basic income or a federal public arts program that gives all Americans, including black Americans who are overrepresented among the poor, the material resources and time free from work that one needs to write. In the Sensitivity Era, black self-determination looks like another book deal for a *New York Times* bestselling author. "The irony of social integration absent class consciousness," reflects sociologist Shamus Khan, "is that elites have been given the tools to more effectively remain elite."[78] Perhaps there is no better tool than one that conflates "black faces in high places" with equality.

When moral entrepreneurs are not demanding a "seat at the table," they are pushing Sensitivity Inc.'s products. The biggest products are new definitions of *racism, homophobia, patriarchy*, and other buzzwords. It is no coincidence that the largest redefinition mills—journalism and academia—cannot function without new content. Despite their dignified postures, journalists and academics are just as much a part of capitalism as people who sell Air Jordans, iPhones, and pornography. They have to constantly produce new content.

This is especially true in the era of fast journalism where op-eds have taken the place of long-form, reported stories that take months to research and write. When a journalist, and I use that term loosely, purports to "unpack" what Stephen King's newest novel really means, by redefining what *ableism* or *misogyny* really mean, they are able to meet their Monday morning deadline. When they write a similar op-ed about what James Patterson's comment about male writers really means, they are able to meet their Tuesday morning deadline. When novelist Bret Easton Ellis tweets about Donald Trump, they have a new topic for their Wednesday morning deadline. At newspapers and magazines with slashed budgets, where fewer writers are responsible for more content, cultural criticism is grist for the mill. At websites where writers have to churn out a dozen or more op-eds per day—this is the model for click-driven advertising dollars—they only have time to write op-eds like "This Fantasy Novel Is Fatphobic."

In the same vein, academia depends on new content. No professor gets tenure for saying there really is nothing new to say about *The Catcher in the Rye*. No graduate student is awarded a PhD for saying there really is nothing new to say about *One Flew Over the Cuckoo's Nest*. If one wants a career, they better say *something*. This is an especially difficult task for people who want to spend their professional lives with texts that have been around forever. Unless one has a hip, new framework to make sense of *Beowulf*—even better if it revolves around a new neologism like "hetero-monstrification" or "transspecies-patriarchalism," which will produce a citation in your name every time it is used thereafter—one might be out of a job. As professor Michael Billig explains in his book *Learn to Write Badly*: "The rewards do not go to those who only write when they have something to say and who then take trouble to write as clearly as possible. This is an age of academic mass publication, and certainly not a time for academic idealists." Anthony Grafton, another professor, compares modern scholarship to fast food restaurants.[79] The "publish or peril" pressure is real.

This pressure is intertwined with the current state of academic publishing. At a moment when even the best university presses are in danger—in 2019, Stanford University's provost announced he would stop funding

Stanford University Press—they must survive on smaller budgets. University libraries, which have historically been a reliable market for niche academic books, have their own budget problems. A lot of university press sales now come from independent purchases on Amazon. As one editor at a top university press explained to me, the era of fiscal conservatism has affected some disciplines more than others. For example, sociologists tend to do well because their books focus on problems that people outside academia care about: #MeToo, police violence, and so on.

By contrast, there is not much of an Amazon market for a three-hundred-page book about sixteenth-century poetry. In the past, university presses could afford to publish books that produce no return on investment. In the era of austere budgets, editors are more careful. The editor I spoke to hopes that English departments will soon allow ebooks to count toward tenure because some books about literature are, literally, not worth the paper they are printed on. That said, if an English professor or a PhD student can connect their book on sixteenth-century poetry to the problems that people do care about—for example, a monograph on Christopher Marlowe that purports to be relevant to #MeToo—they have a greater chance of being published, read, and reviewed.

Other Sensitivity Inc. products focus on the unconscious. In his Robin DiAngelo–inspired manifesto, English professor Philip Nel recommends enrolling publishing employees in a program to help them overcome their unconscious biases.[80] As Nel explains, even African American editors like Andrea Davis Pinkney, who founded the first major African American children's imprint, will benefit. According to Nel, Pinkney's support for *A Birthday Cake for George Washington* reflects "both a lack of racist intent and the normalization of White supremacy in American culture." As such, she should be sent to re-education camp to exorcise the unconscious demons hiding inside her head.

To be clear, these programs already exist. "With the rise of human resources," reflects one of my interview subjects, "all my friends in publishing are just tearing their hair out. We all have to do these online classes, which are so condescending, to teach us about these things. They're just horrible." Contra Nel, those who have the expertise to speak about the empirical value of these interventions have a similar take. Patricia Devin, who runs the Prejudice and Intergroup Relations Lab at the University of Wisconsin–Madison, is hardly alone in her evaluation of the evidence:

"The reality is this multimillion, maybe billion, dollar industry has gotten way far ahead of the evidence. There's sort of a lot of intuition and wishful thinking that goes on."[81] In a moral panic, a lack of evidence is beside the point.

If there is one thing that white "allies" love, it is introspection. *Reading While White*, a blog for white librarians to publicly interrogate their white privilege, also centers DiAngelo as their north star. A typical lament: "As a White person, I can't and won't ever begin to understand the trauma BIPOC have faced and continue to face every day. I can be horrified, devastated, enraged, and justice-focused, and at the end of the day I'm still White. I will always be colluding with racism and benefiting from it. . . . I am a White person of 2020. I am learning, and sharing, and doing my best to fight the anti-Blackness and racism that I'm swimming in and that has been part of my life and this country since forever."[82]

There is a similarity between this "antiracism" and the New Age spiritual circles one finds in San Francisco, Brooklyn, Madison, Boulder, and other places where affluent white liberals in gentrified neighborhoods gather to talk about their feelings. Throughout, one gets the impression that white people are more interested in looking in the mirror—a perennial source of embarrassment for "whiteness studies," given its aspiration to decenter "whiteness"[83]—than doing anything that even vaguely resembles political activism.

In part, this is a problem because professions incentivize this behavior. The aforementioned author lists "contributor to the Reading While White blog" in their professional bio, as if this is a professional accomplishment.[84] Likewise, one finds white professors and their graduate students churning out "mesearch," the new alternative to research, and being rewarded for it with lines on their curriculum vitaes. At a moment when confessing one's "whiteness" on Twitter is as fashionable as posting a beach selfie, some academics note how many Twitter followers they have at the top of their vitaes. Even some academic publishers, who should be least concerned with these popularity contests, ask for this number in their guidelines for book proposals.[85]

Despite the profitability of white liberal psychobabble, a genre more in debt to Robin DiAngelo than Bayard Rustin, not everyone is a fan. Melissa Chen, a cofounder of Ideas Without Borders, a nonprofit that translates books about human rights, laments: "the irony is that the people who decry the 'centering of whiteness' are precisely the ones centering whiteness because they see white supremacy/privilege as the motivating reason for every single thing in life."[86] On a similar note, sociologist Cedrick-Michael Simmons contends that people should ask black Americans "whether they want more diversity trainings or more money in their bank accounts." Based on his knowledge "as a Black student, sociologist, and a person who doesn't come from a wealthy family, [he] would bet at least $70,000 that the vast majority of people would choose 'more money.'"[87]

In his article, Simmons does not talk about redistributing money to the black elites who dominate public conversations about what "Black America" needs. He talks about redistributing money to black people who actually need it. Although his own work focuses on black students, his point is just as true of black writers. I would bet at least $70,000 that most black writers would rather have more money to sustain the time free from work that writing requires, than more diversity trainings at publishing houses, blog posts about "reading while white," and whatever else produces a profit, a "like," or another line for one's curriculum vitae. Ironically, the profits, "likes," and CV lines often go to white people.

Whereas some moral entrepreneurs sell trainings, seminars, weekend retreats, and self-help books that encourage white people to "embrace discomfort" and "do better," other moral entrepreneurs sell the commodities of blackness, gayness, fatness, and transness alongside the idea that their success is a success for the phantom constituencies they purport to represent. Whether one reads tweets by sensitivity readers advertising their services on Twitter, or an interview with Philip Nel in *Esquire*, it should be clear that moral entrepreneurship is not the exclusive terrain of television evangelicals.[88] Secular liberals profit from righteous indignation, too. And the more writers are publicly shamed because they "got it wrong," the more writers will pay ten, eleven, or twelve sensitivity readers to "get it right." From the moral panic over comic books in the 1950s to the moral panic over children's and YA literature right now, moral entrepreneurs do not let moral panics go to waste.

Likewise, the more agents and editors are treated like Hester Prynne, the more they will realize that the best way to avoid a literary scandal, and to virtue signal their commitment to "social justice," is to work with an Own Voices author who, unlike the Own Voices reviewer at *Kirkus*, will not write anything that could possibly provoke this moral crusade. The enterprise of virtue signaling is even shaping how books are marketed. For example, when one compares the short author biography in *Blood Heir* with the longer author biography in *Red Tigress*, Amélie Wen Zhao's second novel, the new emphasis on her "multicultural upbringing," her "deep love" of "cross-cultural perspectives," and her desire to "bring this passion to her stories"[89] reads like a branding exercise—one designed to show other liberals that, after being ruthlessly flagellated on social media, she, too, has heard the Good News.[90] When *Crimson Reign* comes out, her author biography might be even longer. Perhaps she will thank WNDB for helping her exorcise the "unconscious racism" that possessed her. Recall that some people accused of conspiring with the devil in Salem, Massachusetts, became the church's biggest devotees.[91]

Already a number of agents and publishers do not just state their preference for Own Voices authors committed to writing progressive books in their submission guidelines. They actually ask authors if their work is Own Voices. In the world of contemporary literature, authors are forced to illuminate the connection between their lived experiences and the experiences of their fictional characters. On February 17, 2022, Elizabeth Holden tweeted: "I don't typically tweet about agents' rejections (as I also don't tweet about requests). But I received a rejection on a full today, for my 'queer roller derby YA,' because, the agent told me, he'd discovered I am married to a man. Ouch. Despite the agent acknowledging I could be bi, I was told it just wouldn't work, as a business decision, since my novel is partially about first love between two girls."[92]

For author Evelyn Silver, there is a compulsion to perform one's identity: "Nonsense like this makes me feel the need to scream about how queer I am because of how invisible it looks from the outside, and that's . . . that's not how it should be."[93] As agent and author Melissa Colasanti explains, "I don't ALWAYS want to have to explain to everyone that my character, who is bipolar, is being portrayed based on my life exp. as a mentally ill woman. As in, here's my defense as to why I know what I'm doing. Many LGBTQ people don't want to be outed to tell that story."

Yet the market incentivizes agents and publishers to out their authors. One editor, who works at a Big Five publisher, described their experience with Own Voices:

> I think the danger of Own Voices as a selling term, when it isn't put forward by the author themselves, is that it really forces a lot of writers, especially on the

LGBTQIA2S+ spectrum, to out themselves. So, they've written a bisexual protagonist, but if the author hasn't disclosed anything about themselves, people started
being like, well if it's not Own Voices is it worth buying? But to make it Own
Voices, we were forcing those writers to out themselves, which I personally think
is unacceptable.

Like, that's their private business. Especially coming from a platform with a
really international audience, I'm very used to working with creators who are like,
"I'll tell you if you want. But in my country if they found out that I was queer, I
could die. This is the highest stakes there is. This could be a real problem for me."
So, we had a company policy that we would just not disclose it, we would just not
market it that way. But, of course, you know, the audience, the readers, started
expecting those kinds of titles, especially for queer fiction.

Likewise, literary agent Lauren Spieller reflects: "I really, really hate that
we're in a moment that involves demanding people share their personal
business/ identity/ trauma as a way of defending their rights—to create, to
participate, to exist. . . . I HATE that we have to talk about how [my clients]
might have to defend their right to tell their own story."[94] But this is what
happens when moral entrepreneurs like Jackson, Clayton, and others pressure publishers to idolatrize Own Voices. It is, in the words of the agent
who rejected Holden, "a business decision." No one wants to be the next
publisher or agent slammed for supporting a book that departed from the
gospel of lived experience.

Just look at what happened to Haymarket Books. In 2021, an open letter
accused them of ableism, as it demanded to know if the three poets editing
an announced anthology, *Against Ableism*, "publicly identify as neurodivergent or autistic."[95] Illustrative of moral entrepreneurship, the letter writers
describe themselves as "brilliant disabled poets" who can edit this anthology. Because no publisher wants to bring an unsellable book to market,
Haymarket outed their editors as disabled.[96]

To borrow a concept from social psychologist Shoshana Zuboff, "surveillance capitalism" has a distinct meaning in the Sensitivity Era.[97] And
the business of surveillance capitalism extends from Haymarket and other
left-wing publishers all the way to the Big Five publishers. In the words of
one vice president, "Where I'm more privy to what cancel culture has done,
and what the internet has done, is in the acquisition process. We are very
interested in knowing what, in sort of trying to suss out what books will
get a lot of attention on social media—we hope the right kind of attention
on social media—and what kind of books might cause a problem on social

media, which can come back in our faces in terms of sales. Nobody wants to publish a book that social media is going to cancel or an author that is going to get canceled by social media. It's unpleasant, it can be hurtful, it's upsetting, and it's not good for business."

Building on their point about acquisitions, the era's emphasis on everything but economic inequality perpetuates the misguided idea that minority authors are underrepresented, first and foremost, because they are minorities—especially if they are minorities of color. As *Reading While White* puts it, "Race is society's biggest structural organizer, and it is essential to recognize it as such."[98] To be sure, there are agents and publishers who are consciously or unconsciously biased. At the same time, one would be hard-pressed to argue that an industry filled with liberals who love every form of social justice that is not economic justice are the primary reason that an Indigenous author from a reservation has a hard time getting their manuscript published. This author probably has a hard time landing their manuscript, just as they have a hard time landing a spot at Harvard University, or an unpaid internship at a Manhattan literary agency, because generational wealth predicts who ends up succeeding in the literary world and who ends up taking orders at Starbucks.[99]

As one agent told me, "It's been pretty all-white because the salaries are pretty low. A lot of people have parental support. That cuts out a big portion of people who might otherwise be interested in the field." In this respect, a "politics of redistribution," to use philosopher Nancy Fraser's language, would be one of the most useful paths toward a "politics of recognition."[100]

To come back to Jason Allen's point about the Haves and the Have Nots, writing requires time free from work. It is also buttressed by access to resources—early literacy programs, well-funded K–12 classrooms, parents who can fund weekends and summers free from work, professors who have editorial connections, universities that provide scholarships, fellowships, and access to distinguished writers, and so on—that mark the trajectories of so many published writers. Likewise, unpaid and barely paid internships at agencies and publishers, many of which are located in New York City, may as well require a familial safety net. Because Indigenous people, black people, and other groups of people are overrepresented among the poor, it makes sense that they are underrepresented as published authors, agents, and editors. It makes a lot less sense to treat this as a problem that has little or nothing to do with wealth, a problem that will magically disappear with more unconscious-bias training seminars, confessions of white guilt, and other quick fixes.[101] As hooks reflects, "No one wants to talk about class. It is not sexy or cute. Better to make it seem that justice is class-free."[102]

Contrary to the pablum of Kendi, DiAngelo, and the literary critics they inspire, if one reads the memoirs of Steven Pressfield, Stephen King, Chuck Palahniuk, and other white men from poor and working-class backgrounds, they might see how difficult it is to survive as a Have Not. As Princeton's Keeanga-Yamahtta Taylor puts it, they might also see that "the privileges of white skin run very thin in a country where nineteen million white people languish in poverty."[103] In contrast, if one reads about novelist and moral entrepreneur Roxane Gay, a Phillips Exeter Academy graduate whose parents paid her rent until she was thirty years old, one might see that the privileges of wealth run extremely thick regardless of one's race, gender, sexuality, and so on.[104] Or, like the writers at *Time* who describe Gay's background as "ordinary," in their cover story about "ordinary families" and their "extraordinary kids," one might not see these privileges at all.[105] In the Sensitivity Era, not seeing class differences is what the fight for a more inclusive literary culture looks like.

Moral Entrepreneurs on the Right

In 1995, Metropolitan Books published *The Twilight of Common Dreams: Why America Is Wracked by Culture Wars* by sociologist Todd Gitlin. In his book, Gitlin argues that too much of the left is focused on issues that have little or nothing to do with politics. As he explains, since the late 1960s, the left was "marching on the English department while the right took the White House."[106] Five decades later, the left has won all the English departments. Yet, at a moment when the right controls the majority of state governorships, the majority of state senates, the majority of state houses, the US Senate, the US House of Representatives, the Supreme Court, and the Oval Office, progressives still have their eyes focused on literature. In this respect, the Sensitivity Era looks like a parody of Gitlin's era—a parody with real political consequences. Although Karl Marx was wrong about the end of capitalism, he was right about history. It repeats itself, "the first time as tragedy, the second time as farce."[107]

Back then, the right's politicians and pundits exploited the left's struggle for political correctness to win elections. Today, the connection between the left's cultural crusade and the right's political victories is even more apparent. As one case in point, consider the Dr. Seuss brouhaha. After Dr. Seuss Enterprises ceased publication of six "dangerous" books in early 2021, and some public libraries removed these books from circulation, a phalanx of conservatives took up the fight. On Twitter, House Minority Leader Kevin McCarthy posted a video of himself reading *Green Eggs and Ham* (not one of the six books). "I still like Dr. Seuss," he tweeted, "RT if you still like him too!"[108] Senator Ted Cruz posted a screenshot of Dr. Seuss at the top of Amazon's bestseller list, with books in the first eight slots, drawing attention to the disjunction between moral crusaders and the general public. Above the screenshot, he asked, "Could Biden try to ban my book next?"[109] Although Biden did not ban Dr. Seuss's books, he did not mention Dr. Seuss on Read Across America Day. The past two presidents did. Cruz was capitalizing on the moment.

Cruz also started selling copies of Dr. Seuss's work to fund his political campaign.[110] In the first day, he raised $125,000. He credited "lefties losing their minds" for the money that will be used to win his next election. Not to be outdone, Congressman John Joyce introduced the Guarding Readers' Independence and Choice (GRINCH) Act "to safeguard children's access to historic books and characters."[111] The Fox News Channel, which owns thirteen of the fifteen most watched cable news shows, devoted segment after segment to Dr. Seuss.[112] According to one poll, "77 percent of Republican voters reported hearing 'a lot' or 'some' news about Dr. Seuss's estate pulling a few of his books from circulation."[113] As Fox entered week three of their coverage, they warned Americans: "When we start down the road of policing speech that we don't like, we're going down a very dark road."[114] One might think there were more pressing issues during a global pandemic. Though, if the point is to win elections, the right did not miss its mark.

Consider Lucian Gideon Conway III, Meredith A. Repke, and Shannon C. Houck's research on the 2016 presidential election.[115] In their experiment, later published in the *Journal of Social and Political Psychology*, they recruited hundreds of participants from a slightly left-leaning sample of adults. Participants were then asked to respond to questions that assessed their perceptions of Hillary Clinton, Donald Trump, and "norms restricting communication (Political Correctness—or PC—norms)."[116] As these researchers show, participants who were primed to think about restrictive

communication norms displayed more support for Trump than participants who were not primed to think about these norms.

In this respect, exposure to these norms undermined support for Clinton. "In control conditions, Clinton was soundly preferred to Trump," but
"when Political Correctness norms were made salient, this gap virtually disappeared." Political correctness was not irrelevant to the election. To the
contrary, "support for Donald Trump was in part the result of over-exposure
to PC norms."[117] As figure 3.1 suggests, norms that aspire to control what
people write, read, and say fuel support for politicians who challenge these
norms. Importantly, this effect occurred among people who had different
political ideologies.[118]

The feeling of being watched by the PC Police is not a relic of the 2016
election. In the 2020 American National Elections Studies' pre-election
survey, Americans were asked about political correctness.[119] Specifically,
"respondents were asked whether they thought people needed to change
the way they talked to be with the times or whether this movement had
gone too far and people were too easily offended. People being too easily
offended won by a 53% to 46% margin over people needing to change the

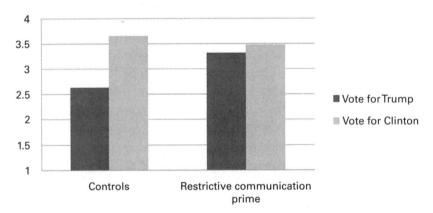

Figure 3.1
Voting likelihood in the 2016 presidential election. Source: Lucian Gideon Conway
III, Meredith A. Repke, and Shannon C. Houck, "Donald Trump as a Cultural Revolt
against Perceived Communication Restriction: Priming Political Correctness Norms
Causes More Trump Support," *Journal of Social and Political Psychology* 5, no. 1 (May
2017): 255. This figure was used via a Creative Commons license: "Attribution 4.0
International Deed," Creative Commons, https://creativecommons.org/licenses/by
/4.0/.

way they talked." This was not a sample of Fox News viewers. Most of the respondents planned to vote, or had already voted, for Joe Biden. Another poll reported that 80 percent of Americans "believe that political correctness has gone too far."[120]

In this context, Ted Cruz's attempt to associate Uncle Joe with canceled Dr. Seuss books makes political sense. According to a 2021 survey, conducted by the Center for American Political Studies at Harvard University and Harris Insights and Analytics, 64 percent of respondents are concerned about "a growing cancel culture" that is "a threat to our freedom."[121] In contrast to the moral crusaders who lobbied Amazon to ban *A Birthday Cake for George Washington*, 60 percent of Americans believe that Amazon should not ban *any* book based on its political viewpoint.[122] Again, this was not a sample of Fox News viewers. The results reflect a nationally representative sample of American voters.

In another poll, conducted in February 2022, "84 percent of adults said it is a 'very serious or 'somewhat serious problem that some Americans do not speak freely in everyday situations because of fear of retaliation or harsh criticism." Notwithstanding the prattle of moral crusaders who continue to give the impression that only racist white people are concerned about this problem, 84 percent of African Americans agreed it is a "very serious" or "somewhat serious" problem.[123] To reiterate a point made throughout *That Book Is Dangerous!*, if you want be profoundly misinformed about what "Black America" thinks, I recommend following the Twitter accounts of the race leaders mentioned in this book.

When College Pulse, the Foundation for Individual Rights and Expression, and RealClearEducation, surveyed 19,969 undergraduate students in the United States, "only about one in nine (12%) students would feel very comfortable expressing their perspective on social platforms; one in three students report that they would be *very uncomfortable* posting it."[124] In another survey of 37,000 college students, "more than 80% of students report censoring their viewpoints at their colleges at least some of the time."[125] An Arizona State University student reflects: "As an English major just about every class I've taken has touched on the 'dangers' of white people and whiteness," and "I often hear students say things like 'X is the only male whose opinion matters' and 'who cares what he thinks he's not even gay' sometimes in front of the whole class and people just seem to accept it as a fundamental truth." Another student, from Amherst College, adds: "Many students at this school are very liberal and I am afraid of being 'cancelled.'"[126]

Today's students are tomorrow's authors, agents, editors, and publishing executives who censor themselves. As one bestselling author told journalist and YA author Kat Rosenfield, under the condition of anonymity, "I'm afraid. I'm afraid for my career. I'm afraid for offending people that I have no intention of offending."[127] This same author scrapped a character of color in her work because, like so many authors and publishing insiders, she felt it was not worth the inevitable backlash. "The potential for reputational damage is real," explained one literary agent, and "no one wants to be called a racist, or sexist, or homophobic. That stink doesn't wash off." Like another agent, who describes himself as someone committed to diversity in publishing, this agent requested that their name not be included in Rosenfield's article.

An agent, who would not allow me to record our interview, said it is not just about canceled books. It is also about authors who lose speaking fees and other income because their Wikipedia page now includes accusations. To borrow PR specialist Ryan Holiday's term, there is a "trading up" effect that happens.[128] A few Goodreads reviewers accuse an author's work of racism, ableism, and so on. Their accusations are amplified by a blogger. Soon, there is a story in *Jezebel*, or *HuffPost*, or *BuzzFeed*. From there, the story is retweeted by the same people who started the controversy. It now seems a lot more important. More prestigious outlets like the *New York Times* and the *Washington Post* jump on the bandwagon. After, if one looks at the Wikipedia page for the author, there is a "controversy" section. Unless this author has thousands of dollars to pay consultants for search engine optimization work, an unflattering Wikipedia link may remain the first link every time their name is googled. This cycle—it often looks as random as the stoning in Shirley Jackson's "The Lottery"—can unfold in a matter of days over something as seemingly unnewsworthy as a picture book about a birthday cake. Another agent told me she has "given up on representing contemporary fiction because of these morality and diversity panics."

In this respect, it is unsurprising that conservative politicians and pundits focus on publishing, college campuses, and other sites where liberal PC norms are the strongest. It is also unsurprising that these norms continually reappear in scholarship on those who voted for Donald Trump. In *Strangers in Their Own Land: Anger and Mourning on the American Right*, sociologist

Arlie Russell Hochschild traveled from her liberal enclave at the University of California–Berkeley to Lake Charles, Louisiana. She wanted to understand how people on the other side of the political spectrum think. As she explains, many conservatives feel "a sense of release from the constrictions of politically correct speech and ideas" when they hear Trump shout "Let's get rid of PC!" "My friends on the right felt obliged to try to modify their feelings," Hochschild explains, "and they didn't like having to do that; they felt under the watchful eye of the 'PC police.'" According to this ethnographer, "it was with joyous relief that many heard a Donald Trump who seemed to be wildly, omnipotently, magically free of all PC constraint.'"[129]

It is not just conservatives who want to be free of PC constraint. This is what makes PC the perfect wedge issue for the right. On the one hand, prominent liberals deny the existence of PC and cancel culture. "Cancel culture is this boogeyman that people have come up with to explain away bad behavior and when their faves experience consequences," explains novelist, *New York Times* contributor, and moral entrepreneur Roxane Gay.[130] For his part, moral entrepreneur and distinguished professor of English Philip Nel, opining in the pages of the *Washington Post*, believes "cancel culture" is just a "white-supremacist fantasy."[131] Because "no government agent has yet appeared at my door demanding that I surrender my copies" of Dr. Seuss's books, explains Nel, there is no "cancel culture." According to Nel, books contain "poison." And what people call "cancel" culture is actually "healing" culture.

Like Gay and Nel, some of the liberals I interviewed had no use for the term. In the words of one agent, "The phrase 'cancel culture' gives me the heebie jeebies. I really hate that phrase. To me, the phrase evokes images of white supremacy and institutionalized racism. For me, it's the perfect excuse to downplay real concerns. It's a very defensive term. There's a lot of 'Oh my God, will I actually be able to write the things I want to write?' It's a totally fake fear." Following the trend of reframing disagreement—some people believe the term is accurate and useful, whereas other people believe the term is neither accurate nor useful—as the difference between safety and danger, this agent also believes "cancel culture" is a "dangerous phrase." Because no progressive wants to be associated with dangerous white supremacists, I understand why many progressives are reluctant to use the phrase.

As Laurent Dubreuil observes, the cancelers are canceling the term "cancel culture."[132] "It's a beautiful thing, the destruction of words," wrote

Orwell in *1984*, "Don't you see the whole aim of Newspeak is to narrow the range of thought? In the end we shall make thoughtcrime literally impossible, because there will be no words in which to express it."[133] The importance of "cancel culture," despite its imperfections and more belligerent uses—for example, Donald Trump's failure to win re-election in 2020 was not "cancel culture"—is that it gives people the language to illuminate a social problem. When a canceler tells people to stop using "cancel culture," it is like a censor telling people to stop using "censorship." You cannot address a problem if you are stripped of the language to discuss it.

The cancelers understand this. Like "cancel culture," they are trying to redefine "censorship" in the narrowest terms possible. Writing in the pages of the *Guardian*, Farah Mendlesohn, the head of the department of English and media at Anglia Ruskin University, asserts that "censorship is when a government or authority prevents someone from speaking or writing. When a business stops producing something because it is faulty, that is product recall." Accordingly, because the US government did not jail the authors of *A Birthday Cake for George Washington*, *The Adventures of Ook and Gluk*, and other books, people should not use the word "censorship." They should use euphemisms.

Literary history is filled with censors who play these language games. For example, the censors in South Africa, from the 1960s through the 1970s, did not describe censorship as censorship. Euphemistically, they described it as "publications control." "Censorship," reflects novelist J. M. Coetzee, "was a word it preferred to censor from public discourse about itself."[134] The current push to redefine "censorship" as "government censorship," and the push to eliminate the term "cancel culture" from discussions about cancel culture, are the latest moves in the Newspeak playbook. In Nel's words, offensive books are like cars without seat belts. Cars are "recalled." They are not "censored." This is not a "cancel culture." It is a "healing culture."

On the other hand, this view is *wildly* out of touch with public opinion. In response to a Morning Consult poll conducted from July 1 through July 6, 2021, thousands of respondents were asked about cancel culture.[135] The majority of people in every single age group—Generation Z (born 1997–2008), Millennials (born 1981–1996), Generation X (born 1965–1980), and Baby Boomers (born 1946–1964)—had a negative view of it. Members of Gen Z, who range from thirteen to twenty-four years old, had the most negative view of it; 55 percent reported a negative view, whereas just 8 percent reported a positive view. The youngest members of Gen Z, thirteen- to sixteen-year-olds, are even less sympathetic. A whopping 59 percent reported a negative view of cancel culture.

At the end of 2020, The Learning Network at the *New York Times* issued a writing prompt to Gen Z.[136] The results were remarkably similar. "While a number of students spoke to the potential insight, growth and accountability that can come from calmly and gently 'calling in' someone," reported *The Times*, "the overwhelming majority expressed, in no uncertain terms, serious concern for cancel culture's impact on society." Perhaps these young people's brains have been "poisoned" by offensive books, and that is why they do not celebrate this "healing" culture. Or perhaps they have a sober view of reality. A few of their responses:

We shut people down when we sense what is considered 'immoral behavior,' but in fact, tearing someone down and getting 'rid' of them is what should be regarded as immoral.

—Chloe B, Miami Country Day School

Cancel culture is often extremely toxic (specifically on the internet, not the way it is in our personal lives) and I think there are simply better and more mature ways to deal with situations as such.

—Mercy V, IPoly High School

When I think of cancel culture, I can't help but think of old religious groups who would execute members of other religions.

—Javier Aristy, Hoggard High School

More interestingly, Gen Z also has the least positive view of capitalism.[137] In contrast to Baby Boomers, 54 percent of whom reported a positive view of capitalism, just 22 percent of Gen Z respondents reported the same view. As the pollsters reflect, "Those respondents ages 13–24 who grew up in the aftermath of the Great Recession are more likely to harbor negative attitudes toward the capitalist economy than toward the latest cultural flash point, especially when compared to many of their elders." In contrast to the tenured professors and bestselling authors who lead the moral crusade on #KidLit and #YATwitter, jumping from one cultural flash point to the next, this generation has actual problems to confront.

Aside from the grim realities of capitalism, which look like they belong in a Kim Stanley Robinson novel, there is another explanation for the attitudes of Gen Z. They are more likely to know the pain of cyberbullying. Unlike all the adults who grew up without Facebook, Twitter, and TikTok, many young adults were born into the panopticon of social media. According to one dataset from 2020, over 20 percent of parents said that a child or young adult in their household, aged ten to eighteen, had been cyberbullied.[138] In another dataset from UNICEF, which polled thirteen- to fourteen-year-olds, "more than a third of young people in 30 countries report being a victim of online bullying."[139] As one college student and book blogger reflects, #YATwitter "feels like being in high school again," a place where bullies reign over others.[140] Just as we should not tolerate cyberbullying from children and teenagers, we should not tolerate it from adults.

The data from Morning Consult is not an outlier. According to another recent poll conducted by Yahoo News/YouGov, "most (56%) Americans think that cancel culture in the United States is a very big (28%) or somewhat big (28%) problem."[141] When most Americans think cancel culture is a big problem, and prominent liberals writing for the *New York Times*, the *Washington Post*, and other places deny that it even exists—or they call you a white supremacist for believing that it exists—you do not have to be a Republican mastermind to see the opportunity right in front of your eyes. Republican pundits, pollsters, and politicians understand that most Americans will defend free speech, including speech that is offensive and upsetting. As public opinion analyst Harry Enten explains, criticism of cancel culture is one of the "best political plays" for the right because "fear of cancel culture and political correctness isn't something that just animates the GOP's base."[142] It is "the rare issue that does so without alienating voters in the middle."

This is one reason why the right devotes so much attention to canceled books. As one progressive literary agent, who used to work for *The Nation*, reflects:

> The Left needs political pragmatists to sit these people down and say, "Not only do we have to park it, but we're paying an awful political price." It elects people like Donald Trump. The resentment toward political correctness. People will vote for anybody who announces their repugnance to it. It's just killing us. It's killing local elections. It's killing schoolboards. It's so unproductive. Way before Tucker Carlson, this was Roger Ailes's red meat. He loved nothing like going to Ivy League universities and pointing out prissy, overly sensitive politically correct instruction. It's a long tradition. The right wing has had great fun with the left wing. It is a real drag. Much of what they say is correct.

This is also why the right is so effective at cultivating the next generation of conservatives. When journalist Robby Soave attended Turning Point USA's High School Leadership Summit in 2018, he was struck by how many teenagers showed up with concerns about political correctness. "One gets the sense from talking with these kids that the most important issue—aside from illegal immigration, perhaps—is political correctness." As Soave describes it, many young Americans are concerned about social media mobs. According to one fifteen-year-old girl, the summit was not just a "welcome relief," but a "reminder that she wasn't alone."[143] Never one to waste a culture war, education secretary Betsy Devos delivered a speech that implored these teenagers to focus on persuading those with whom they disagree. For Devos, politics is about power. While many liberals are, to use Halberstam's language, huddled together bonding in their self-righteousness, a lot of conservatives, including those who are not even old enough to vote, are out in their communities talking to people, changing their minds, and winning elections.

Electoral politics aside, political correctness has a distinct relationship with the "alt-right." In her book *Kill All Normies: Online Culture Wars from 4Chan and Tumblr to Trump and the Alt-Right*, Angela Nagle examines the PC liberalism that exists in online space on the left. Sifting through posts and tweets, she explains that these spaces promote a "cult of suffering, weakness, and vulnerability."[144] At the same time, they confuse cancellation and self-flagellation with political work. From Twitter to Tumblr, these are spaces where "lightly thrown claims of misogyny, racism, ableism, fatphobia, transphobia and so on" abound.[145]

Like #YATwitter and #KidLit, these spaces are marked by the belief that people have the right to not be offended. As Nagle explains, "the hysterical liberal call-out produced an online backlash of irreverent mockery and anti-PC,"[146] which turned provocateurs like Milo Yiannopoulos and Steve Bannon into cultural icons and political advisers. It also turned Reddit, 4chan, and other websites into recruitment centers for those who see the left as hypersensitive, humorless, and snobbish little clicktivists. As recently as 2009, Bill O'Reilly decried the fringe website 4chan as "a far-left website."[147] Less than a decade later, the *New York Times* decried it as an "alt-right breeding ground."[148] As of June 15, 2022, 4chan is now one of the five hundred most trafficked websites in the United States.[149] A central part of that rapid transformation was the equally rapid influx of disdain for political correctness, cancel culture, and liberal elites who treat their fellow Americans as a "basket of deplorables."

The same year Zero Books published Nagle's broadside, Data & Society, an independent nonprofit research organization, published a report about media manipulation and disinformation. In its discussion of radicalization, the report concludes: "Far-right movements exploit young men's rebellion and dislike of 'political correctness' to spread white supremacist thought, Islamophobia, and misogyny through irony and knowledge of internet culture. This is a form of radicalization happening primarily through forums, message boards, and social media targeting young men immersed in internet culture."[150]

To be sure, some leftists are trying to counter the alt-right with their own brand of irreverent humor, irony, and knowledge of internet culture. "Reclaiming vulgarity from the Trumps of the world is imperative," argues activist Amber A'Lee Frost, or "we will find ourselves handicapped by our own civility."[151] *The Michael Brooks Show* on YouTube and the *Chapo Trap House* podcast are two examples of the "Dirtbag Left."[152] Notwithstanding these interventions, the alt-right has been a lot more successful at capitalizing on the anti-PC wave.

Just look at the books that are quoted, turned into memes, and joked about on websites like 4chan. Books like *American Psycho* and *Fight Club*, which could be referenced to make fun of Wall Street bankers and politicians like Trump, are referenced to make fun of liberals. In part, this is because some liberals—always ready to hector you about the "heteronormativity," "toxic masculinity," and so on in whatever you like to read—deride these popular books. Think about this take on Chuck Palahniuk's magnum opus and its film adaptation published in *Esquire*:

> *Fight Club* popularized a version of toxic machismo. . . . Plenty has been written about *Fight Club* not holding up in a society where we're reckoning with how shitty white men bumble through the world. . . . *Fight Club* doesn't go any deeper than a high school essay. . . . *Fight Club* feels so hilariously juvenile. Perhaps it's the clunky unsubtle source material, but *Fight Club*—for the most part—is a joyless two-hour mansplaining of modern capitalist America. So, perhaps it's best to leave *Fight Club* back in 1999. We've matured as individuals, as a society (hopefully). America is in a different place, and as beloved as *Fight Club* is to most people still today, we just don't need it anymore. Let's just follow the first rule of *Fight Club*, and just never talk about *Fight Club* again.[153]

Building on the work of those studying the radicalization of young men, you might get blowback if you are looking down on a popular book and film that many young men love, one with strong populist themes, in the pages of an upscale magazine that publishes articles like "The 13 Best Rolex Watches for Men" and "The Gucci Basket Puts a Luxury Stamp on 80s Basketball Shoe Style"—articles that suggest a lot about who actually reads *Esquire*. Certainly, the alt-right can be forgiven for associating PC with affluent liberal snobs.

In contrast to mainstream Republicans, the alt-right has no "coherent commitment to conservative thought or politics."[154] Yet a commitment to conservative thought and politics is not the point. As Nagle explains, "What we now call the alt-right is really this collection of lots of separate tendencies that grew semi-independently but which were joined under the banner of anti-PC cultural politics."[155] When Trump is applauded by those in alt-right spaces, he is not applauded because these spaces are full of dyed-in-the-wool Republicans who love the flag, family values, Christianity, and free market capitalism.

To the contrary, the alt-right includes antiwar activists, atheists, Occupy Wall Street veterans, and other people who might have ended up on the other side of the political divide. In large part, Trump is applauded because he goes out of his way to publicly violate what Hochschild calls the liberal "feeling rules," what Conway and his colleagues call "political correctness norms," and what Nagel calls "Western liberal performative politics."[156] Moreover, his proposals—including his proposal to defund colleges and universities that restrict free speech—actually address the nonpartisan concerns about PC that recur in poll, after poll, after poll.

The same is true of Fox News's humorist Greg Gutfeld. As of 2021, Gutfeld had higher ratings than Stephen Colbert and Trevor Noah—leaving the liberal media establishment scratching its head in confusion.[157] With a mountain of content that mocks PC norms (the kind of content that would get Colbert and Noah canceled), is anyone actually confused by Gutfeld's broad appeal? Is anyone confused by the rapid ascent of Steven Crowder, J. P. Sears, and other right-wing humorists who have taken over YouTube with viral videos like, "How to be a Woke White Person" and "Dr. Seuss BANNING Bonanza!" Nagle's words are truer now more than ever: pro-censorship liberals have "done damage that will prove long-lasting."[158]

Here, one is reminded of the "backfire effect." As Conway and his colleagues explain, the effect has two elements. First, people might suppress or change what they say in the short term to avoid sanctions from others, but this can be counterproductive in the long term.[159] Just because people suppress or change their views in public, to avoid the ire of the PC Left, does not mean their views magically disappear. It is one thing to disagree; it is quite another to be deprived of the right to disagree. Much like alcohol during Prohibition, private views can, and often do, become stronger when they go underground. Second, emotional reactance is real. "Freedom of choice is a valued psychological commodity," explain Conway and his colleagues, "and so we often will deviate from others' expectations—both in belief and in action—in order to re-assert our right to choose."[160] At its core, the moral crusade over literature believes that children, teenagers, and even adults should be deprived of the right to choose their own books.

Even within the terrain of literature itself, one sees the blowback. From *Triggered: How the Left Thrives on Hate and Wants to Silence Us* by Donald Trump Jr., to *The Authoritarian Moment: How the Left Weaponized America's Institutions against Dissent* by Ben Shapiro, the *New York Times* bestselling follow-up to his other bestseller *Bullies: How the Left's Culture of Fear and Intimidation Silences Americans*, to *Don't Burn This Book: Thinking for Yourself in an Age of Unreason* by Dave Rubin, yet another *New York Times* bestseller, there is a growing library of popular literature that depicts liberals as snobs, idiots, and cultural authoritarians. Some of this literature, like *Woke: A Guide to Social Justice* by Titania McGrath (the pseudonym of playwright and comedian Andrew Doyle) is satirical.[161] In *Woke*, Doyle writes from the perspective of a "radical intersectionalist poet" on the "forefront of online activism."[162] Her manifesto for social justice begins, "I am a much better person than you." Today, Titania, an Oxford University graduate who wrote a dissertation on "the corrosive nature of cis-masculine futurity," has more than seven hundred thousand Twitter followers. The most interesting aspect of Doyle's ongoing experiment in satire is that some tweeters still think Titania is real. They cannot distinguish her from the affluent, highly educated, and perpetually outraged white liberals she satirizes.

In addition to the books, there are new magazines that position the right as the sane alternative to the PC Left. *Quillette* was founded in 2015, the same year that Cynthia Leitich Smith coined #DiversityJedi. Whereas Smith remains an opinion leader in the world of literature for young people, with about twenty thousand followers, *Quillette* has more than two hundred thousand followers. In fact, it has more followers than *The New Republic*, *The Progressive*, *CounterPunch*, *AlterNet*, *The Baffler*, *Dissent* and other left-wing magazines that have existed for decades. *Quillette*'s articles include "Young Adult Fiction's Online Commissars," "The Problem with Sensitivity Readers," and "If You Want to Save the Planet, Drop the Campaign against Capitalism." Like *Tucker Carlson Tonight*, their website mixes criticism of the moral crusade over literature with paeans to the free market. At a time when democratic socialism is more popular than ever in the United States, it is one of those magisterial moves that understands what a position on a wedge issue is supposed to accomplish. It is supposed to attract people who might otherwise be unsympathetic to your other positions.

Despite the long-standing effectiveness of this approach, some progressive editors are committed to the polar opposite approach. Undeterred by the widespread unpopularity of cancel culture in the United States, the *New Republic* has published tracts like "The Case for More Cancelling" and "The 'Cancel Culture' Con" alongside more thoughtful articles that link capitalism to climate change. Given the reality that this magazine has been around since 1914—recall their proclamation during the comic book crusade that "every hour spent in reading comics is an hour in which all inner growth is stopped"—their editorial board should be thoroughly embarrassed to see *Quillette* build a larger following in just a few years. The disconnect between a New York City magazine that arrogantly dismisses "cancel culture" as a "joke"[163] and the overwhelming majority of American voters who describe it as a "threat to our freedom"[164] is a disconnect that is entirely unhelpful to the left. It is almost as if the *New Republic*'s editorial board consulted pollsters and political strategists before screaming, "We don't care! This is a hill we're willing to die on!"

None of this is to suggest that other issues—abortion, violent crime, the US-Mexico border, and so on—are less important to the right's appeal. Nor is it to suggest that conservatives are leading the fight against literary censorship. To the contrary, they are leading the legislative fight to censor books they dislike. Even a cursory glance at data from the American Library Association (ALA) will familiarize readers with the conservative crusade to ban children's and YA books in libraries and schools. Whereas many liberals are driven by essentialism and presentism, many conservatives are driven by nostalgia for a moment when books were less progressive and authors and their characters were less diverse.[165] To quote one of the many reports published by ALA's Office for Intellectual Freedom, "Out of the 2015 Top Ten Most Frequently Challenged Books, nine of them contained diverse content," and "86 books on this list include content by or about people of color, LGBT people and/or people with disabilities."[166]

The conservatives trying to censor Alex Gino's *George* because it does not reflect "the values of our community,"[167] and the liberals trying to censor *Blood Heir* because it does not reflect the values of their community, are two sides of a moral panic. Depending on the side, books are turning young people into gays, Marxists, homophobes, witches, or racists. As one of my interview subjects, a *New York Times* bestselling author widely celebrated for her contributions to Latin/x literature, told me: "Everyone comes at it saying they're doing this for the children. Everybody claims to be doing the best thing for the children. We could talk all day about how I disagree with the idea of books turning young people into one thing or the other." Another one of my interview subjects, a Pulitzer Prize finalist, was even more succinct in our interview: "The Left has become the Right in certain ways."

However, the right rarely devours its own. Moreover, their crusade has not made publishers bend at the knee. "The rage on the right concerning texts that they deem to be offensive to their world," one Big Five president explained to me, "doesn't seem to impinge in the same way." As far as I can tell, the right's rage is irrelevant, if not a source of personal pride for the liberals who run publishers, agencies, award committees, and other areas of literary culture. Above all, the right's crusade has not provoked the same backlash. Whether it is Barack Obama lamenting the "woke" culture of liberal clicktivists obsessed with "purity"—in the first black president's words, "That's not activism"[168]—or Donald Trump Jr. lamenting this same culture while presenting conservatism as the sane alternative, the most discernible effect of PC liberalism is retaliation from Americans on all sides of the political spectrum.

To reiterate the point, just because people are afraid to express themselves in public does not mean liberal PC norms are popular. Like a volcano, it might mean that dissent is brewing just beneath the surface, and it may explode in ways—like the election of Donald Trump—that pose actual threats to a more diverse and tolerant future.[169] If you cry wolf long enough, a real wolf will eventually step out of the woods.

On the rare occasion when liberals target conservative authors, instead of one another, their playbook is the same. Though, the results are much different. Inside Penguin Random House, some staffers tried to stop the publication of Jordan Peterson's self-help book, *Beyond Order: 12 More Rules for Life*, because of his political views.[170] In a meeting, some of these adults cried. Given Peterson's enormous following, it is unsurprising that his publisher did not cancel his book because liberal tears hit the floor. It is also unsurprising that Simon and Schuster went forward with their multimillion-dollar book deal with former vice president Mike Pence after an open letter from some of their employees accused them of standing "on the wrong side of justice."[171] Whereas *Poetry* is willing to retract this or that poem, major publishers are not willing to sacrifice gargantuan profits. After all, they are businesses. One vice president explains: "At the management level, people are very supportive. I would say anyone who is incentivized to make money is in support of conservative imprints because they have tended to be very lucrative. That's the reason they continue to exist. But, if you put it to an internal vote, it wouldn't even be close. It would be 8–1 in favor of disbanding the conservative imprint or banning, you know, *Fox* personalities and Republican politicians. In production and other departments, people are very unhappy about having to work on the books."

When a conservative author does lose a publisher in response to crying liberals, they just find another one. For example, Josh Hawley's *The Tyranny of Big Tech* was picked up by Regnery Publishing after he lost his contract with Simon and Schuster.[172] The publicity around his lost contract was such a media boon that his book debuted as an Amazon bestseller in three different categories. Journalist Andy Ngo experienced the same media boon.[173] Before Hachette published his book *Unmasked: Inside Antifa's Radical Plan to Destroy Democracy*, protesters gathered at the famous Powell's City of Books in Portland, Oregon. They demanded that the world's largest independent bookstore, which refused to sell the book in their store, also remove it from their website. In the words of PEN America, "Bookstores play an essential role in ensuring the public's right to access information."[174] But, due to safety risks, Powell's closed early every day during the week of January 11, 2020. It is hard to imagine better publicity for a book about threats to democracy. *Unmasked* hit number three on *The New York Times* nonfiction bestseller list.

Public relations specialists pray to the PR gods for this kind of attention. For example, Ryan Holiday defaced a billboard for *I Hope They Serve Beer in Hell*, an adaptation of his client Tucker Max's book. He then distributed photographs of the vandalism, wrote fake tweets, and posted fake comments to articles online. He wanted to create the impression that there was "a real protest movement against Max's sexism."[175] After, a real protest movement against Max's sexism emerged. Holiday, the provocateur, could not have been happier. "The writer who is gagged today," writes J. M. Coetzee in *Giving Offense*, "is famous tomorrow for having been gagged."[176] As the poet Ben Johnson put it back in 1603:

> Nor do they aught, that use this cruelty
> Of interdiction, and this rage of burning;
> But purchase to themselves rebuke, and shame,
> And to the writers an eternal name.[177]

4 The Future of the Sensitivity Era

The Campus Epicenter

When one searches "moral panic" and "moral crusade" in the flagship journals of the Children's Literature Association, which is an organization devoted to the academic study of literature for children and young adults, not one article uses these concepts to describe what is going on in the culture of children's and YA literature today.[1] By contrast, "racism" returns 323 results.[2] In large part, this field of scholarship has turned "reading literature into a whack-a-mole game of spot the 'problematic'-ism."[3] For example, a recent article on Paddington Bear, published in *Children's Literature Association Quarterly*, argues: "The Paddington texts are problematic in that, while ostensibly arguing for sympathy for migrants, they nonetheless affirm certain models of English identity which are tied to whiteness, imperialism, empiricism, [and] the English language."[4] Recent conference presentations, dissertations, course descriptions, and job advertisements suggest that the next generation of children's and YA literature scholars will be whacking moles, too.

Although professors and graduate students should be familiar with the moral crusade directed at comic books—it is not every week that the US Senate holds a hearing on literature written for young people—it is possible that no one notices the similarities between the past and the present. It is also possible that no scholar wants to be pilloried by the authors, agents, editors, and other scholars who participate in the current crusade.[5] With an influx of English PhDs, and relatively few tenure-track jobs available for the graduates who hold these degrees, no one wants to be stigmatized as a "problematic" literary critic. For that matter, no one wants to be stigmatized as a "problematic" author, agent, or editor either. As one children's book agent told Kat Rosenfield, "None of us are willing to comment publicly for fear of being targeted and labeled racist or bigoted."[6] In the Sensitivity Era, if a scholar wants to avoid blowback, they should stick to whack-a-mole. To wit, crusaders targeted *New York Magazine* when they heard Rosenfield was writing an article critical of their crusade. They said her article would endanger someone's life.[7]

Much has been written about censorship on college campuses in the past decade, but few scholars have paid attention to the fact that many writers, if not the overwhelming majority of writers, are now trained on campus. In his book *The Program Era: Postwar Fiction and the Rise of Creative Writing*, Mark McGurl documents the ongoing boom in creative writing programs. Whether one wants to pursue a bachelor of arts in Creative Writing at the University of Arizona, or a master of fine arts in Children's Book Writing and Illustrating at Hollins University, there are now hundreds of programs to choose from.[8] As novelist Poe Ballantine reflects, the old path of "quitting your job, selling your car, and hustling like an old hooker with a toothache" has been "replaced by taking out a student loan and enrolling in the nearby university."[9]

A few years after Harvard University Press published *The Program Era* in 2009, scholars of higher education noticed something strange happening on college campuses. Although the demands to censor professors and other students were not new, the demands were becoming medicalized.[10] In yesterday's creative writing classroom, a draft of a novel might have been considered poorly written or maybe even offensive. Today, it creates a "dangerous" and "harmful" classroom that is not a "safe space."

This is why some professors ask their students to include "trigger warnings" at the top of their work, or to simply avoid writing about any topic that might "trigger" another student in the room. As Oberlin College put it in their guidelines for faculty, trigger warnings "show students that you care about their safety."[11] In an era of mandatory sensitivity training programs, anonymous bias-reporting systems, and other measures instituted by campus bureaucrats, who are rapidly outpacing tenured professors, one can only imagine what it is like to be a novelist, poet, or playwright on a college campus.[12]

At Williams College, visiting professor Misha Chowdhury, a queer Bengali playwright, was working on a production of Aleshea Harris's *Beast Thing*.[13] The play attempts "to step into and explode certain archetypal stories and characters in American culture that are inevitably marked as white." As opening night approached, the theater department canceled all scheduled performances. In his statement of resignation, Chowdhury reflects:

> It angers and saddens me deeply that the conversation about care and trauma that is taking place at Williams, which aspires, I believe, toward a better ethics, is resulting in artists of color being silenced and pushed away from campus. . . . I witnessed a Black playwright and a Black video designer and a Black actor being asked to revise their project or their image or their performance because it would cause harm to Black audience members. Generalizing people's traumas in that way troubles me.
>
> There is a profound irony at play. I experienced many instances in which people imposed fragility and fear onto bodies of color and, couched in the language of care, policed what people of color are allowed to do and make and say. . . . I will be pulling out of my candidacy for the tenure-track position in the department next year. The climate at Williams that resulted in the cancellation of Beast Thing makes it very difficult for me to create the kind of work I value here.[14]

Around the same time, plays were canceled at Knox College, Kenyon College, Brandeis University, the University of Utah, and other colleges and universities. At the University of Michigan, professors and students demanded that Bright Sheng, a professor in the School of Music, Theatre and Dance, be removed from his course after he screened an adaptation of William Shakespeare's *Othello*. "I was shocked that [Sheng] would show something like this in something that's supposed to be a safe space," exclaimed one student.[15] His apology was then accused of further insensitivities.

Although Sheng survived the Cultural Revolution in China, he did not remain the professor of his own course. A few weeks into the fall 2021 semester, he was replaced. When students are revered for reporting their professors, it is hard not to be reminded of China as well as the Soviet Union. Under Stalin, "every schoolchild had to learn the story of the boy Pavlik Morozov, who was celebrated for turning in his parents for holding anti-Soviet attitudes."[16] Similar to "anti-Soviet attitude," "safety" is a watchword without a clear definition. Used to justify the overreach of campus bureaucrats, it is like "terror" in the "war on terror."

Writing in *Research in the Teaching of English*, the flagship research journal of the National Council of Teachers in English, Deborah Appleman reflects:

> Examples abound of the chilling effects of trigger warnings on literature instruction. . . . A women's studies professor who included *The Bluest Eye* by Toni Morrison on her syllabus was confronted by her students even before her class began.

"We won't read this book under any conditions," they told her. "It has incest in it, and that is triggering." The professor found herself in a profound pedagogical, even moral, dilemma. On one hand, she didn't want to harm or revictimize any of her students. On the other hand, she fervently believed that the novel has a critically significant place in our (finally) diversifying literary heritage and deserves to be read.

What complicated her decision was that the students (as is sometimes the case) were arguing from a place of deeply held principle rather than personal traumatic experience. . . . Can literature be read without triggering, or, in fact, is part of the role of literature *to* trigger—that is, to wake and engage our complex set of emotions and experiences? While it is, of course, imperative to consider our students' well-being and to teach sensitively, I worry that these considerations will banish some significant texts into silence.[17]

Whereas the old era of "solidarity" revolved around doing political work to help people who face injustices that one is insulated from (for example, white Americans working in solidarity with African Americans to topple Jim Crow), the new era of "allyship" revolves around the institutionalization of neurosis. For the neurotic, reading is not like revictimization. It is revictimization. In an unexpected plot twist, censoring Toni Morrison is now a feminist act. If you have a hard time staying up to date with the twists and turns of the Sensitivity Era, it is only a matter of time before you, too, are accused of insensitivities. Unlike political solidarity, cultural allyship can look confusing to anyone unfamiliar with the abstruse, always changing guidelines for safety.

On campus, even journalism has to be a "safe space." According to Northwestern University's newspaper: "While our goal is to document history and spread information, nothing is more important than ensuring that our fellow students feel safe."[18] Infamously, Northwestern also put Laura Kipnis, a tenured professor in their School of Communication, through a Title IX investigation because she wrote a *Chronicle of Higher Education* article "suggesting there are too many Title IX investigations." She was the subject of a second Title IX investigation for writing "a book about being investigated for saying there are too many Title IX investigations."[19]

At Princeton University, hundreds of faculty members and staff signed a letter that asked their university to form a committee to "oversee the investigation and discipline of racist behaviors, incidents, research, and publication on the part of faculty."[20] At a moment when "racist" means whatever anyone wants it to mean, it will be interesting to see what thoughtcrimes turn up in the work of Princeton's poets, novelists, playwrights, journalists, and scholars. After all, Joyce Carol Oates, a professor of creative writing at Princeton, was admonished for criticizing sensitivity readers.[21] According to one critic, Oates "spewed a lot of racist tweets about how if people don't like the stories, don't read them, and they should start their own publishing houses to get their books published."[22] Because this is what counts as "racism" in the Sensitivity Era, Princeton's investigators will surely find more "racism" in Oates's fifty-eight novels. Likewise, people accused Princeton poet Michael Dickman of "racism" after he wrote a poem, "Scholls Ferry Rd.," that included a racist character. *Poetry* retracted his poem. In response, Tracy K. Smith, another Princeton poet, spoke of "developing a formalized process for addressing accountability and making reparations in situations of this kind."[23] Whereas most Americans associate reparations with African American slavery and the displacement of Native Americans, the twenty-second Poet Laureate of the United States believes they are relevant if someone wrote a poem you did not like.

A mountain of recent books—*Speak Freely: Why Universities Must Defend Free Speech*; *Safe Enough Spaces: A Pragmatist's Approach to Inclusion, Free Speech, and Political Correctness on College Campuses*; *What's Happened to the University? A Sociological Exploration of Its Infantilization*; and so on—suggest that the problems of free speech at Williams College, the University of Michigan, Princeton University, and elsewhere are not distinct to these colleges and universities. Across the country, institutions of higher education look less like the University of California in the 1960s, where the left's Free Speech Movement ascended, and more like the pseudo-therapeutic spaces of Goodreads and Bookstagram. Because higher education is what David Fenza, the executive director of the Association of Writers and Writing Programs, calls "the largest system of literary patronage for living writers the world has ever seen,"[24] its infantilization is central to the infantilization of literary culture.

As English professor Jack Halberstam, a seminal figure in queer studies who also goes by Judith (and who does not, in his words, "police" what people call him[25]), reflects: "I rarely go to a conference, festival or gathering anymore without a protest erupting about a mode of representation that triggered someone somewhere. And as people 'call each other out' to a chorus of finger snapping, we seem to be rapidly losing all sense of perspective."[26] Many of the moral crusaders discussed in *That Book Is Dangerous!*

(Reese, Clayton, Nel, Bowles, Lindblom, Vivian, Gay, et al.) teach or have taught on campus. "There was a time when emotionally fragile individuals who could not withstand the stresses of daily living headed off, on reaching adulthood, to a covenant or monastery," writes philosophy professor William B. Irvine. "These days, they might instead go to a college campus."[27]

An insular culture of hypersensitive people who accuse one another of "harm" is great fodder for dystopian literature. It is terrible for literary culture. It might be most terrible for historically underrepresented writers who do not get the feedback they deserve. One recent MFA graduate recalls a typical experience workshopping what they considered a heavy-handed, sermon-like story:

> There was no way I was going to stand up and be like, "Hey, I think maybe you need to tone down the political messaging for the sake of your story. There's a story here. I want to just hear your story, which will have in it these important social issues. But when it starts to stray into the grandstanding, the preaching, it actually takes away from the impact." In the interest of the exact message this writer wants to get across, I would like to make this recommendation. But there's no chance I'm going to say it. I'm just opening myself up to a world of shame. Also, nobody says it. So, this writer isn't getting the feedback that they probably need to make this piece better.
>
> As an MFA program, you're kind of doing your black writers a disservice without telling them that it's sort of more clever to hide your politics, not because you should hide yourself. That would be how that would be received if I said it. They'd be like, "You just want to suppress this person's radical black politics." No, not at all. But being sneaky about that stuff is just more effective. It's always been that way. It works better when I'm immersed in that experience, instead of having it talked about to me in these very moralistic terms. Books that are pedantic are boring, and nobody wants to read them.
>
> Nobody could ever say that in that room, except maybe another person of color. And there's no room for nuance. I'm not going to be able to make my point understood because I'm probably not going to say it that well the first time. I'm just a person who's trying to get my point across. It's fine if you make a little misstep, and people cringe a little, and you go, "No, that's not what I meant," as long as there's room for pretty rapid forgiveness when people realize you're not saying that, you're saying something else. But there isn't. It just feels like it's bad for everybody.

Another writer I interviewed describes this workshop climate as the "racism of low expectations."

John McWhorter, a black English professor, reflects: "White people calling themselves our saviors make black people look like the dumbest, weakest, most self-indulgent human beings in the history of our species, and teach black people to revel in that status and cherish it as making us special."[28] Another anecdote from a top-ranked MFA program illustrates McWhorter's point:

> We had a black writer turn in this truly beautiful essay. Everybody was so admiring of it. We were in the complimentary phase of the workshop, and the professor said, "This is just such an ambitious thing you've brought in. It's taking on so many different topics, and it's so exciting." Then one of the other students, a white student, made a point of stopping the professor, and saying, "Just so you know, the word 'ambitious,' especially when applied to women and people of color, is deeply insulting because you're saying that she's sort of stepping beyond her capabilities, that she's trying to do more than she can, than she's capable of as a black woman." After, the professor spent two minutes doing the standard penance. But everyone's so tight after that because you're like, Jesus, this guy just complimented her writing.

MFA programs reward students who spot morally problematic issues in other's students' work, in other students' comments, and even in their professors' compliments. "There's social points awarded for each identification of something problematic," explained one recent MFA graduate, "it happens all the time." How much time this leaves for elements of craft, like how to write an inciting incident or a climax, is beside the point.

As I interviewed writers, I was reminded of a scene in *One Flew Over the Cuckoo's Nest* by Ken Kesey (a novelist who had inimical experiences as a graduate student in Stanford's creative writing program): "The flock gets sight of a spot of blood on some chicken and they all go to *peckin'* at it, see, till they rip the chicken to shreds, blood and bones and feathers. But usually a couple of the *flock* gets spotted in the fracas, then it's their turn. And a few more gets spots and gets pecked to death, and more and more. Oh, a peckin' party can wipe out the whole flock."[29] In MFA programs, the peckin' party spills over into the Office of Diversity and Inclusion, which investigates professors and students who have been anonymously reported by their peers.

It also spills over into Twitter, Facebook, and other platforms where MFA students and their professors accuse writers of harm. In this scene, the MFA is worn like a sheriff's badge. It is both an exclusive status symbol—at the top programs, rejection rates sit at just under one 100 percent—and an indication that one knows how to enforce the laws of "literary citizenship." Meghan Daum, who was a faculty member in the MFA Writing Program at Columbia University, describes the scene:

I've come to see the MFA in writing as the educational equivalent of a draft dodge. If the annual Association of Writers & Writing Programs (AWP) conference is any indication, getting an MFA in writing has little to do with actual writing and nearly everything to do with finding a place in a social clique. This clique, which convenes mostly online, seems less interested in the values or dynamics of any particular program (Iowa, Ohio, Pacific's low-residency; it's all the same) than in something called literary citizenship, a term I didn't hear until probably 2017. Separate from caring about literature, literary citizenship implies adherence to an unspoken moral code, one that pays lip service to equity and inclusion while still making gossip and exclusivity the main event. In the literary body politic, an MFA confers an almost mystical authority. I've noticed that many Twitter bios list MFA alongside things like nonbinary or neurodivergent, as if studying creative writing at the graduate level is an identity category.[30]

To build on Daum's point, the consistency between programs—Iowa, Ohio, Columbia, it does not matter—might be the most salient aspect of "the largest system of literary patronage for living writers the world has ever seen." The teaching is predictable. The writing is predictable, too. In the words of one black novelist who teaches on campus,

I don't like workshops. I think a workshop is a stupid way to teach people to write. But I can't come up with anything better. I can take you to a bookstore now, and we can go find a book of stories, and I can say, "This person went through an MFA program." All the stories look the same. They all sound the same. They all have the same shape. And why wouldn't they? They're trying to write for eleven other people sitting in a room, and it's art by committee. There's never going to be an edge on it. Workshops, the MFA programs, have done American letters no favors.

That's not to completely put them down. I teach in a graduate program. My students are very talented. But we're making art. It's not factory work. Now, back to your question about what goes on in the workshops. It's the same thing that goes on when someone comes in my office, and they start talking about their problems. And I always say, "Is it on this paper?' Is it written down right here?" Because if we're not talking about a story you're trying to sell me, make me believe, then I don't care. There's counselors on campus. You go talk to them. But I am not a psychotherapist. I cannot help you.

While this novelist spoke, I was reminded of Vladimir Nabokov. Nabokov, whose work has been banned as obscene in more than one country, said: "I do not write for groups, nor approve of group therapy."[31] It is hard to imagine a perspective less amicable to the MFA program.

To quote Dan Franklin, the director of Jonathan Cape, which has published Salman Rushdie and other giants: "I wouldn't publish [Nabokov's] *Lolita*. What's different today is #MeToo and social media—you can organize outrage at the drop of a hat. If *Lolita* was offered to me today, I'd never be able to get it past the acquisition team—a committee of thirty-year-olds, who'd say, 'If you publish this book, we will all resign.'"[32] Regrettably, a novel ranked by *Time* as one of the hundred best English-language novels published since 1923 will not make it past the slush pile today. The new gatekeepers, many of whom graduated from MFA programs, will not allow it.

In the United States, colleges and universities also publish the most prestigious literary journals. These are the journals where writers cut their teeth. They are also the journals where agents find new writers to represent. As one agent told me, "It's pretty darn hard to sell something, fiction or non-fiction, for someone who hasn't been publishing somewhere that has some prestige." When one reads submission guidelines for places that do have prestige, one would think the point of literature is agitprop. One would also think every editor has a clinically diagnosed case of PTSD. A few examples:

> "We are here to champion writing that upsets systems of power & dominance. Our magazine isn't going to destroy the cis-heteronormative white-supremacist ableist patriarchy. But we are going to try, & we seek to celebrate art that is trying alongside us. Above all, we seek work that is self-aware & avoids the risk of harm. . . . Because we value the wellbeing of our editors (who in turn value the wellbeing of our readers), we request content warnings & recommend sensitivity readers."
> —*Hunger Mountain Review*, Vermont College of Fine Arts[33]

> "We will not consider submissions that include prejudice, racism, xenophobia, classism, sexism, ableism, fat-shaming, homophobia, gratuitous violence, etc. We reserve the right to reject such submissions outright and no longer read submissions from that author. We also reserve the right to remove content from our journal if an author is known to be harassing or abusive."
> —*Redivider*, Emerson College[34]

> "We welcome the work of writers and artists from marginalized communities, identities, and traditions. . . . We do not tolerate submissions that contain hate speech, bigotry, discrimination, or racist, sexist, homophobic, transphobic, or ableist language or violence of any kind."
> —*Denver Quarterly*, University of Denver[35]

> "The magazine is an accomplice to the LGBTQIA+ community, Black Lives Matter, and abolitionist movements wherever they may be found. . . . We are not interested in reading racist, misogynistic, ableist, homophobic, transphobic,

xenophobic, or any otherwise hateful work. Nor are we interested in white savior narratives. . . . If you're wondering if your submission needs a content warning, go ahead and add it to your document and know that we appreciate your care. If you imagine your piece could be hurtful to any specific segment of the population, please find another venue."

—*Passages North*, Northern Michigan University[36]

The first guidelines inflate their own importance. *Hunger Mountain Review* is not just a literary journal; it is a force that aspires to "destroy" the "cis-heteronormative white-supremacist ableist patriarchy." Ironically, their editors' will be crushed by something as small as a poem without a trigger warning. Put otherwise, stopping their revolution will not take much effort. (As an aside: those who use the most militant rhetoric—vowing to "destroy," "dismantle," "topple," and "overthrow" this or that "structure" or "system"—are, given their fetishistic focus on their own emotional fragility, the very last people you would want on your side when doing real political work. In the future, I will refer to this phenomenon as "militant fragility.") The second and third guidelines raise the question of how anyone can write a story about, for example, the Trump administration if they are not allowed to include prejudice, bigotry, violence, and other uncomfortable topics. *Redivider*'s guidelines also look like they were copied and pasted from a morality clause, as they allow the journal to censor writers accused of vaguely defined offenses. The last guidelines, written with the same vagueness, prohibit writing that might trigger someone somewhere. If Titania McGrath were to parody these guidelines, I am not sure what would look different.

On and off campus, the trigger warnings themselves are getting stranger. They began with race, gender, and sexuality. Now they encompass identities that most people have never even heard of. In the February 2023 issue of *Library Journal*, a publication that helps librarians decide what books to purchase for their libraries, a reviewer recommended *Mushrooming: An Illustrated Guide to the Fantastic, Delicious, Deadly, and Strange World of Fungi* by Diane Borsato and Kelsey Oseid. But that recommendation came with a warning: "Readers who experience trypophobia, a fear of holes, should note that images throughout the book detail the spots, frills, and holes in mushrooms."[37]

Whereas literary culture celebrates trigger warnings, psychologists have a much different take on the subject. In "Helping or Harming? The Effect of Trigger Warnings on Individuals with Trauma Histories," Payton J. Jones,

Benjamin W. Bellet, and Richard J. McNally, three researchers in the department of psychology at Harvard University, had trauma survivors read passages from literature. Some survivors received trigger warnings. Other survivors did not. Harvard's team concluded: "We found no evidence that trigger warnings were helpful for trauma survivors, for participants who self-reported a posttraumatic stress disorder (PTSD) diagnosis, or for participants who qualified for probable PTSD, even when survivors' trauma matched the passages' content. We found substantial evidence that trigger warnings countertherapeutically reinforce survivors' view of their trauma as central to their identity."[38]

Yet submission guidelines give the impression that trigger warnings are exactly what these readers need, despite the reality that "avoiding triggers is a *symptom* of PTSD, not a treatment for it."[39] They also give the impression that publishing poems, plays, and short stories is like working at the Consumer Product Safety Commission. Whereas this government agency is charged with "protecting the public from unreasonable risks,"[40] these journals charge themselves with protecting readers from the "risk of harm." The "risk of harm" includes anything that "could be hurtful to any specific segment of the population." To be "safe," today's writers should stick to stories about playing with kittens, watering organic vegetable gardens, and hosting Fairtrade potlucks in the park. Notwithstanding all the blather about "resistance," "rebellion," and "revolution," if I were to pick one word to describe the literature published in the Sensitivity Era it would be "anodyne."

From Hurt Feelings to State Censorship

Unlike the past, moral crusaders no longer depend on traditional media gatekeepers to raise the alarm. Nor do they depend on these gatekeepers to keep the siren at full volume. Today, anyone with an internet connection can be a moral crusader. Moreover, research shows that expressions of moral anger and disgust, two emotions central to moral crusades, are associated with more retweets.[41] In this respect, Twitter is the perfect platform for a moral crusade. Abetted by Facebook, Goodreads, and other vanity presses, even the most uninformed readers—those who never read the book—have an audience. As sociologist Karen Sternheimer reflects in *Pop Culture Panics*, "there has possibly never been a better time to launch a moral crusade, from a media perspective."[42]

Historically, the importance of these new platforms cannot be over-stated. In the past, there were comparatively few places to publish book reviews. Outlets like the *New York Review of Books* and *Harper's Magazine* are not vanity presses. A person cannot slop together some sentences about fighting a book in a Walmart parking lot and expect to be published there. Professional reviews were, and often still are, written by people who are themselves published authors. In these places, there is a sense that another author might one day review your book. Hence, many authors were, and often still are, reluctant to trash the work of other authors. As one well-reviewed author and occasional reviewer explains, "I think [having published a book and been reviewed] gives you a certain respect for the work at hand. It's not easy to write a book and it's not easy to get a book published and so long as the author has good intentions, which they almost always do, in my review I honor those good intentions. Also other writers may review *me* one day. So as I see it there's no point in being needlessly critical or uselessly dismissive."[43]

Yet needlessly critical and uselessly dismissive is the very grist of book reviews on Twitter, Goodreads, and other platforms. These reviews consist of not just overlooking an author's good intentions but also ascribing malevolent intentions where there are none. More to the point, most of these reviewers are not authors themselves. They have no understanding of how hard it is to write a book, much less a book that is published. They have no understanding of the work at hand. Many do not include their full names when they write their reviews. It is the costume ball of no repercussions for people who burn books they have or, as is more often the case, have not read.

Twitter, Goodreads, and other platforms are to literary culture what Yelp is to restaurant culture. Whereas a chef confronts the vicious customer who cannot even boil water, today's author confronts the vicious reader who cannot even write a coherent sentence. As Bradbury puts it, "Those who don't build must burn," and "the world [is] full of burning of all types and sizes."[44] Like Yelp, angry reviews go viral, regardless of whether they have any relationship to reality. Given the review's place between author and prospective readers, the new platforms are central tools of the Sensitivity Era.

They also require no effort to use. In his introduction to *The Best of Me*, a collection of his best work, David Sedaris reflects: "It used to be that you'd write a letter of complaint, then read it over, wondering, *Is this really worthy a twenty-five-cent stamp?* With the advent of email, complaining became free. Thus, people who were maybe a tiny bit offended could, at no cost whatsoever, let you know that they were NEVER GOING TO BUY ANY OF YOUR BOOKS EVER AGAIN!!!"[45] With the advent of social media, they can tell everyone else not to read your books, too. To raise the alarm, they do not even have to get off the couch.

Publishers are aware of the power of influencers on Goodreads, Booksta-gram, BookTok, and other platforms. To quote one Big Five vice president at length:

> The model for a long time was publishers would publish books and buy up space, whether it's the bestseller slot at certain accounts, whether it's the supermarket, or Borders, or whatever. You know, pay for play. People would go in the book-store and look around. They'd be drawn in by certain displays and how things were marketed to them that way.
>
> The majority of books now, whether they're print books or ebooks, are sold online. Discoverability is different. Whether it's book bloggers, or reading group guide websites, we're catering to this audience. We're finding readers where they are. Social media has really opened up a whole new world to this.
>
> Now people are talking among themselves and creating names for themselves. There's so many different types of Bookstagrammers now. People who have cre-ated big followings by doing book reviews, taking really pretty photos of books, and creating a little personality of themselves as book arbiters. Goodreads is another community.
>
> These are things that did not exist ten years ago. There are clearly readers out there; it's finding where they are. Publishers now are really on the side of trying to now work with these individuals and do more direct-to-consumer marketing. A generation ago, we didn't have to do that.

The power of influencers is compounded by the fact that it is more diffi-cult for publishers to get the kind of publicity they used to get from print media. Inevitably, they have to play ball with Goodreads influencers, Book-stagrammers, BookTokers, BookTubers, and other people in the new literary ecosystem. As one editor at a Big Five publisher explained to me:

> There is shrinking book coverage. Book sections are tiny, if not completely deci-mated from papers. We can't even get interviews for our authors. I have a book that's come out. Oh, my God. A brilliant writer. A book that feels so topical. So great. Something that people want to read. Starred review. Reviews galore. But we can't get any media for it. Because there's just no space for it.
>
> On the one hand, I'm so glad there's these different forums. As our traditional spots for coverage, reviews, exposure are shrinking, it's great there are these other

places to showcase our books. Especially if it's where everyone is hanging out. YouTube and Instagram and TikTok and all of that. We see the tremendous value. We see it in sales.

However, it's not journalism. People like a sensationalized story in our new world. An opinion can spread so quickly. I had a conversation last week about what we can do about Goodreads. How do we even know a review is real? It's crazy. If it's a negative response, it could kill a book.

During our interview, this editor talked about a recent experience with Net-Galley, which provides digital versions of advance reader copies to reviewers. Before we spoke, a review came in from a person who acknowledged they could not read the book because there was something wrong with the file. They still reviewed the book.

The prevalence with which people freely admit they never read, nor have any intention of ever reading, books they passionately criticize is another indicator of how decrepitly anti-intellectual literary culture has become. In the past, publicly announcing you have no idea what you are talking about, because you never encountered the object of discussion, would have been an embarrassing omission. Even the food critics on Yelp stick to reviewing restaurants they ate at. Today, that omission is worn as a badge of pride. Above all, *That Book Is Dangerous!* is a case for reading books. That one has to make a case for reading books should indicate the stakes of this moral panic.

But reading poses a problem for moral crusaders who want to turn the public against books. "The more we know the more we are prey to the contradictions of thought," wrote dystopian novelist Anthony Burgess in his response to *1984*, "the less we know the better able are we to act."[46] For this reason, the decline of reading—through skim reading, rushed reading, or not reading at all—is a perennial feature of the dystopian genre.[47] To avoid the contradictions of a novel, poem, or play is to avoid the contradictions of being human. Moral crusades wage war. A person who recognizes contradictions, inconsistencies, nuances, and ambiguities (in a text, in an author, or even in a moment) is unfit for battle. "Ignorance is Strength." That is The Party's slogan in *1984*.

The ignorance is so strong that the book burners are now burning pieces of literature that do not even exist. They build literary effigies for their Two Minutes Hate. One poet describes their experience: "Somebody rewrote my whole poem, from some fascist perspective, and sent it around Twitter. One guy, I remember, he said, 'Can you believe this?' He thought that was my poem. But it was a fake. Then somebody told him, 'No, that's not the actual poem.' He's like, 'Well, that's a moot point.' I was like, 'Really? That's a moot point?'" In war, the first casualty is truth. In the digital age, untruths circulate with a speed that past moral crusaders could not have dreamed.

The current crusade is also intertwined with other developments that are not going to disappear anytime soon. For example, the term "sensitivity reader," which was not mentioned on Twitter until 2016, can now be found all over Twitter. These self-declared experts, who ensure literature is not offensive, are now being hired by Penguin Random House, HarperCollins, and other leaders in publishing. Dhonielle Clayton, the YA author who pilloried Brooke Nelson, Kosoko Jackson, the YA author who pilloried Amélie Wen Zhao, and Anna María, the editor who called on her Twitter followers to violently assault J. K. Rowling, belong to this new profession that grows in direct proportion to moral outrage. When Kosoko Jackson got "absolutely massacred"—as one sensitivity reader I spoke to put it—it could not have been better business for other sensitivity readers. In this climate, even sensitivity readers have their work read by sensitivity readers. Just as more homeowners buy disaster insurance after a natural disaster, so, too, with authors and their publishers after a literary blowup.

As another case in point, Zhao only decided to publish *Blood Heir* after she and her publisher brought in sensitivity readers to fix her writing.[48] The same was true for Keira Drake and *The Continent*. Sensitivity readers are so popular that some agents and publishers now require them before they will even look at a manuscript. Like the edited books in *1984*, the published versions of *Blood Heir* and *The Continent* do not acknowledge that the novels' publication dates were delayed, and the books themselves were rewritten, to appease the authorities on Twitter. What Orwell said of Oceania is just as true of the Sensitivity Era: "Books, also, were recalled and rewritten again and again, and were invariably reissued without any admission that any alteration had been made."[49] Some books, like *A Birthday Cake for George Washington* and *The Adventures of Ook and Gluk*, were recalled but never reissued. The point is clear: literary culture does not need Big Brother when Little Brothers produce the same chilling effects.

In an eerie throwback to film censorship in the 1920s, publishers have also started to include "morality clauses" in their contracts.[50] For example, the same year that NewSouth Books published bowdlerized editions of *The Adventures of Tom Sawyer* and *The Adventures of Huckleberry Finn*, *Adweek* reported on a new clause that was appearing in HarperCollins contracts.

According to the clause, this publisher may terminate a contract if "Author's conduct evidences a lack of due regard for public conventions and morals, or if Author commits a crime or any other act that will tend to bring Author into serious contempt, and such behavior would materially damage the Work's reputation or sales."[51]

Much like the language of a 1921 Universal Studios clause and the language of the 1954 Comics Code, the language of this clause is so vague that it gives HarperCollins the right to terminate contracts for virtually any reason. Similar clauses have appeared in contracts written by Simon and Schuster, Penguin Random House, and other publishers. Those who notice similarities between this secular moralism and religious fundamentalism might be interested to know that these clauses were first used by Christian publishers before they appeared in contracts written for children's authors.[52]

Back in 2008, a few years before the *Adweek* report, the Society of Authors' Children's Writers and Illustrators Group warned people about a new clause that Penguin Random House was inserting into its standard contract for children's books: "If you act or behave in a way which damages your reputation as a person suitable to work with or be associated with children, and consequently the market for or value of the work is seriously diminished, and [sic] we may (at our option) take any of the following actions: Delay publication / Renegotiate advance / Terminate the agreement."[53] Like "authenticity," "suitable" is one of the Sensitivity Era's vague watchwords that can mean anything anyone wants it to mean.

Since then, sensitivity readers, morality clauses, and other interventions have spread from literature written for children and young adults to literature written for adults. Today, the Society of Authors, not just it's Children's Group, is "alarmed at the proliferation of these clauses in publishing contracts."[54] Omnisciently, *The Nation* forecasted what this would look like. In a 1949 issue, it argued: "Comic books are an opening wedge. If they can be 'purified'—that is, controlled—newspapers, periodicals, books, films, and everything else will follow."[55] Not content to eliminate the "danger" in literature written for children and young adults, today's crusade hopes to purify everything that has or will ever be written. Like the crusaders of the past, the self-appointed guardians of public morality believe adults need their protection, too. In fact, insatiability is a defining feature of moral crusades. As crusaders achieve victories, they expand the scope of their crusade.

In 2020, members of the New York Times Union pressured the paper of record to hire sensitivity readers. Among others, Glenn Greenwald, the Pulitzer Prize-winning journalist who worked with Edward Snowden to expose the National Security Agency's domestic surveillance program, rebuked their demand. A gay progressive, he had choice words for the self-appointed protectors who purport to protect people like him from harm: "As creepy as 'sensitivity readers' are for fiction writing and other publishing fields, it is indescribably toxic for *journalism*, which necessarily questions or pokes at rather than bows to the most cherished, sacred pieties. For it to be worthwhile, it must publish material—reporting and opinion pieces—that might be 'potentially objectionable' to all sorts of powerful factions, including culturally hegemonic liberals. But this is a function which the New York Times Union wants not merely to avoid fulfilling themselves but, far worse, to deny their fellow journalists."[56]

The Times also established a sensitivity hotline for journalists to report one another. Like Big Brother, Kathleen Kingsbury, editor of the opinion section, is watching: "Any piece of Opinion journalism—including headlines or social posts or photos or you name it—that gives you the slightest pause, please call or text me immediately."[57] In the Sensitivity Era, even journalism must make liberal readers feel comfortable.

Around the time *Science* adopted sensitivity readers, and *Nature Communications* adopted Own Voices reviewers, writers at the *New Yorker* were taken back when they found a morality clause in their contracts.[58] According to the clause, Condé Nast can terminate their agreement with a writer if the writer "becomes the subject of public disrepute, contempt, complaints or scandals."[59] Masha Gessen, a Russian American journalist, and author of *The Future Is History: How Totalitarianism Reclaimed Russia*, which won the National Book Award, refused to sign her contract. Jeannie Suk Gersen, a law professor at Harvard University, also refused to sign her contract. As she put it, "No person who is engaged in creative expressive activity should be signing one of these." Like Gessen, who has criticized the excesses of the #MeToo movement as a "moral panic," Gersen's work has offended some liberals. Although Gessen and Gersen were able to renegotiate their contracts, most writers are not a National Book Award winner or an Ivy League professor. Most writers do not have the power to rewrite a contract designed to control their expression.[60]

As the Authors Guild, the oldest and largest professional organization for American writers, described it in their Winter 2018–Spring 2019 bulletin:

> The Authors Guild objects to publishers' new and increasing use of so-called "morals clauses"—or "morality clauses"—in book contracts. . . . What constitutes behavior "subject to widespread public condemnation," "moral turpitude" or similar terms used in these clauses varies widely and often has as much as anything to do with a nation's current sociopolitical climate. Before McCarthyism came to an end in 1954, it destroyed the careers of a significant number of writers, filmmakers, artists, academics and other left-leaning intellectuals. In 1990, before the courts declared such pledges unconstitutional, the National Endowment for the Arts, bowing to pressure from cultural conservatives, mandated that grant applicants had to sign "obscenity pledges," promising not to use public funds to create works of a morally questionable nature. Now publishers apparently want the ability to terminate authors' contracts for failing to predict how their words will be received by a changing public. This is a business risk like any other, yet publishers are attempting to lay the risk solely at the feet of authors. Worst of all, morals clauses chill free speech.[61]

According to Richard Curtis, a literary agent and former president of the Association of Authors' Representatives, these clauses were "seldom found in contracts until recently, when social media made public accusations more common." He continues, "As a literary agent I've never felt the need to perform a background check on my clients. . . . Unfortunately, your personal life is becoming our business."[62] In the words of an agent I interviewed, "I'm not sure I'm going to continue working in the literary world. I used to work for someone whose husband had been blacklisted in the movie business during McCarthyism. He said to me, 'Gosh, this feels just like those times.'"

At a moment when the Murdoch family owns HarperCollins, having just spent hundreds of millions of dollars to acquire the trade division of Houghton Mifflin Harcourt, too, and other conservatives work in the upper echelons of other publishing houses, liberals might think twice about championing morality clauses, sensitivity readers, and other interventions that give publishers even tighter control over their authors. Right now, it is profitable to genuflect to liberals. In the future, it might be more profitable to listen to the conservatives who purchase books, too. These conservatives might not want to read a children's book that celebrates Black Lives Matter, a YA novel that humanizes a gay teenager, or an adult memoir written by an antifa protester. Anyone alive on September 11, 2001, should remember how swiftly American culture shifted. Back then, antiwar writers were pilloried by the public. They were the source of "harmful" and "dangerous" ideas. As Donald Trump put it in an April 2021 statement about "woke cancel culture," "We can play the game better than them."[63]

Like their counterparts on the right, some moral crusaders on the left now want the United States government to intervene. With hate speech laws in other countries as their reference points, these crusaders believe the United States should have hate speech laws, too. These laws, they argue, will protect the public from literature that includes harmful stereotypes, harmful language, and harmful ideas.

Yet, around the world, these laws have been used to censor the very people they were designed to protect. For example, African American feminist bell hooks had 1,500 copies of her book *Black Looks: Race and Representation* seized by Canadian Customs officers who considered it a "dangerous" and "racist, sexist book."[64] By the same token, campus speech codes, which were institutionalized to protect minorities from offensive speech, have been used to censor minorities and progressive speech. Before anyone proposes more laws, campus speech codes, publishing policies, and other interventions designed to restrict speech in the name of progressive values, they should familiarize themselves with the historical record of these interventions.

In addition to hate speech laws, other liberals have proposed other legislation. In their article about the misguided outrage hurled at Rebecca Roanhorse's adult novel, *Trail of Lightning*, which revolved around accusations of "cultural appropriation" and "spiritual harm," Northern Cheyenne Two Spirit journalist and fiction writer Adrian L. Jawort laments the direction of literary culture. They are especially concerned about the embrace of state censorship among authors:

> Many people will outright agree with and defend the statement by Joy Harjo, a Muscogee Creek and US poet laureate, who wrote in a 2017 blog post entitled "Erasure," "What about enlarging the purview of the Indian Arts and Crafts Act of 1990 to include the literary?" This act was initially proposed to prevent forgeries of Native arts and crafts. The penalty for a first-time offense is a fine of up to $250,000 in addition to a five-year prison term; a business could face up to a $1 million fine for producing counterfeit crafts. Suggesting that the IACA apply to literature would put potentially controversial art under the government's microscope. Unenrolled tribal descendants who don't appease the colonized concepts of blood quantum requirements would fall under this act—unless they

catered to political pressure to appease cultural committees like Saad Beez Hózhǫ's propaganda-like definition of art should be [sic]. . . . Consider the optics of the US poet laureate advocating government control of literature-as-crime.[65]

Jawort explains that Native authors and academics who defended Roanhorse in private were afraid to defend her in public. As fiction writer Sterling HolyWhiteMountain reflects, "When artists are becoming afraid to speak, that's something we should be deeply concerned about, and we need to take a close look at the social conditions that are causing this fear."[66] Historically, even the dumbest crusades eventually reach the government. New York City banned pinball from 1942 to 1976.[67] Like the criticism now hurled at literature, Supreme Court justice Aaron J. Levy warned Americans about these "vicious contraptions."[68] After that ban was lifted, the US Senate held a hearing in which rock music was linked to Satanism.[69] Even if the government never intervenes, there are more than enough clicktivists to ensure that children's, YA, and now adult literature are "safe" for public consumption.

Just as novelist Daniel Defoe, after he became the subject of a literary controversy in the eighteenth century, was more concerned about being pilloried than imprisoned or fined, the reputational damage of public degradation remains real.[70] In place of eggs and rotten fruit, the digital pillory is marked by tweets, memes, scathing reviews, blocking, reporting, and doxing in what seems like a never-ending purge. In the words of playwright Carmen Aguirre, a Chilean refugee who joined the resistance movement against Augusto Pinochet as a teenager:

> Decolonizing as a form of dismantling our own internalized mythologies could start with rejecting the mythology that if other people don't think like me, they must be bad and therefore purged from the commons. . . . The time of the great purge has been led by the notion that there is an absolute truth, and that absolute truth is my opinion on any given subject. And usually these absolute truths are tied to my identity. . . . And people who don't adhere to my absolute truth need to be canceled, fired, disposed of, mobbed, publicly humiliated, shamed, and, essentially, sent to the Far Right. Because that's what we're risking. Sending those who don't agree with us to the Far Right. Is this what we want? The time of the great purge, led by the identitarian Left. . . . is not being ordered or overseen by the state, but rather by members of our own community who engage in an impenetrable wall of elitist language games. We are all constantly being called upon to be accountable for our use or misuse of language by the purgers who demand it from their victims. . . . Their defense for purging is usually around offended sensibilities and hurt feelings.[71]

Many leaders in the moral crusade trying to purge children's and YA books are leaders in the moral crusade now trying to purge adult books. Recall that David Bowles—the "disgusting worms" guy from chapter 1— speaks for young people. This moral entrepreneur also speaks for "wholly authentic Latinx voices."[72] When Macmillan published *American Dirt* by Jeanine Cummins, Bowles was at the center of the moral panic. His outrage landed him a *New York Times* op-ed[73] (one journalist describes Bowles's criticism as so "riddled with unfair inaccuracies and distortions" that "he either read it very hastily or is lying about what is and isn't in it"[74]), an interview on National Public Radio, and a private meeting with Macmillan. As the petition, demanding that Oprah retract her Book Club seal, puts it: "Good intentions do not make good literature, particularly not when the execution is so faulty, and the outcome so harmful. . . . In a time of widespread misinformation, fearmongering, and white-supremacist propaganda related to immigration and to our border, in a time when adults and children are dying in US immigration cages, we believe that a novel blundering so badly in its depiction of marginalized, oppressed people should not be lifted up."[75]

Just as the 1950s crusaders associated comic books with adults and children dying from violence, these crusaders associate *American Dirt* with adults and children dying from violence. At the same time, Cummins's book tour was canceled because of "specific threats to booksellers and the author."[76] Because moral crusaders regard books as physical violence, they consider physical violence a proportionate response to books. In the words of Richard Ovenden, author of *Burning the Books*, "We should all see attacks on books as an 'early warning' signal that attacks on humans cannot be far behind."[77]

Furthermore, we should all see changes in America's literary landscape as an early warning signal that changes in the literary landscapes of other countries cannot be far behind. When Germans paint over a poem printed on the side of a building because "a line that translates as 'avenues and flowers and women and an admirer' portrays women as objects of male desire,"[78] or when a British publisher inserts a morality clause into their contract, or when a French publisher hires a sensitivity reader (*lecteur en sensibilité*), it is like Starbucks opening another location across the pond. As one UK agent put it, in respect to publishers, "Whatever happens in the US eventually ends up in London because these are global companies."[79]

It eventually ends up in Sydney, Toronto, and other cities where American publishers have offices. To put this in terms that moral crusaders will understand, cultural imperialism still exists.

According to Nigerian novelist and feminist Chimamanda Ngozi Adichie, American liberals are spreading their "cruel" and "cannibalistic" culture of self-righteous indignation to other cultures.[80] As she puts it, "I think in America the worst kind of censorship is self-censorship, and it is something America is exporting to every part of the world."[81] For novelist, poet, and National Book Critics Circle member Anis Shivani, what is happening in literary culture resembles what was happening during the Maoist Cultural Revolution. As he reflects, the current moment is marked by "increasingly subtle inquiries into subterranean prejudice"; "an unceasing process of reeducation"; public trials, confessions, and self-flagellations; uncritical self-righteousness; strict adherence to anti-intellectual orthodoxies; essentialist ideas about identity; a "never-ending game of identity one-upmanship"; and the "exuberant joy" displayed by those who expose and punish others. Above all, the moment is marked by a Manichean understanding of power: "One is either a victim or a victimizer; there is no third option. This is the idea that wants to take over literature."[82]

The Path Out of the Sensitivity Era

Today, the "social justice" approach to literature looks a lot like the "broken windows" approach to crime. Throughout the 1980s and 1990s, criminologist George L. Kelling, political scientist James Q. Wilson, and other academics popularized the idea that there is a link between low-level offenses like throwing a rock through the window of an abandoned building and more serious crimes like assault.[83] According to them, if society was more responsive to these small transgressions, there would be less violent crime down the road. Far from a fringe academic theory, their theory has influenced everything from the "tough on crime" policies of Mayor Rudy Giuliani to the "law and order" promises of president Donald Trump. From stop-and-frisk on the streets to mandatory minimum sentences in the courtroom, the broken windows approach to crime epitomizes the surveillance and punishment culture that so many activists on the left aspire to end.

For the moral crusade over literature, there is no crime that is too petty and undeserving of a swift and severe punishment. Like politicians and pundits on the right, the crusaders on the left believe that punishing small offenses is how you solve large-scale social problems that have little or nothing to do with these offenses. Hence, ending the career of an author who called another author a "dick" on Twitter is how you topple white supremacy and the "systemic power imbalance" that permeates the United States.[84] In short, the left's approach to literature looks like the right's approach to crime. On both sides, adults see themselves as punitive moral leaders who protect the rest of us from harm. To reiterate a point made by literary critic Gary Saul Morson and economist Morton Schapiro, there is nothing distinctly right wing about fundamentalism.[85] Moral certainty, intolerance for those who think differently, and rituals of punishment also mark the historical record of the left.

These liberals are a real problem for the progressive movement. As cognitive linguist and political consultant George Lakoff explains, there is a culture war between the punitive moral framework of the right and the compassionate moral framework of the left. On the right: "Not to show overwhelming strength is immoral, since it will induce evildoers to perform more evil deeds, because they'll think they can get away with it. . . . As Newt Gingrich puts it on the Fox network, 'retribution is justice.'"[86] According to Lakoff, it is important for progressives to offer an alternative to the punitive moral framework—a framework that includes the "shouting and name calling and put-downs"[87] that one finds all over the Fox network and, increasingly, all over Left Twitter. To put the matter bluntly, if one actually wants to do something about the discipline and punishment culture that permeates everything from public schooling to mass incarceration, then changing how one communicates is, as Lakoff suggests, not the worst place to start.

Like Oceania, where "not even the smallest deviation of opinion on the most unimportant subject can be tolerated,"[88] even young people have been caught in the crosshairs of the PC cops. When she was an undergraduate student at Northern State University, Brooke Nelson did not want to select any of Sarah Dessen's YA novels for her university's Common Read program. "She's fine for teen girls," Nelson said. "But definitely not up to the level of Common Read. So I became involved simply so I could stop them from ever choosing Sarah Dessen."[89] Nelson helped the committee select *Just Mercy* by attorney Bryan Stevenson, a memoir about injustice in the American judicial system that won the NAACP Image Award for Outstanding Literary Work. When Dessen came across Nelson's comment in the *Aberdeen News*, she screenshotted it for her 268,000 Twitter followers.[90] "I'm having a really hard time right now," she moaned, "this is just mean and cruel." One critical comment from one college student in one local newspaper was simply too much for this number one *New York Times* best-selling author to bear.

As expected, a degradation ceremony erupted. Angie Thomas, Jenny Han, N. K. Jemisin, and other *New York Times* bestselling authors directed their thousands of followers to the latest folk devil. YA author Siobhan Vivian tweeted: "Fuck that fucking bitch," to which Dessen replied, "I love you." Dhonielle Clayton, the COO of We Need Diverse Books, showcased her own writing skills as a sensitivity reader and fellow YA author: "Can I add a few more choice words for Siobhan's brilliance . . . fuck that RAG-GEDY ASS fucking bitch."[91] Vivian responded with a clapping emoji. As is typical of moral crusades, Nelson was reduced to a villain who might have belonged in a banned comic book from the 1950s. Bestselling author Rox-ane Gay, who has her own imprint at Grove Atlantic (Roxane Gay Books), called Nelson a "nemesis," while fellow bestseller Thomas tweeted at the university.

Another bestselling author, Jodi Picoult, believed there was "something more sinister at work." According to Picoult's Humpty Dumpty idea of what it means to be a feminist: "To not speak up about this incident isn't just demeaning to Sarah. It's demeaning to women, period."[92] ("'When *I* use a word,' Humpty Dumpty said in a rather scornful tone, 'it means just what I choose it to mean,'" wrote Lewis Carroll, that master of literary nonsense.[93]) If Thorstein Veblen were still alive, he could use this incident to write a coda to his *Theory of the Leisure Class*.[94] After all, the conspicuous waste of time is central to his theory. In this Wonderland of rich liberals with hurt feelings, Northern State University tweeted an apology to Dessen. In response to the harassment, Nelson deactivated her social media accounts.[95]

Yet, in a textbook example of what media theorist Kate Eichhorn describes in *The End of Forgetting: Growing Up with Social Media*, the first page of Google will continue to remind Nelson of what she went through. For Eichhorn: "To not be tethered to the past by one's own memories—or worse yet, reminders from someone's else memories—is to have the freedom to reimagine oneself in the present and the future. It is precisely because for-getting and freedom are linked that the end of forgetting is of such great consequence, above all for young people."[96] Whereas a college student who was bullied in the campus dining hall does not have to relive their bullying every time they search their name on the internet, the folk devils on #KidLit and #YATwitter do. In an era of digital stigma, this raises real problems for any person trying to move on with their life. As Eichhorn and others argue, moving on is central to psychological health, and not just for young people.

At this point, one might reasonably wonder why any self-respecting adult would participate in these degradation ceremonies. *1984* offers one hypothesis: "All this marching up and down and cheering and waving flags. . . . If you're happy inside yourself, why should you get excited about Big Brother and the Three-Year Plans and the Two Minutes Hate and all the rest of their bloody rot?"[97] In the same vein, if you are happy inside yourself, why would one college student's remark about what you wrote be enough to crush you? If you are happy inside yourself, why are you sitting on Twitter calling a college student you have never met a raggedy-ass fucking bitch? Although it is beyond the purview of this book, the research suggests that low self-esteem is not irrelevant to understanding why people act like this.[98]

Typically, those on the sidelines who resent these degradation ceremonies in private remain silent in public.[99] "To say 'there be no witches,'" wrote Arthur Miller, "is to invite charge of trying to conceal the conspiracy and to discredit the highest authorities who alone can save the community!"[100] But, as this ceremony erupted, people actually spoke up. Ebony Elizabeth Thomas, a black professor of education at the University of Michigan, and the author of *The Dark Fantastic: Race and the Imagination from Harry Potter to the Hunger Games*, tweeted: "If your life and career is about young people, you'd know that's bullying." Tressie McMillan Cottom, a black sociologist of education at the University of North Carolina, and the author of *Lower Ed: The Troubling Rise of For-Profit Colleges in the New Economy*, added: "It's a student on a common book committee. It's a thing that stings to read but it is not a political statement. This is so wrong."[101] As Mia Wenjen, an Asian American children's author and cofounder of Multicultural Children's Book Day, put it: "When I think of what happened to Brooke Nelson, I realize that what Sarah Dessen did could have happened to anyone. It could have happened to my own teen daughters."[102]

To build on Thomas's point, I think some crusaders know they are bullies; at least a few of them must have a modicum of self-awareness. I also think at least some of them would never permit someone to bully a family member, friend, or colleague they care about. But what Emory University psychologist Philippe Rochat calls "moral acrobatics" is a stable feature of social life. As he describes it, "Our ability to switch moral codes depending on people and situations is the most unsettling issue of moral psychology." For Rochat, individuals think "the world in black and white to avoid the heavy psychological cost of moral ambiguity."[103] This is also the cost of "cognitive dissonance."[104] One might stand up to the person who insults their best friend, but this same person might have no reservation about insulting someone whom they have never met. The psychological act of reducing a stranger to a bitch, a raggedy-ass fucking bitch, or a witch makes it easier to dole out punishment. To reiterate the point, people who see the world in shades of gray, and who refuse to villainize others, are unfit to participate in a moral crusade.

In the end, some of these crusaders apologized, which speaks to the potential for a self-correcting dynamic in literary culture—if people speak up.[105] Here, Dan Kahan's research on cultural credentials is pertinent.[106] Along with other researchers involved in the Cultural Cognition Project at Yale University, Kahan showed participants arguments from fictional experts. These experts, whom the participants believed were real, had different political commitments. One expert was described as the author of *The Immigrant Invasion: Threatening the American Way of Life* and *The War On American Manhood*. Another expert was described as the author of *Three Social Evils: Sexism, Racism, and Homophobia*. As Yale's team learned, people are more sympathetic to arguments when the arguments come from experts who share their values.

In the world of #Kidlit and #YATwitter, identities matter, too. When experts like Thomas, Cottom, and Wenjen—as opposed to, say, a conservative, cisgender, heterosexual, white male like Tucker Carlson—stand up to the bullies, it encourages other members of this liberal community to stand up, too. What social psychologists call "reactive devaluation," a phenomenon in which "people devalue arguments and positions simply because of their source," is real.[107] This is the reason I mention people's political and social identities in *That Book Is Dangerous!* It is also the reason why people who have the "right" identities are so crucial to ending this moral panic.

In the words of Jonathan Rauch, the openly gay author of *Gay Marriage: Why It Is Good for Gays, Good for Straights, and Good for America*: "When offended people devote their energies to shutting someone up or turning him out or getting him fired, rather than trying to show that he is wrong or trying to be thicker skinned, we should be in the habit of telling them to grow up. That's all. No demands will be met, no punishments meted out."[108] One should also add that there will be no confessions, self-flagellations, and promises to "do better" when no one did anything wrong.

In *Fahrenheit 451*, a retired English professor warns us: "I saw the way things were going, a long time back. I said nothing. I'm one of the innocents who could have spoken up and out when no one would listen to the 'guilty,' but I did not speak and thus became guilty myself. And when finally they set the structure to burn the books, using the firemen, I grunted a few times and subsided, for there were no others grunting or yelling with me, by then. Now, it's too late."[109]

To echo Wenjen, what happened to Brooke Nelson, Jessica Cluess, Kosoko Jackson, Amélie Wen Zhao, Keira Drake, Laura Moriarty, Laurie Forest, Ramin Ganeshram, Vanessa Brantley-Newton, Andrea Davis Pinkney, Dav Pilkey, Emily Jenkins, Sophie Blackall, Alexandra Duncan, E. E. Charlton-Trujillo, and countless others—the "guilty" list gets longer each month —could happen to anyone.

In this respect, the task for progressives is the same as it has always been. Writing in the 1990s, black cultural theorist Stuart Hall grappled with liberals who tried to control what other people wrote, read, and said. In his essay "Some 'Politically Incorrect' Pathways Through PC," he laments the rise of a "small but dedicated band" who, in their enthusiasm for moral self-righteousness and public punishment, remind him of latter-day Puritans.[110] "As I write," reflects Hall, "I can hear the thumbscrews being unpacked, the guillotine sharpened, the pages of the Dictionary of Political Correctness being shuffled, the tumbrils beginning to roll."[111] Like other progressives, Hall believed that their PC panic grew in the soil of political defeat, most epitomized by the ascendance of Ronald Reagan in the United States and Margaret Thatcher in the United Kingdom. It is no coincidence that the return of political correctness has coincided with the ascendence of Donald Trump.

Hall, who was the first editor of *New Left Review*, recognized culture as an important site of struggle for the left. Yet he was taken aback by the issues this cultural crusade focused on (for example, antiracists tried to ban "Baa, Baa, Black Sheep" from schools), its fetish for punishment over persuasion,

and its inability to build the broad constituencies needed to enact meaningful change. He was also disturbed by its essentialist ideas about race,
which closely resembled the ideas of actual racists, and its denial of the
multiple meanings inherent in language. According to Hall, real progressives must remain committed to the struggle against racism and other intolerances; they have to reveal the way the right uses these culture wars to
its advantage; and they have to distance themselves from the "undeniable
idiocies committed in the name of 'anti-racism' or 'anti-sexism' or 'anti-
homophobia'" and so on. As he succinctly put it, in what could be the epi-
graph to *That Book Is Dangerous!*, "Our enemies are bad enough; God save
us from our friends."[112]

In the end, "to call something a moral panic is not to deny that something exists."[113] Books are racist, Islamophobic, and otherwise terrible. Some
of these books make readers feel awful about themselves. As Zadie Smith,
writing about her own experiences as a young reader, reflects: "me, aged
twelve, in my little corner of London, looking for some form of cultural
reflection, any kind at all, but finding only distorted mirrors, monstrous
cliché, debasing ridicule, false containment."[114] However, if anything can
be learned from literary history, it is that there are always multiple interpretations to a text. Crusades that seek to enforce their interpretations on
everyone else, through public pressure and de facto censorship, raise real
problems for writers and readers. Like Smith, one can support the movement for better books while criticizing the punitive culture that makes her
story "Now More Than Ever" read less like satire and more like realism. In
fact, if the movement for more diverse and sensitive books is to have any
future at all, it will have to stop alienating the very people who want to
write and read these books.

Acknowledgments

At a conference, a professor in the audience once asked me who I model my writing style after. Somewhat flippantly, I told him Suge Knight at the 1995 Source Awards. In all seriousness, there is no one whom I have ever tried to emulate. My writing style has been more influenced by my passions—the Ultimate Fighting Championship, bodybuilding, skateboarding, mosh pits, rap music, stand-up comedy, and my blue-collar upbringing—than any writer. That said, to borrow Isaac Newton's words, "If I have seen further, it has only been by standing on the shoulders of giants."[1]

When Eric Cheyfitz told me he didn't earn a BA because he instead chose to play in a rock band, I knew we would get along. At Cornell University, he was a perennial source of support and a constant reminder that real gangsters don't genuflect to the haters.

One of my colleagues traveled to Princeton University with Michael Macy, and he said he was flocked by Princetonians asking him what it's like to work with Michael, like he was some kind of rock star. Michael *is* a rock star, and there's not another person who I've exchanged as many emails with while writing this book.

Shiyu Ji is the quantitative sociologist par excellence, and I'm grateful I've had the opportunity to work with him to explore the culture wars, such as in our *Newsweek* article about the impact of *The Joe Rogan Experience* on book sales, which I imagine will evolve into a book about Joe Rogan's impact on American culture.[2]

I owe a debt to my Cornell colleagues Neil Saccamano, who pushed me to think in more sustained terms about the history of literary censorship, and Laura Niemi, who introduced me to more than one pertinent psychology paper, for reading excerpts of this book. My dinners with Tyrell Stewart-Harris, as I wrote this book, were indispensable to my time in Ithaca.

I had an interview subject for another book I'm writing refuse to let me interview them because they said my dissertation advisor is a "batshit crazy woke feminist." Jane Juffer deserves every teaching and mentoring award she has already received and undoubtably will receive in the future. She is patient, erudite, generous with her time, and more interested in helping her students than in molding them into little Jane Juffers.

Shamus Khan was once asked, "If you ran a gang, which sociologists would you make 'Gang Leader for a Day'"?[3] Mustafa Emirbayer was at the top of the list. As far I'm concerned, Mustafa is the OG. A brilliant scholar in his own right, he's also the wizard behind the curtain helping so many scholars I'm enamored by. I'm grateful that he has continued to help me, even when it could not have been less fashionable for him to do so.

Harvard University's Program on the Study of Capitalism, led by the intellectual powerhouse Sven Beckert, exposed me to a lot of historians doing impressive historical work. Although I don't think this book is a history book, it's definitely a book that has been made better by my time hanging out with historians. In my head I will forever hear Sven's thick German voice asking the question of the hour, "If you're right, then what does it mean for how we understand the history of capitalism?" Publishing, and this book, is one part of that history.

Writing requires material support, and I'm thankful to Cornell University, especially the Department of Literatures in English, for offering me multiple years of it. I'm also thankful that, while working on this book, I was surrounded by professors and students who shared my commitment to truth seeking. Indeed, it was President Martha Pollack who made the theme of our 2023–2024 academic year not safe spaces, but free expression.

Tim Dayton once said that if he pushed a bookcase on me, and the bookcase broke my nose, my broken nose wouldn't be a "social construct." He also once said he has no use for Plato's "Forms," having never seen one himself. "Aristotle," he continued, "is a man I can work with." Tim, and his wife Angela Hubler, are the real deal English professors, seemingly immune to each new and increasingly idiotic fad in their discipline. I'm grateful to call them my friends.

If it wasn't for Randall Knoper's seminar on Mark Twain, which I took when I was an undergraduate student at the University of Massachusetts Amherst, I might have remained a business major. If I had remained a business major, I probably would have ended up like the protagonist in *Fight*

Club. If you have read that novel, you can thank Randall for the fact that my life went in a different direction.

Through the trials and tribulations of my academic career, Gordon Fraser has shared his Yoda-like wisdom. If I had one word to describe Gordon, it would be "mensch."

Nadine Strossen's *Hate: Why We Should Resist It with Free Speech, Not Censorship* should be required reading. Nadine personifies the old-school spirit of the ACLU, which has since devolved into the ACLUFLO, the American Civil Liberties Union for Liberals Only. Unlike the organization she used to lead, Nadine's nonpartisan commitment to free speech is indefatigable.

For someone who started a publishing house called Heresy Press, Bernard Schweizer is, for real, one of the nicest guys I know. It is a true sign of the times that publishing great literature—the kind that "heaves, manifests, and lasts," to use Toni Morrison's words—is now considered a heretical act.[4] In the literary landscape, Heresy Press is a lighthouse in a dark ocean. It deserves all the praise it has received and will continue to receive.

Both through their work, and through their conversations with me, the *Nonsite* crew has influenced how I think about politics and culture in the United States. That crew includes political scientists Cedric Johnson and Adolph Reed Jr., literary critics Walter Benn Michaels and Ken Warren, and historian Touré F. Reed. Their penchant for trenchant analysis is matched by their incisive, entertaining, and infinitely quotable prose.

Speaking of writing styles, I owe a debt to Erik Olin Wright.[5] He personified the "no bullshit" approach to sociological analysis that he preached. Perhaps the most influential sociologist of his generation, Erik always encouraged his students to write with clarity, free of academese, so their critics would know why they disagreed with them. It was a real honor to be the last student he took on.

While on the subject of students, I would be remiss not to shout out my own. To the students in "American Literature and Culture: 1865 to Present," "True Stories," and, especially, "Culture Wars: The Struggle to Define America," which I based on the themes in this book, you were the highlight of my time at Cornell. Vis-à-vis the Ivy League stereotype, you helped me create classrooms that were defined by rigorous and—not infrequently—contentious discussions. After I was awarded the Deanne Gebell Gitner '66 and Family Annual Prize for Teaching, I was asked to write about what this prize meant to me. What could I say? *Veritas numquam perit.*

Chad Alan Goldberg and Gay Seidman are two more sociologists with whom I have had more than one conversation about politics and culture. Given the belligerent circus that the University of Wisconsin–Madison has devolved into, especially its sociology department, I'm glad there's at least a few sober minds who have tenure on that campus.[6]

As a journalist, I'm grateful to all the editors with whom I have worked. At the *Guardian*, Jess Reed opened the door for me to write my first reported feature (which ultimately took home the second-place prize for Best General Feature from the Society for Features Journalism). At *Newsweek*, Batya Ungar-Sargon always gives me a platform and, more importantly, she continues to give a platform to people on all sides of the political spectrum (even those with whom she disagrees). Jacob Brogan at the *Washington Post* is another gift to the journalistic world. Across the board—at the *Boston Globe*, the *Nation*, the *Miami New Times*, *Vice*, *Slate*, *Salon*, *Jacobin*, and the *Progressive*, among other newspapers, magazines, and websites—I've grown as a writer by working with so many great editors.

I'm also grateful to all the people I've interviewed over the years, including Chuck Palahniuk, Theo Von, Steve-O, and other freaks, misfits, rebels, rejects, rabble-rousers, and troublemakers. As Hunter S. Thompson, a writer who no doubt would have cut through the Sensitivity Era's horseshit with his rhetorical shotgun shells (and, if we're going to be honest, perhaps a few real shotgun shells) famously put it in a 1974 article for *Rolling Stone*: "When the going gets weird, the weird turn pro." As he less famously put it, "There is a bond, among pros, that needs no definition."[7]

I'm especially grateful to the people I interviewed for this book. You revealed that the problem is worse than I thought.

Hannah Doyle at Oxford University Press is an all-star. Perhaps we'll work together on another book.

Noah Springer, Elizabeth Agresta, Debora Kuan, Anthony Zannino, Nicholas DiSabatino, Zubin Meer, Sheila Hill, and the rest of the MIT Press team—you all have been nothing but wonderful. I can't imagine a better press for this book.

Nancy and Martin Vazquez have been like second parents to me. My apologies for my precarious sense of adventure as a kid (my own double-speak for deviant behavior)—but, look, I turned out all right.

My best friend Matt Vazquez has had my back for twenty-five years. At a moment when anything even remotely masculine is declared "toxic," Quez personifies the best a man can be. I love you, dude.

Bryan Martin, another legacy brother of twenty-five years, provided me space by the pool, in between our visits to the Comedy Mothership, to wrap up the final edits on this book. This is the same B. Martin who tried to get me to laugh in court when we were teenagers. Like many of my friends, he reminds me that even the most serious things shouldn't be taken *too seriously*.

Andy Tran's commitment to his family, his business, and his personal development is inimitable. Sweating it out in your sauna and freezing to death in your cold plunge have become necessary side quests during my trips to Austin.

Steve Vien and Pat Curley, you guys are depraved. There are perhaps no other people who appreciate the music of B-Fish, the physiques of Lats and Abu, and *American Psycho* more than us. "Impressive, very nice. Let's see Paul Allen's card."

The 1117 crew keeps me sane, especially during the winter, when I might otherwise turn into Jack from *The Shining*. "Sideshow" Zach Buckholtz and Isabella Heffron Neuhold, you both were recent—but absolutely necessary—additions to my life. I have talked to you guys about everything under the sun—which, not frequently appears during the winter season in Wisconsin.

Brian Davis is my intellectual brother from another mother. There is not a person with whom I have shared more conversations—and laughs—about the culture wars. He continues to remind me that many of the brightest minds aren't in the Ivory Tower.

Aside from being my photographer, Emma Lee Davis is also one of my best friends. Intelligent, pragmatic, compassionate, and irreverent, she's the sister I never had. Writing, and for that matter living, can be lonely. Like a great novel, Emma has always made me feel a little less alone.

Ashe Davis has never tired of asking me what I'm doing on the front porch (the answer is almost always reading, writing, meditating, or conspiring). If Ashe continues to remind me that it's possible to overflow with happiness over the most mundane occurrences, I continue to remind him that cool people, unlike his dad, rock Vans, nose rings, and backwards snapback hats.

At the end of the day, I would go insane if I was strapped to a desk all day. Lifting heavy things up and then putting them back down has been an absolutely crucial ying to the yang of writing. Scott "Caveman" Magerer (where are your veins, dude?), Sho (I still don't know your last name), and the rest of the original Gold's Gym crew have played an irreplaceable role in my life. If you're not willing to quit during a set of twenty-rep squats, you're not going to quit while going through the long, laborious process of writing a book. I've learned more valuable lessons in the squat rack and on the deadlift platform—at Gold's Gym, at Ford's Gym, at Metroflex, and at Westside Barbell, where the late and great Louie Simmons spilled his blood on me—than I ever did in a classroom.

Ray Tse, who, in his words, thought I would "end up in a ditch" after college, and who became my friend despite my questionable sense of gym attire (camo shorts, Timberlands, and, as he distinctly remembers, *two* wifebeaters)—I'm glad I've proved your premonitions wrong. Of all the gym bros, Chris Fields deserves the biggest shoutout for helping me recover from injury after injury via, and he hates when I use this term, his "telehealth" visits. A modern-day Renaissance man with a 500+ pound squat and near encyclopedic knowledge of everything from human anatomy to postmodern fiction, his poetry journal, *Neologism*, is worth checking out.

Before I started bodybuilding and powerlifting, I wrestled. As Dan Gable puts it, "Once you've wrestled, everything else in life is easy."[8] That includes writing a book. Moreover, after wrestling with concussions, a deviated septum, and stitches under my eye that were so gnarly I had to wear a protective mask, I can't imagine a situation in which I would break down crying, like the employees at Penguin Random House, because somebody wrote a book that I'm not interested in reading. If I hadn't interviewed someone who was in the room, I would have thought that scene involving Jordan Peterson's *Beyond Order: 12 More Rules for Life* and buckets of liberal tears was a *Saturday Night Live* sketch.

My Kansas homies—Tom Webb, Cormac Badger, and Rob Probst—have always provided me space to air my ideas and annoyances about the Sensitivity Era. Thank you for allowing me to consistently redirect the conversation back to my gripes about the latest cancellation. The stand-up comedian Bill Hicks described himself as "Chomsky with dick jokes."[9] That's how I describe these guys. If one of us ever "goes woke," and releases our Zoom conversations and texts, we will all surely be unemployed.

"Intellect is a great servant, but a lousy master," said Ram Dass.[10] I'm grateful to him, Jack Kornfield, Jon Kabat-Zinn, Sensei Rick Smith, and other folks I've had the pleasure of sitting with on meditation retreats over the years, folks who've helped me quiet, focus, and otherwise tame my monkey mind. If more people went on retreats, like S. N. Goenka's vipassana ten-day, there would be a lot less political polarization and fewer culture wars. There would also be a lot fewer people having public meltdowns on Twitter.

Jean-Paul Sartre wrote that "Life begins on the other side of despair."[11] On that note, I owe a special debt to Jonathan Sandler. He has, more than once, helped me get to the other side.

There's a reason so many writers—Ernest Hemingway, Joyce Carol Oates, the list is as long as Jack Kerouac's scroll of *On the Road*—have cats. If you don't know the reason, you're probably not a writer with cats. Little Bear and Nahko Bear were the only company I had while writing most of this book, and I'm grateful for their affection (and their antics). They are, in Hemingway's words, "purr factories" and "love sponges."[12]

Notwithstanding the Sensitivity Era's unwavering commitment to describing anything even mildly unpleasant as "trauma," and then manufacturing an all-encompassing identity out of it, identifying as a victim was, in my house, and the houses of all my friends in the housing projects the next street over, never something that was cool. I thank my dad Adam, an immigrant who blew out his back and knees on the job before he died, and my mom Suzanne, who washed dishes in an old folks' home, as well as my brother Travis, who gave me my first bloody nose, for never permitting me to self-identify as a victim.

To end with a quote from Karl Marx, "Men make their own history, but they do not make it just as they please; they do not make it under circumstances chosen by themselves, but under circumstances directly encountered, given, and transmitted from the past."[13] I'm thankful that the circumstances of my upbringing were not the same as many of the elites discussed in this book.

Notes

Introduction

1. Alexandra Alter, "She Pulled Her Debut Book When Critics Found It Racist. Now She Plans to Publish." *New York Times*, April 29, 2019, https://www.nytimes.com/2019/04/29/books/amelie-wen-zhao-blood-heir.html.

2. Quoted in Kat Rosenfield, "The Toxic Drama on YA Twitter," *Vulture*, August 7, 2017, https://www.vulture.com/2017/08/the-toxic-drama-of-ya-twitter.html.

3. Adiba Jaigirdar, "Books by Muslims to Support Instead of Reading *American Heart*," *Book Riot*, October 12, 2017, https://bookriot.com/books-by-muslims-instead-of-american-heart/.

4. Suzanne Perez Tobias, "Best-Selling Kansas Author Faces Backlash for Writing Muslim Character," *Wichita Eagle*, January 21, 2018, https://www.kansas.com/entertainment/books/article195856114.html.

5. Emma Nolan, "J.K. Rowling Book Burning Videos Are Spreading Like Wildfire across TikTok," *Newsweek*, September 16, 2020, https://www.newsweek.com/jk-rowling-books-burned-tiktok-transgender-issues-1532330.

6. Anna María (@annamaria), "I hope JK Rowling gets punched in the face today (: I hope her nose breaks and it gushes all over her clothes (: I hope her teeth get knocked out . . ." X, August 29, 2020, https://x.com/ripx4nutmeg/status/1299781026512867328.

7. "Scholastic Needs to Apologize for Publishing a Children's Book Filled with Racist Imagery," Change.Org, started March 24, 2021, https://www.change.org/p/scholastic-inc-scholastic-needs-to-apologize-for-publishing-a-children-s-book-filled-with-racist-imagery.

8. Mark Kennedy, "'Captain Underpants' Book Pulled for 'Passive Racism' Against Asians," *Los Angeles Times*, March 29, 2021, www.latimes.com/entertainment-arts/books/story/2021-03-29/captain-underpants-book-pulled-passive-racism.

9. Quoted in Jeffrey A. Trachtenberg, "Dr. Seuss Books Deemed Offensive Will Be Delisted from eBay," *Wall Street Journal*, March 4, 2021, https://www.wsj.com/articles/dr-seuss-books-deemed-offensive-will-be-delisted-fromebay11614884201.

10. To be clear, librarians weed books with low circulation. With limited space, librarians cannot keep books that no one wants to read. However, the Dr. Seuss books were in high demand. For example, at Chicago Public Library "all six of the Dr. Seuss books [were] checked out, with more people in line to borrow the books after that." Although the library honored those in line, it also decided to withhold indefinitely these books from the public until it could decide what to do with them. When private companies like eBay ban the sale of a book, we are in trouble. When public institutions are not doing everything they can to secure open access to those banned books, we are in deep trouble. Madeline Kenney, "Chicago Public Library System to Pull Six Dr. Seuss Books from Circulation Due to Racist Imagery," *Chicago Sun Times*, March 6, 2021, https://chicago.suntimes.com/2021/3/6/22316983/dr-seuss-chicago-public-library-racist-imagery-circulation.

11. "Remove 'A Birthday Cake for George Washington' from Amazon.Com," Change. Org, started January 14, 2016, https://www.change.org/p/amazon-com-remove-a-birthday-cake-for-george-washington-from-amazon-com.

12. Quoted in Kat Rosenfield, "What Is #OwnVoices Doing to Our Books?" *Refinery29*, April 9, 2019, https://www.refinery29.com/en-us/2019/04/228847/own-voices-movement-ya-literature-impact.

13. I do not capitalize "black" for the same reason that other writers do not capitalize "black." In his preface to *Revolutionaries to Race Leaders: Black Power and the Making of African American Politics*, political scientist Cedric Johnson, himself a black writer, elaborates: "My usage reflects the view that racial identity is the product of historically unique power configurations and material conditions. This view contradicts the literary practice common to much Black Power radicalism, where racial descriptors are capitalized to denote a distinctive, coherent political community and assert an affirmative racial identity." Cedric Johnson, *Revolutionaries to Race Leaders: Black Power and the Making of African American Politics* (Minneapolis: University of Minnesota Press, 2007), xvii.

14. Quoted in Kevin Shalvey, "Ted Cruz Has Been Selling Signed Copies of the Dr. Seuss Book 'Green Eggs and Ham,' and Raised $125,000 in 24 Hours," *Business Insider*, March 13, 2021, https://www.businessinsider.com/sen-cruz-sells-signed-dr-seuss-books-green-eggs-and-ham-2021-3.

15. Aila Slisco, "Kevin McCarthy Slams Democrats on House Floor for Outlawing Dr. Seuss—They Didn't," *Newsweek*, March 2, 2021, https://www.newsweek.com/kevin-mccarthy-slams-democrats-house-floor-outlawing-dr-seussthey-didnt-1573327.

16. Mark Joyella, "Fox News Sweeps Week's Top Five Most-Watched Shows in Cable News," *Forbes*, August 3, 2021, https://www.forbes.com/sites/markjoyella/2021/08/03/fox-news-sweeps-weeks-top-five-most-watched-shows-in-cable-news/.

17. Quoted in Sean Illing, "'Wokeness Is a Problem and We All Know It': James Carville on the State of Democratic Politics," *Vox*, April 27, 2021, https://www.vox.com/22338417/james-carville-democratic-party-biden-100-days.

18. Claire Armitstead, "Morality Clauses: Are Publishers Right to Police Writers?" *Guardian*, June 13, 2018, https://www.theguardian.com/books/2018/jun/13/junot-diaz-sherman-alexie-morality-contract-publishers.

19. Glenn Greenwald, "The New York Times Guild Once Again Demands Censorship of Colleagues," *Intercept*, October 11, 2020, https://theintercept.com/2020/10/11/the-new-york-times-guild-once-again-demands-censorship-for-colleagues/.

20. Judith Shulevitz, "Must Writers Be Moral? Their Contracts May Require It," *The New York Times*, January 4, 2019, https://www.nytimes.com/2019/01/04/opinion/sunday/metoo-new-yorker-conde-nast.html.

21. Nylah Burton, "Cancel Culture Is Real, but adrienne maree brown Says We Should Be Careful about Throwing People Away," *shondaland*, February 9, 2021, https://www.shondaland.com/inspire/books/a35452132/adrienne-maree-brown-we-will-not-cancel-us/.

22. Salman Rushdie, "Notes on Writing and the Nation," in *Burn This Book: Notes on Literature and Engagement*, edited by Toni Morrison (New York: HarperCollins, 2012), 80.

Chapter 1

1. "Books by and/or about Black, Indigenous and People of Color (All Years)," Cooperative Children's Book Center, last updated March 20, 2024, https://ccbc.education.wisc.edu/literature-resources/ccbc-diversity-statistics/books-by-about-poc-fnn/.

2. See Malinda Lo's articles, "Diversity in 2013 *New York Times* Young Adult Bestsellers," *Diversity in YA*, April 2014, https://web.archive.org/web/20140503052944/http://www.diversityinya.com/2014/04/diversity-in-2013-new-york-times-young-adult-bestsellers/; "Diversity in YALSA's Best Fiction for Young Adults: Updated for 2014," *Diversity in YA*, February 2014, URL no longer available.

3. Richard Jean So and Gus Wezerek, "Just How White Is the Book Industry?" *New York Times*, December 11, 2020, https://www.nytimes.com/interactive/2020/12/11/opinion/culture/diversity-publishing-industry.html.

4. Jim Milliot, "The PW Publishing Industry Salary Survey, 2019," *Publishers Weekly*, November 15, 2019, https://www.publishersweekly.com/pw/by-topic/industry-news/publisher-news/article/81718-the-pw-publishing-industry-salary-survey-2019.html.

5. "Literary Agent Demographics and Statistics in the US," *Zippia*, 2021, https://www.zippia.com/literary-agent-jobs/demographics/; "The Lee & Low Diversity Baseline Survey 2.0," *Lee & Low Books*, 2020, https://blog.leeandlow.com/2020/01/28/2019diversitybaselinesurvey/.

6. Clayton Childress, *Under the Cover: The Creation, Production, and Reception of a Novel* (Princeton, NJ: Princeton University Press, 2019), 75.

7. Rudine Sims Bishop, "Mirrors, Windows, and Sliding Glass Doors." *Choosing and Using Books for the Classroom* 6, no. 3 (Summer 1990), https://scenicregional.org/wp -content/uploads/2017/08/Mirrors-Windows-and-Sliding-Glass-Doors.pdf.

8. Bishop, "Mirrors."

9. Elizabeth Gettins, "Rare Book of the Month: W.E.B. Du Bois' Brownies," Library of Congress Blogs, February 1, 2017, https://blogs.loc.gov/loc/2017/02/rare-book-of -the-month-w-e-b-du-bois-brownies/.

10. "Council on Interracial Books for Children (CIBC)," Social Justice Books, 2017, https://socialjusticebooks.org/council-on-interracial-books-for-children-cibc/.

11. Nancy Larrick, "The All-White World of Children's Books," *Saturday Review*, September, 1965, 63–65, 84–85.

12. Philip Nel, *Was the Cat in the Hat Black? The Hidden Racism of Children's Literature, and the Need for Diverse Books* (Oxford: Oxford University Press, 2019), 136.

13. Bishop, "Mirrors."

14. Christine Jenkins and Michael Cart, quoted in Derritt Mason, *Queer Anxieties of Young Adult Literature and Culture* (Jackson: University Press of Mississippi, 2020), 8.

15. Mason, *Queer Anxieties*, 7.

16. Walter Dean Myers, "Where Are the People of Color in Children's Books?" *New York Times*, March 15, 2014, https://www.nytimes.com/2014/03/16/opinion /sunday/where-are-the-people-of-color-in-childrens-books.html.

17. Nel, *Was the Cat in the Hat Black?*, 171.

18. Ebony Elizabeth Thomas, *The Dark Fantastic: Race and the Imagination from Harry Potter to the Hunger Games* (New York: New York University Press, 2019), 2.

19. Nel, *Was the Cat in the Hat Black?*, 169.

20. Robin Chenoweth, "Rudine Sims Bishop: 'Mother' of Multicultural Children's Literature," Ohio State University, September 5, 2019, https://ehe.osu.edu/news /listing/rudine-sims-bishop-diverse-childrens-books.

21. Bishop, "Mirrors."

22. Frantz Fanon, *Black Skin, White Masks* (London: Pluto Press, 2008), 42–43.

23. Corinne Duyvis, "#OwnVoices," accessed November 4, 2024, www.corinneduy vis.net/ownvoices/.

24. W. E. B. Du Bois, *The Souls of Black Folk* (Oxford: Oxford University Press, 2007), 8.

25. Editor Tom Beer, email correspondence, November 22, 2020. "About Kirkus Collections," *Kirkus Reviews*, www.kirkusreviews.com/diversity/about/.

26. Vicky Smith, "Unmaking the White Default," *Kirkus Reviews*, May 4, 2015, https://www.kirkusreviews.com/news-and-features/articles/unmaking-white-default/.

27. Marjorie Ingall, "Confessions of a Sensitivity Reader," *Tablet*, March 8, 2019, https://www.tabletmag.com/sections/community/articles/confessions-of-a-sensitivity-reader.

28. There are over five hundred federally recognized tribes in the United States alone, so one might wonder what it means to be a sensitivity reader for "Native American representation." "Sensitivity Readers," Firefly Creative Writing, accessed November 4, 2024, https://fireflycreativewriting.com/sensitivity-readers.

29. Katy Waldman, "Is My Novel Offensive?" *Slate*, February 8, 2017, https://slate.com/culture/2017/02/how-sensitivity-readers-from-minority-groups-are-changing-the-book-publishing-ecosystem.html.

30. Oleander Chevalier (@oleanderwrites), "Friendly reminder that I'm a sensitivity reader for the following things: trans (FtM) issues, ADHD, anxiety, depression, and fibromyalgia . . ." X, September 1, 2020, https://x.com/oleanderwrites/status/1300929781425410048; Madeline Dau (@Madeline_Dau), "Hi Friends! Looking for a #SensitivityReader to read a spec fic short story (about 3500 words) featuring a trans side character. I want to make sure I'm not . . ." X, September 8, 2020. https://x.com/Madeline_Dau/status/1303329521412771841.

31. Salt and Sage Books, "Sensitivity & Expert Consultants," https://www.saltandsagebooks.com/sensitivity-expert-consultants/.

32. Hannah-Esmeralda Figueras, "Sensitivity Readers," *Unsuitable: Conversations about Women, History & Popular Fiction @Duke University* (blog), 2018, https://sites.duke.edu/unsuitable/sensitivity-readers/.

33. Ingall, "Confessions."

34. Alexandra Alter, "In an Era of Online Outrage, Do Sensitivity Readers Result in Better Books, or Censorship?" *New York Times*, December 24, 2017, https://www.nytimes.com/2017/12/24/books/in-an-era-of-online-outrage-do-sensitivity-readers-result-in-better-books-or-censorship.html.

35. Quoted in Alter, "Online Outrage."

36. For related discussions, see Mustafa Emirbayer and Mathew Desmond's discussion of the "insider doctrine" and Rogers Brubaker's discussion of "epistemological insiderism." As Emirbayer and Desmond argue, "We disagree that an insider's vantage point *in and of itself* leads to scientific discoveries unavailable to the outsider. After all, one would be hard pressed to find a thinker who applied the insider doctrine to members of dominant groups—who argued, for example, that only

capitalists can advance knowledgeable claims about capitalists, or men about men." For Brubaker, "epistemological insiderism not only stakes out certain domains as belonging to persons with certain identities; it also risks boxing persons with those identities into specific domains." These sociologists recognize the importance of lived experience; but they do not fetishize it.

Mustafa Emirbayer and Mathew Desmond, *The Racial Order* (Chicago: University of Chicago Press, 2015), 38. Rogers Brubaker, "The Uproar over 'Transracialism,'" *New York Times*, May 18, 2017, https://www.nytimes.com/2017/05/18/opinion/the -uproar-over-transracialism.html.

37. Jane C. Hu, "Gut Check: Working with a Sensitivity Reader," *Open Notebook*, January 21, 2020, https://www.theopennotebook.com/2020/01/21/gut-check-working -with-a-sensitivity-reader/.

38. Adolph Reed Jr., *Class Notes: Posing as Politics and Other Thoughts on the American Scene* (New York: New Press, 2001), 71.

39. Quoted in Alison Flood, "Vetting for Stereotypes: Meet Publishing's 'Sensitivity Readers,'" *Guardian*, April 27, 2018, https://www.theguardian.com/books/2018 /apr/27/vetting-for-stereotypes-meet-publishings-sensitivity-readers.

40. Waldman, "Is My Novel Offensive?"

41. Quoted in Erec Smith, "Free Black Thought: A Manifesto," *Persuasion*, May 5, 2021, https://www.persuasion.community/p/free-black-thought-a-manifesto.

42. Alice O'Connor, *Poverty Knowledge: Social Science, Social Policy, and the Poor in Twentieth Century U.S. History* (Princeton, NJ: Princeton University Press, 2001).

43. Karen E. Fields and Barbara J. Fields, *Racecraft: The Soul of Inequality in American Life* (New York: Verso Books, 2014), 102.

44. Kenneth W. Warren, *What Was African American Literature?* (Cambridge, MA: Harvard University Press, 2011), 110.

45. Touré F. Reed, "'Jess La Bombalera' and the Pathologies of Racial Authenticity," *Jacobin*, September 6, 2020, https://jacobin.com/2020/09/jess-la-bombalera-and-the -pathologies-of-racial-authenticity.

46. "Writing With Color," Tumblr, https://writingwithcolor.tumblr.com/post/9478 4330111/whenever-i-write-non-white-characters-i-get-a-lot.

47. Back cover of Fields and Fields, *Racecraft*.

48. Quoted in Lila Shapiro, "What the Job of a Sensitivity Reader Is Really Like," *Vulture*, January 5, 2018, https://www.vulture.com/2018/01/sensitivity-readers-what -the-job-is-really-like.html.

49. Don Lee, "The Freedom to Mislead: An Interview with Don Lee," interview by Anis Shivani, *New Letters* 79, no. 1 (Fall 2012–2013): 80.

50. Alisa Valdes-Rodriguez, "Auntie Sandra's Cabin: Why No One Should Be Surprised Sandra Cisneros Endorsed American Dirt," 2020, https://web.archive.org /web/20210616111616/https://www.alisa-valdes-rodriguez.com/post/auntie-sandra -s-cabin-why-no-one-should-be-surprised-sandra-cisneros-endorsed-american-dirt.

51. Quoted in Everdeen Mason, "Publishers Are Hiring 'Sensitivity Readers' to Flag Potentially Offensive Content," *Chicago Tribune*, February 15, 2017, https://www .chicagotribune.com/2017/02/15/publishers-are-hiring-sensitivity-readers-to-flag -potentially-offensive-content/.

52. David Bromwich, *Politics By Other Means: Higher Education and Group Thinking* (New Haven, CT: Yale University Press, 1992), 26.

53. Zadie Smith, "Fascinated to Presume: In Defense of Fiction," *New York Review of Books*, October 24, 2019, https://www.nybooks.com/articles/2019/10/24/zadie -smith-in-defense-of-fiction/.

54. Valdes-Rodriguez, "Auntie Sandra's Cabin."

55. Quoted in Nicole Martinez, "Author David Sedaris on Political Correctness and 'Painfully Chic' Miami," *Miami New Times*, April 19, 2017, https://www.miaminew times.com/arts/david-sedaris-author-of-theft-by-finding-to-read-at-miamis-arsht -center-9284416.

56. Quoted in "The Age of Outrage," *America Inside Out with Katie Couric*, season 1, episode 6, *National Geographic*, 47:29, 2018, https://www.nationalgeographic.com /tv/episode/2ef396cc-a078-45f1-b6ab-5f72ec01708c/playlist/PL553044961.

57. Angie Thomas does not always explicitly mark her characters as black. Yet, as Starr, explains, "You rarely see white people in Garden Heights." When white people do appear, Thomas goes out of her way to mark them. "We find a table next to some white guys" is one passage where white characters appear in Garden Heights. In other passages, it is assumed that the characters are, like Starr and her family, black. For example, *Kirkus Reviews* describes Starr's neighborhood as "her black neighborhood." Review of *The Hate U Give* by Angie Thomas, *Kirkus Reviews*, February 28, 2017, https://www.kirkusreviews.com/book-reviews/angie-thomas/hate-u-give/; Angie Thomas, *The Hate U Give* (New York: Balzer + Bray, 2017), 46.

58. Melina Abdullah and Patrisse Khan-Cullors, "Why 'The Hate U Give' Is Not a Black Lives Matter Movie," *Los Angeles Sentinel*, October 18, 2018, https://lasentinel .net/why-the-hate-u-give-is-not-a-black-lives-matter-movie.html.

59. The novel ends with a moment of noblesse oblige. "We ain't gotta live there to change things, baby," explains Big Mav, "we just gotta give a damn." Thomas, *Hate U Give*, 436.

60. Taylor Thomas, "'Hate U Give' Author's Latest Serves Up Inspiring Tale of Rap and Redemption," *Pittsburgh Post-Gazette*, February 2, 2019, https://www.post-gazette

.com/ae/books/2019/02/02/Angie-Thomas-On-The-Come-Up-book-review/stories
/201902030002.

61. Tiff, "Giveaway Contest: The Hate U Give by Angie Thomas," *Mostly YA Lit*,
August 25, 2017, https://www.mostlyyalit.com/2017/08/giveaway-contest-the-hate-u
-give-by-angie-thomas.html.

62. Anisaa, "Review: The Hate U Give by Angie Thomas," *Bookstacked*, September 8,
2017, https://bookstacked.com/reviews/book-reviews/review-the-hate-u-give-by-angie
-thomas/.

63. Percival Everett, *Erasure* (Minneapolis: Graywolf Press, 2001), 39–40, 53.

64. Elizabeth Ellen, "Alex Perez on The Iowa Writers' Workshop, Baseball, Growing
Up Cuban-American in Miami & Saying Goodbye to the Literary Community,"
Hobart, September 29, 2022, https://www.hobartpulp.com/web_features/alex-perez
-on-the-iowa-s-writers-workshop-baseball-and-growing-up-cuban-american-in-america.

65. "About," *Adroit Journal*, accessed November 4, 2024, https://theadroitjournal.org
/about/.

66. Smith, "Unmaking the White Default."

67. Vicky Smith, "The Road to Heck . . . : Misreading Race in This Children's Book,"
Kirkus Reviews, March 8, 2016, https://www.kirkusreviews.com/news-and-features
/articles/road-heck/.

68. Marina Watts, "In Smithsonian Race Guidelines, Rational Thinking and Hard
Work Are White Values," *Newsweek*, July 17, 2020, https://www.newsweek.com
/smithsonian-race-guidelines-rational-thinking-hard-work-are-white-values-151
8333.

69. Everett, *Erasure*, 28.

70. Robert Wood, "Why Authors Need to Take Care When Writing Outside Their
Gender (UPDATED AND IMPROVED)," *Standout Books*, September 21, 2015, https://
web.archive.org/web/20240414205423/https://www.standoutbooks.com/writing
-gender/.

71. Ibram X. Kendi, *How to Be an Antiracist* (New York: Penguin Random House,
2019), 9.

72. "What is #Disrupt Texts?," #DisruptTexts, accessed November 4, 2024, https://
disrupttexts.org/lets-get-to-work/.

73. Lorena's Baby Sol is here! (@nenagerman), "Did ya'll know that many of the
'classics' were written before the 50s? Think of US society before then & the values
that shaped this nation afterwards . . ." X, November 30, 2020, https://archive.is/7U
v2I#selection-3819.12-3819.165.

74. David Bowles (Mācuīl Ehēcatl) (@DavidOBowles), "Nobody with a shitty, reactionary, regressive take on the classics in the classroom today . . . . . . actually knows a GODDAMN THING about literacy . . ." X, November 30, 2020, https://archive.md /VkdRm.

75. Amna Khalid and Jeffrey Snyder, "Poverty of the Imagination," *Arc Digital*, January 12, 2021, https://medium.com/arc-digital/poverty-of-the-imagination-624c 51f6026b.

76. Ellen Oh Hell No (@ElloEllenOh), "We should do a WORST CLASSICS BOOKS EVER list and why they should not be taught in K–12 schools anymore because they legit cause kids to hate reading . . ." X, November 20, 2020, URL no longer available.

77. Godspeed you! White/Puerto Rican Emperor (@olmsted_frank), "we can't allow this thought process to spread," X, December 1, 2020, https://x.com/olmsted_frank /status/1333779560962400257.

78. Padma Venkatraman, "Weeding Out Racism's Invisible Roots: Rethinking Children's Classics," *School Library Journal*, June 19, 2020, https://www.slj.com/story /weeding-out-racisms-invisible-roots-rethinking-childrens-classics-libraries-diverse -books.

79. On the importance of public libraries, I recommend Eric Klinenberg, *Palaces for the People: How Social Infrastructure Can Help Fight Inequality, Polarization, and the Decline of Civic Life* (New York: Broadway Books, 2018). If the Sensitivity Era is, at least in part, a product of polarization, then public libraries, per Klinenberg, might be part of the solution.

80. WTVC/Associated Press, "Chattanooga Library Fires Worker Who Burned Library Books by Conservative Authors," News Channel 9 ABC, February 19, 2020, https://newschannel9.com/news/local/library-worker-accused-of-burning-conserva tive-books.

81. Rage against the Machine, "Bulls on Parade," track 2 on *Evil Empire*, Genius, April 16, 1996, https://genius.com/Rage-against-the-machine-bulls-on-parade-lyrics.

82. Philip Thody, "The Power of the Story: Fiction and Political Change," *Modern Language Review* 92, no. 2 (April 1997): 415–417.

83. George Orwell, *1984* (New York: Signet Classics, 1977), 200.

84. *The Discussion Guide to the Inaugural Poem*, Penguin Classics, March 2021, https:// storage.googleapis.com/classroom-portal-production/uploads/2021/03/1ad72aa2 -the-hill-we-climb_discussionguide.pdf.

85. Quoted in Khalid and Snyder, "Poverty of the Imagination."

86. Those familiar with Tony Bennett's work will be reminded of his discussion of the teacher/critic as an "ethical exemplar," one who engages the student/reader in

an "unending process of ethical self-correction." Tony Bennett, *Outside Literature* (London: Routledge, 1990), 190.

87. Morton O. Schapiro and Gary Saul Morson, *Minds Wide Shut: How the New Fundamentalisms Divide Us* (Princeton, NJ: Princeton University Press, 2021), 198.

88. Fyodor Dostoevsky, quoted in Schapiro and Morson, *Minds Wide Shut*, 115.

89. Chuck Palahniuk, *Fight Club* (New York: Norton, 2005), 200, 14.

90. Quoted in Joel Best, *Is That True? Critical Thinking for Sociologists* (Berkeley: University of California Press, 2021), 55.

91. John M. Ellis, *Literature Lost* (New Haven, CT: Yale University Press, 1997), 34–35.

92. Philippe Rochat, *Moral Acrobatics: How We Avoid Ethical Ambiguity by Thinking in Black and White* (Oxford: Oxford University Press, 2021), 141.

93. Harold Bloom, *The Western Canon: The Books and School of the Ages* (London: Riverhead Books, 1995).

94. Yes, the cookies are real. Alex Damen, "Cookies for a Cause Is Not *Just* a Cookie Business, It's a Movement," We Are Women Owned, December 4, 2018, https://www.wearewomenowned.com/cookies-for-a-cause-is-not-just-a-cookie-business-its-a-movement/.

95. Quoted in Khalid and Snyder, "Poverty of the Imagination."

96. Eibhlis Gale-Coleman, "The Hidden Dangers of the Literary Canon," *Curiosity Shots*, June 15, 2021, URL no longer available.

97. "Word of the Year 2018: Shortlist," Oxford Languages, 2018, https://languages.oup.com/word-of-the-year/2018-shortlist/.

98. Erin Spampinato, "How Does the Literary Canon Reinforce the Logic of the Incel?" *Guardian*, June 4, 2018, https://www.theguardian.com/books/2018/jun/04/incel-movement-literary-classics-behind-misogyny.

99. Ellis, *Literature Lost*, 12.

100. Quoted in Laurent Dubreuil, "Nonconforming," *Harper's Magazine*, September 2020, https://harpers.org/archive/2020/09/nonconforming/.

101. Dubreuil, "Nonconforming."

102. Stanley Fish, *Is There a Text in This Class? The Authority of Interpretive Communities* (Cambridge, MA: Harvard University Press, 1982).

103. Eviatar Zerubavel, *Social Mindscapes: An Invitation to Cognitive Sociology* (Cambridge, MA: Harvard University Press, 1999), 47.

104. Greg Lukianoff and Jonathan Haidt, *The Coddling of the American Mind: How Good Intentions and Bad Ideas Are Setting Up a Generation for Failure* (New York: Penguin Press, 2018), 7.

105. William B. Irvine, *A Slap in the Face: Why Insults Hurt—And Why They Shouldn't* (Oxford: Oxford University Press, 2017).

106. Lukianoff and Haidt, *Coddling*, 10.

107. Lukianoff and Haidt, *Coddling*, 30.

108. Paraphrased in Allyson Waller, "Howard Students Protest Cut of Classics Department, Hub for Black Scholarship," *New York Times*, April 25, 2021, https://www.nytimes.com/2021/04/25/us/howard-classics-department.html.

109. Samantha Lock, "'To Kill a Mockingbird,' Other Books Banned From California Schools over Racism Concerns," *Newsweek*, November 13, 2020, https://www.newsweek.com/kill-mockingbird-other-books-banned-california-schools-over-racism-concerns-1547241.

110. "Stop Burbank Unified School District's Ban on Anti-Racist Books," Change.Org, started October 22, 2020, https://www.change.org/p/burbank-unified-school-district-s-board-of-education-stop-burbank-unified-school-district-s-ban-on-anti-racist-books.

111. Fields and Fields, *Racecraft*, 90.

112. Martin Luther King Jr., "Letter from a Birmingham Jail," African Studies Center, University of Pennsylvania, April 16, 1963, https://www.africa.upenn.edu/Articles_Gen/Letter_Birmingham.html.

113. Roosevelt Montás, *Rescuing Socrates: How the Great Books Changed My Life and Why They Matter for a New Generation* (Princeton, NJ: Princeton University Press, 2021).

114. Kevin Gregory, "Dr. Glenn Loury: 'Tolstoy Is Mine. Dickens Is Mine.'" YouTube video, 2:06, November 15, 2021, https://youtu.be/Pza_L0ZzRnU.

115. Khalid and Snyder, "Poverty of the Imagination."

116. Quoted in Warren, *African American Literature?*, 119–120.

117. Smith, "Fascinated to Presume."

118. Henry Louis Gates Jr., "'Authenticity,' or the Lesson of Little Tree," *New York Times Book Review*, November 24, 1991, https://www.nytimes.com/1991/11/24/books/authenticity-or-the-lesson-of-little-tree.html.

119. Matt Seybold, "Put the Reader Through Hell: In Memory of Toni Morrison, Twain Scholar," Center for Mark Twain Studies, August 6, 2019, https://marktwainstudies.com/put-the-reader-through-hell-in-memory-of-toni-morrison-twain-scholar/.

120. Toni Morrison, "Introduction," in *The Oxford Mark Twain: Adventures of Huckleberry Finn*, edited by Shelley Fisher Fishkin (Oxford: Oxford University Press, 1996), 153, 160.

121. Barack Obama, "Here's Why I'm Celebrating Banned Books Week," *Medium*, September 23, 2022, https://barackobama.medium.com/heres-why-i-m-celebrating -banned-books-week-f42e3513f613.

122. Randall Kennedy, *Nigger: The Strange Career of a Troublesome Word* (New York: Vintage, 2003), 104, 143.

123. Orwell, *1984*, 34.

124. David Goggins, *Can't Hurt Me: Master Your Mind and Defy the Odds* (Austin, TX: Lioncrest Publishing, 2018), 11.

125. "Whitewash," Oxford Learner's Dictionary, accessed November 4, 2024, https://www.oxfordlearnersdictionaries.com/us/definition/english/whitewash_2.

126. Abigail Johnson Hess, "It Costs Over $69,000 a Year to Go to Cornell—But This Is How Much Students Actually Pay," *CNBC*, May 25, 2019, https://www.cnbc .com/2019/05/23/heres-how-much-students-actually-pay-to-go-to-cornell.html.

127. Quoted in Armani Syed, "The Trouble with the Rewrites to the James Bond Books," *Time*, February 27, 2023, https://time.com/6258547/james-bond-books -rewritten/.

128. Quoted in Keith Allan and Kate Burridge, *Forbidden Words: Taboo and the Censoring of Language* (Cambridge: Cambridge University Press, 2006), 24.

129. William Marx, *The Hatred of Literature* (Cambridge, MA: Harvard University Press, 2018), 130, 147–148.

130. Nel, *Was the Cat in the Hat Black?*, 69–70.

131. Quoted in D. L. Ashliman, "Censorship in Folklore," University of Pittsburgh, October 17, 2021, https://sites.pitt.edu/~dash/censor.html.

132. Alan Gribben, "Introduction," in *Adventures of Tom Sawyer and Huckleberry Finn: The NewSouth Edition* (Montgomery, AL: NewSouth Books, 2011), 9.

133. Gribben, "Introduction," 10.

134. Orwell, *1984*, 42.

135. Alan Gribben, "Huck Finn and Tom Sawyer Go Back to School," Independent Publisher, 2021, https://www.independentpublisher.com/article.php?page=1439& urltitle=Huck.

136. Jim Zwick, *Mark Twain's Weapons of Satire: Anti-Imperialist Writings on the Philippine-American War* (Syracuse, NY: Syracuse University Press, 1992).

137. Quoted in Benedicte Page, "New Huckleberry Finn Edition Censors 'N-Word.'" *Guardian*, January 5, 2011, https://www.theguardian.com/books/2011/jan/05/huckle berry-finn-edition-censors-n-word.

138. Kennedy, *Nigger*, 111–112.

139. Allan and Burridge, *Forbidden Words*, 25.

140. "Examples of Literary Works Altered on New York State Regents English Language Arts Examinations," National Coalition Against Censorship, June 11, 2002, https://ncac.org/update/examples-of-literary-works-altered-on-new-york-state -regents-english-language-arts-examinations.

141. Metamorphosis Literary Agency, URL no longer available.

142. Thomas Chatterton Williams (@thomaschattwill), "One of the reasons it's so difficult to take seriously the idea that translators must or *should* be of the same "racial" identity as authors . . ." X, March 11, 2021, https://x.com/thomaschattwill /status/1370030260129910796.

143. Quoted in Miriam Berger, "White Translator Removed from Amanda Gorman Poem, Amid Controversy in Europe," *Washington Post*, March 11, 2021, https://www .washingtonpost.com/world/2021/03/11/amanda-gorman-white-translator-spain/.

144. Ingall, "Confessions."

145. Johnson, *Revolutionaries to Race Leaders*.

146. Political scientist Dean E. Robinson argues that black nationalism is not "a transhistorical, and hermetically sealed, phenomenon." Instead, it "tends to draw upon intellectual and political currents in American society." Robinson, *Black Nationalism in American Politics and Thought* (Cambridge: Cambridge University Press, 2001), 4, 88.

147. Adolph Reed Jr., "Black Particularity Reconsidered," *Telos* 39 (March 1979): 86.

148. Salman Rushdie calls this "the New Behalfism." Rushdie, "Notes on Writing and the Nation," in *Burn This Book: Notes on Literature and Engagement*, edited by Toni Morrison (New York: HarperCollins, 2012), 80.

149. Quoted in Ingall, "Confessions."

150. Madeline Pine (@Madeline_Pine), "Gotta laugh at the peeps who say they'd 'never subject their books to a sensitivity reader!' Go ahead, get things wrong then . . ." X, June 30, 2020, https://x.com/Madeline_Pine/status/1278044633612746753.

151. L.R. Lam (@LR_Lam), "No one's being censored. It's another step like hiring an astrophysicist to make sure a space opera isn't getting the science completely backwards . . ." X, December 25, 2017, https://x.com/LR_Lam/status/9453484388 99773440. URL unavailable because account owner limits who can view their posts.

152. Natalia Sylvester, "What a Sensitivity Reader Is (and Isn't) and How to Hire One," *Writer Unboxed*, March 3, 2017, https://writerunboxed.com/2017/03/03/what-a-sensitivity-reader-is-and-isnt-and-how-to-hire-one/.

153. (@MFOrpwood), "If I were writing about a doctor, I'd get a doctor to beta [read] it to make sure I got it right. Same difference," URL unavailable because X account has since been deleted.

154. Stephen Jay Gould, *The Mismeasure of Man*, 2nd ed. (New York: Norton, 1996).

155. George Lakoff and Mark Johnsen, *Metaphors We Live By* (Chicago: University of Chicago Press, 2003).

156. Quoted in Rosenfield, "#OwnVoices."

157. Randall L. Kennedy. "Racial Critiques of Legal Academia." *Harvard Law Review* 102, no. 8 (June 1989): 1777.

158. Tom Nichols, *The Death of Expertise: The Campaign Against Established Knowledge and Why it Matters* (Oxford: Oxford University Press, 2018), 35.

159. Wyatte Grantham-Philips, "A White Professor Says She Pretended to Be Black, Afro-Latina for Her Entire Career," *USA Today*, September 4, 2020, https://www.usatoday.com/story/news/nation/2020/09/04/white-george-washington-university-professor-faked-black-identity/5714726002/.

160. Jonathan Capehart, "The Damage Rachel Dolezal Has Done," *Washington Post*, June 12, 2015, https://www.washingtonpost.com/blogs/post-partisan/wp/2015/06/12/the-damage-rachel-dolezal-has-done/.

161. Peter Aldhous, "She Claimed to Fight for Survivors of Sexual Harassment in Science. But for Many, She Added to the Pain," *BuzzFeed News*, August 29, 2020, https://www.buzzfeednews.com/article/peteraldhous/bethann-mclaughlin-metoostem-harassment-activism.

162. Lisa Page, "When Writer Hache Carrillo Died, the World Discovered His True Identity. What Does That Mean for His Legacy?" *Washington Post*, July 6, 2020, https://www.washingtonpost.com/entertainment/books/when-writer-hache-carrillo-died-the-world-discovered-his-true-identity-what-does-that-mean-for-his-legacy/2020/07/06/4e7b9706-b489-11ea-aca5-ebb63d27e1ff_story.html; Casey Chalk, "Writer Makes Career Pretending to Be Hispanic, Gets Excused Because He's a Leftist," *Federalist*, May 28, 2020, https://thefederalist.com/2020/05/28/writer-makes-career-pretending-to-be-hispanic-gets-excused-because-hes-a-leftist/.

163. For a book-length treatment of authorial impostors, see Christopher L. Miller, *Impostors: Literary Hoaxes and Cultural Authenticity* (Chicago: University of Chicago Press, 2018), 18. Miller's study covers "many cases where readers *claim* they could tell the author was not what he/she pretended to be, but they almost always make this claim only *after* the imposture has been revealed."

164. Smith, "Free Black Thought."

165. Harry G. Frankfurt, *On Bullshit* (Princeton, NJ: Princeton University Press, 2005), 63–64.

166. "Episode 97: Alberto Gullaba Jr. Thought He Might Be Headed for Literary Stardom—Then His Agent Found Out His Race," *Blocked and Reported* (podcast), 1:39:38, January 9, 2022, https://www.blockedandreported.org/p/episode-97-alberto-gullaba-jr-thought.

167. Quoted in Martinez, "Author David Sedaris."

Chapter 2

1. Erich Goode and Nachman Ben-Yehuda, *Moral Panics: The Social Construction of Deviance*, 2nd ed. (Hoboken, NJ: Wiley-Blackwell, 2009) 2.

2. Goode and Ben-Yehuda, *Moral Panics*, 9.

3. Amy Kiste Nyberg, *Seal of Approval: The History of the Comics Code* (Jackson: University Press of Mississippi, 1998), 3–4.

4. Karen Sternheimer, *Pop Culture Panics: How Moral Crusaders Construct Meanings of Deviance and Delinquency* (New York: Routledge, 2015), 93.

5. Quoted in Nyberg, *Seal of Approval*, 112.

6. Nyberg, *Seal of Approval*, 31.

7. Goode and Ben-Yehuda, *Moral Panics*, 9–11.

8. Goode and Ben-Yehuda, 11.

9. "The Comics Code," Comic Book Legal Defense Fund, http://cbldf.org/the-comics-code/.

10. Nyberg, *Seal of Approval*, 113.

11. Nyberg, 114.

12. Nyberg, 115.

13. Goode and Ben-Yehuda, *Moral Panics*, 11.

14. Quoted in Goode and Ben-Yehuda, 11.

15. Sternheimer, *Pop Culture Panics*, 78.

16. Quoted in Susan M. Squier, "Comics in the Health Humanities: A New Approach to Sex and Gender Education," in *Health Humanities Reader*, edited by Therese Jonese et al. (New Brunswick, NJ: Rutgers University Press, 2014), 231.

17. Sternheimer, *Pop Culture* Panics, 83.

18. "Don't step on the toes of the dog-lovers, the cat-lovers, doctors, lawyers, merchants, chiefs, Mormons, Baptists, Unitarians, second-generation Chinese, Swedes, Italians, Germans, Texans, Brooklynites, Irishmen, people from Oregon or Mexico. . . . All the minor minorities with their navels to be kept clean. Authors, full of evil thoughts, lock up your typewriters. . . . It didn't come from the Government down. There was no dictum, no declaration, no censorship to start with, no! Technology, mass exploitation, and minority pressure carried the trick, thank God. Today, thanks to them, you can stay happy all the time." Ray Bradbury, *Fahrenheit 451*, 60th anniversary ed. (New York: Simon and Schuster, 2013), 54–55.

19. Thomas F. O'Connor, "The National Organization for Decent Literature: A Phase in American Catholic Censorship," *Library Quarterly: Information, Community, Policy* 65, no. 4 (October 1995); 386–414.

20. In his 1956 article, "Conditions of Successful Degradation Ceremonies," Harold Garfinkel argues that a degradation ceremony is "any communicative work between persons, whereby the public identity of an actor is transformed into something looked on as lower in the local scheme of social types." According to Garfinkel, these ceremonies emerge when someone denounces someone else. Crucially, the denouncer does not just denounce the alleged deviant. They call upon other members of their tribe to denounce them, too. To be effective, the denouncer must present their indignation as more than a personal indignation. As Garfinkel puts it, "The denouncer must make the dignity of the supra-personal values of the tribe salient and accessible to view, and his denunciation must be delivered in their name." In this respect, the devaluation of a person's status reinforces the solidarity of the group. For this reason, Garfinkel describes degradation ceremonies as a form of secular communion. Garfinkel, "Conditions for Successful Degradation Ceremonies," *American Journal of Sociology* 61, no. 5 (March 1956); 420, 423, https://doi.org /10.1086/221800.

21. Nyberg, *Seal of Approval*, 27.

22. Amy Kiste Nyberg, "Comic Book Censorship in the United States," in *Pulp Demons: International Dimensions of the Postwar Anti-comics Campaign*, edited by John A. Lent (Madison, NJ: Fairleigh Dickinson University Press, 1999), 56.

23. David Hadju, quoted in Sternheimer, *Pop Culture Panics*, 99.

24. Sternheimer, *Pop Culture Panics*, 98.

25. Les Daniels, quoted in Sternheimer, *Pop Culture Panics*, 99; Michelle Ann Abate, *Funny Girls: Guffaws, Guts, and Gender in Classic American Comics* (Jackson: University Press of Mississippi, 2019), 136.

26. Sternheimer, *Pop Culture Panics*, 99–100.

27. Quoted in David R. Stone, "News for the Record," *Journal of Intellectual Freedom and Privacy* 4, no. 1 (Spring 2019): 71.

28. Quoted in Jesse Singal, "How a Twitter Mob Derailed an Immigrant Female Author's Budding Career." *Tablet*, January 31, 2019, https://www.tabletmag.com /sections/news/articles/how-a-twitter-mob-destroyed-a-young-immigrant-female -authors-budding-career.

   Jesse Singal (@jessesingal), "6/ place in, 'oppression is blind to skin color,' as per the book's PR materials. The argument seems to be that because oppression isn't blind to skin color . . ." X, January 29, 2019, https://x.com/jessesingal/status /1090474479850016768.

29. Quoted in Jesse Singal, "Twitter Mob."

30. Richard Hellie, "Russian Slavery and Serfdom, 1450–1804," in *The Cambridge World History of Slavery*, vol. 3, *AD 1420–AD 1804*, edited by David Eltis et al. (Cambridge: Cambridge University Press, 2011), 275–295.

31. Amélie Wen Zhao (@ameliewenzhao), "To The Book Community: An Apology," X, January 30, 2019, https://x.com/ameliewenzhao/status/1090706315440242688.

32. Ruth Graham, "Wolves," *Slate*, March 4, 2019, https://slate.com/culture/2019 /03/ya-book-scandal-kosoko-jackson-a-place-for-wolves-explained.html.

33. "A Place for Wolves," Goodreads, accessed November 4, 2024, https://www .goodreads.com/book/show/38271712-a-place-for-wolves.

34. Kosoko Jackson, *A Place for Wolves*, advanced reader's edition (Naperville, IL: Sourcebooks, 2019), 298.

35. Kosoko Jackson (@KosokoJackson), "From me to the Book Community: I'm Sorry," X, February 28, 2019, https://web.archive.org/web/20190301091837/https:// twitter.com/KosokoJackson/status/1101180233913376773.

36. Quoted in Graham, "Wolves."

37. Kat Rosenfield, "*Kirkus* Editor-in-Chief Explains Why They Altered That *American Heart* Review," *Vulture*, October 19, 2017, https://www.vulture.com/2017/10 /american-heart-review-kirkus-editor-on-why-they-changed-it.html.

38. Alter, "Online Outrage."

39. Orwell, *1984*, 40.

40. Rosenfield, "*Kirkus* Editor-in-Chief."

41. "A Note from the Editor in Chief," *Kirkus Reviews*, https://www.kirkusreviews .com/statement/laura-moriarty/american-heart/.

42. "American Heart," *Kirkus Reviews*, January 30, 2018, https://www.kirkusreviews .com/book-reviews/laura-moriarty/american-heart/.

43. Rosenfield, "*Kirkus* Editor-in-Chief."

44. "Note from the Editor in Chief."

45. "The Review Marina," Tumblr, November 5, 2016, https://bookphile.tumblr.com /post/152271075894/there-is-an-incredibly-racist-upcoming.

46. Keira Drake, "When Social Media Goes After Your Book, What's the Right Response?" *New York Times*, February 6, 2019, https://www.nytimes.com/2019/02 /06/books/amelie-wen-zhao-blood-heir-keira-drake-continent-jonah-winter-secret -project.html.

47. "The Continent," Goodreads, accessed November 5, 2024, https://www.good reads.com/book/show/30075733-the-continent.

48. "Continent."

49. John McWhorter, *Woke Racism: How a New Religion Has Betrayed Black America* (New York: Penguin Random House, 2021).

50. Of course, if the confident person belongs to an outgroup—say, Donald Trump speaking to a room full of liberals—their confidence may not boost their influence. Instead, it may undermine their influence. Cass R. Sunstein, *Conformity: The Power of Social Influences* (New York: New York University Press, 2019), 14–15.

51. Cass R. Sunstein, *On Rumors: How Falsehoods Spread, Why We Believe Them, and What Can Be Done* (Princeton, NJ: Princeton University Press, 2014), 89.

52. In *Copycats and Contrarians: Why We Follow Others . . . and When We Don't*, Michelle Baddeley considers issues of herd behavior in depth. As she reflects, "In our modern, computerized, globalized and deeply interconnected world—in which money, information and expectations move so fast—herds can build enormous momentum which is difficult to monitor and control." Baddeley, *Copycats and Contrarians: Why We Follow Others . . . and When We Don't* (New Haven, CT: Yale University Press, 2018), 259.

53. Everdeen Mason, "This Book is ~~Racist Damaging~~ Rewritten," *Washington Post*, May 19, 2018, https://www.washingtonpost.com/graphics/2018/entertainment/books /keira-drake-the-continent-book-comparisons/.

54. "Continent."

55. Sunstein, *On Rumors*, 7.

56. "Continent."

57. Quoted in Mason, "This Book Is ~~Racist~~."

58. Drake, "Social Media."

59. Nathaniel Hawthorne, *The Scarlet Letter* (New York: Penguin Random House, 201), 186.

60. Erving Goffman, *Stigma: Notes on the Management of Spoiled Identity* (New York: Simon and Schuster, 1986).

61. Justin Tosi and Brandon Warmke, *Grandstanding: The Use and Abuse of Moral Talk* (Oxford: Oxford University Press, 2020), 54, 45.

62. This is what separates *deviance* from *deviation*. "Whereas the number of standard deviations from the mean is a strictly statistical matter," writes Eviatar Zerubavel, "whether or not we consider an act (or, for that matter, a person) 'deviant' is a pronouncedly moral (as such, cultural) one." Zerubavel, *Taken for Granted: The Remarkable Power of the Unremarkable* (Princeton, NJ: Princeton University Press, 2018), 35.

63. Michel Foucault, *Discipline and Punish: The Birth of the Prison* (New York: Vintage, 1995), 201–206.

64. Australian Broadcasting Corporation, "Patricia Cornwell—Scarpetta, Helicopters, Trolls and Same Sex Marriage," *Life Matters* (podcast), 53:00, October 31, 2016, https://www.abc.net.au/listen/programs/lifematters/patricia-cornwell-scarpetta -helicopters-trolls-and-gay-marriage/7982610.

65. Quoted in Stephen Wynn-Davies and Stewart Carr, "Everybody's So Worried about Offending Everybody," *Daily Mail*, November 15, 2021, https://www.daily mail.co.uk/news/article-10200807/Crime-writer-Patricia-Cornwell-reveals-frustra tion-using-politically-correct-words-writing.html.

66. Angie Thomas (@angiecthomas), "Dear #AmericaInsideOut and @katiecouric, @ brownbookworm is more than a sensitivity reader. It would've been nice for you to refer to her as more than that . . ." X, May 16, 2018, https://x.com/angiecthomas /status/996947181897740288.

67. Orwell, *1984*, 11, 14.

68. Orwell, 309.

69. Roger Fowler et al., *Language and Control* (New York: Routledge, 2019), 20.

70. Katie Couric (@katiecouric), "I'm sorry we didn't mention Dhonielle's books, because she is more than a sensitivity reader! She is the author of The Belles, Tiny Pretty Things, and . . ." X, May 16, 2018, https://x.com/katiecouric/status/996960999 747055617.

71. Garfinkel, "Degradation Ceremonies," 422.

72. In their article "A Person-Centered Approach to Moral Judgment," moral psychologists Eric L. Uhlmann, David A. Pizarro, and Daniel Diermeier argue that the consequentialist and deontological theories of moral judgment cannot account for numerous empirical findings. In contrast to act-based theories, the authors contend that a person-centered theory can help explain the disjunction between the moral evaluation of an action and the moral evaluation of the person who commits the

action. As they explain, "Certain transgressions elicit especially negative reactions not because they are unusually wrong in-and-of-themselves, but because they are seen as highly diagnostic of an individual's moral character." It is not just that Couric made a mistake, if one can seriously call it that. It is that her mistake reveals how immoral she is. Uhlmann, Pizarro, and Diermeier, "A Person-Centered Approach to Moral Judgment," *Perspectives on Psychological Science* 10, no. 1 (January 2014): 72.

Psychologists define hostile-attribution bias as "the tendency to interpret ambiguous behavior of others as hostile." In one meta review, researchers conclude that this bias "predicts both aggressive tendencies and aggressive behavior." Stéphanie Klein Tuente, Stefan Bogaerts, and Wim Veling, "Hostile Attribution Bias and Aggression in Adults—A Systematic Review," *Aggression and Violent Behavior* 46 (2019): 61–81.

73. Quoted in Rosenfield, "Toxic Drama."

74. "Remove 'A Birthday Cake.'"

75. E. Lockhart, "This is Emily Jenkins," comment on "On Letting Go," *Reading While White* (blog), November 1, 2015, http://readingwhilewhite.blogspot.com/2015 /10/on-letting-go.html?showComment=1446389284847#c7763644794125015907.

76. M. Duphorne, "Probably the most honest review of the BOOK itself" (customer review), Amazon, June 18, 2016, https://smile.amazon.com/gp/customer-reviews /RGEFIEPSZID8U.

77. J. Fern, "Stop the Censorship of A Birthday Cake for George Washington" (customer review), Amazon, February 28, 2016, https://smile.amazon.com/gp/customer -reviews/R27LTMWMQ6PE5T.

78. Associated Press in New York, "George Washington Slave Cake Book's Author Had Concerns With Scholastic," *Guardian*, February 11, 2016, https://www.the guardian.com/us-news/2016/feb/11/george-washington-slave-cake-scholastic-book -author-objected-illustrations.

79. Ramin Ganeshram, "My Book on George Washington Was Banned. Here's My Side of the Story," *Guardian*, February 18, 2016, https://www.theguardian.com/books /2016/feb/18/my-book-on-george-washington-was-banned.

80. Nard the Bard, "great with a little parental guidance" (customer review), Amazon, July 8, 2016, https://smile.amazon.com/gp/customer-reviews/RYY1XVSA2V05P.

81. Yuki Noguchi, "Why Borders Failed While Barnes & Noble Survived," *NPR*, Jul 19, 2011, https://www.npr.org/2011/07/19/138514209/why-borders-failed-while-barnes -and-noble-survived.

82. For a longer treatment of Amazon's impact on literature, see Mark McGurl, *Everything and Less: The Novel in the Age of Amazon* (New York: Verso Books, 2021).

83. Kennedy, "'Captain Underpants.'"

84. "Scholastic Needs to Apologize."

85. Dav Pilkey, "Dav Pilkey Apology," YouTube video, 0:45, March 25, 2021, https://youtu.be/At1e7buY2Nw&t=2s.

86. "Scholastic Needs to Apologize."

87. Barbara Goldberg, "Six Dr. Seuss Books Pulled from Publication Due to Racist Imagery," *Reuters*, March 2, 2021, https://www.reuters.com/business/media-telecom /six-dr-seuss-books-pulled-publication-due-racist-imagery-2021-03-02/.

88. Bradbury, *Fahrenheit 451*.

89. David Buckingham, *After the Death of Childhood* (Cambridge: Polity, 2000), 4.

90. Christopher Myers, "Young Dreamers," *Horn Book*, August 6, 2013, https://www .hbook.com/story/young-dreamers.

91. Raymond Williams, *Problems in Materialism and Culture* (New York: Verso Books, 1980), 170–195.

92. Neil Gaiman, "Introduction," in *Fahrenheit 451*, xii.

93. Katha Pollitt, "Dr. Seuss's Mistakes Are the Least of Our Troubles," *Nation*, April 1, 2021, https://www.thenation.com/article/culture/banning-books-historical -context/.

94. Much of the empirical work that comes out of Moral Foundations Theory (MFT) suggests that conservatives have a stronger inclination toward purity and disgust. For example, some conservatives resent premarital sex, sex that is not heterosexual, etc. as impure and disgusting. That said, the fear of moral contamination is central to the liberal crusade over literature. Future work in the vein of MFT might use this crusade to complicate some of the conclusions about purity-based morality as it relates to different ends of the political spectrum. Spassena P. Koleva et al. "Tracing the Threads: How Five Moral Concerns (Especially Purity) Help Explain Culture War Attitudes," *Journal of Research in Personality* 46, no. 2 (2012): 184–194, https://doi .org/10.1016/j.jrp.2012.01.006; Jesse Graham, Jonathan Haidt, and Brian A. Nosek, "Liberals and Conservatives Rely on Different Sets of Moral Foundations," *Journal of Personality and Social Psychology* 96, no. 5 (May 2009); 1029–1046, https://doi.org /10.1037/a0015141.

95. Marx, *Hatred of Literature*.

96. Quoted in Marx, *Hatred of Literature*, 147.

97. Ray Bradbury, "Coda," in *Fahrenheit 451*, 209.

98. Jonathan R. Eller, "The Story of Fahrenheit 451," in *Fahrenheit 451*, 185.

99. In his "Coda" to *Fahrenheit 451*, Ray Bradbury writes: "If Mormons do not like my plays, let them write their own. If the Irish hate my Dublin stories, let them

rent typewriters. If teachers and grammar-school editors find my jawbreaker sentences shatter their mushmilk teeth, let them eat stale cake dunked in weak tea of their own ungodly manufacture. . . . In sum, do not insult me with the beheadings, finger-choppings, or the lung-deflations you plan for my works" (210).

100. Nel, *Was the Cat in the Hat Black?*, 1.

101. NCAC, PEN, and the First Amendment Committee of ASJA, "*A Birthday Cake for George Washington*: The Problem with Banishing Books," Scribd, January 22, 2016, https://www.scribd.com/document/296336046/NCAC-A-Cake-for-George -Washington.

102. Alter, "Debut Book."

103. Sternheimer, *Pop Culture Panics*, 96–97.

104. Quoted in Russell Jacoby, *The Last Intellectuals: American Culture in the Age of Academe* (New York: Basic Books, 2000), 63.

105. Anders Walkers, "'Blackboard Jungle': Delinquency, Desegregation, and the Cultural Politics of 'Brown,'" *Columbia Law Review* 110 (December 2010): 1917, available at https://scholarship.law.slu.edu/faculty/166/.

106. Quoted in Jacoby, *Last Intellectuals*, 64.

107. Mason, *Queer Anxieties*, 9.

108. Roderik Rekker et al., "Moving In and Out of Poverty: The Within-Individual Association between Socioeconomic Status and Juvenile Delinquency," *PLOS One* 10, no. 11 (November 2015), https://doi.org/10.1371%2Fjournal.pone.0136461; Jennifer Lansford et al., "Early Physical Abuse and Later Violent Delinquency: A Prospective Longitudinal Study," *Child Maltreatment* 12, no. 3 (August 2007), https://doi.org/10.1177%2F1077559507301841.

109. Nel, *Was the Cat in the Hat Black?*, 1.

110. Schapiro and Morson, *Minds Wide Shut*, 183.

111. As one of innumerable cases in point, consider *Kids on YouTube: Technical Identities and Digital Literacies*. In her book, ethnographer Patricia G. Lange reflects: "the impact and meaning of comments are often analyzed in media studies without regard to girls' own interpretations of them." In her research, Lange illuminates a "lack of correspondence between comments and video makers' interpretations of them." Unlike other scholars, Lange actually interviews young people. With both her feet firmly planted on the ground, she is critical of the "magic bullet" theory in media studies—which, in the words of Shearon Lowery and Melvin L. DeFleur, assumes that "the media have direct, immediate, and powerful effects of a uniform nature on those who pay attention to their content." Lange, *Kids on YouTube: Technical Identities and Digital Literacies* (Walnut Creek, CA: Left Coast Press, 2014), 83, 87.

112. Nel, *Was the Cat in the Hat Black?*, 225.

113. Nel, 133–134.

114. In *Higher Superstitions: The Academic Left and Its Quarrels With Science*, Paul R. Gross and Norman Levitt observe the tendency for humanities scholars to make far-reaching claims in areas of expertise other than their own. In numerous instances, these scholars fail to display even an elementary understanding of basic questions, methods, and research in these areas of expertise. This problem was satirized by Alan Sokal, when he had his nonsense paper—"Transgressing the Boundaries: Towards a Transformative Hermeneutics of Quantum Gravity"—accepted by Duke University Press's *Social Text*. It was again satirized a few years ago when Peter Boghossian, James A. Lindsay, and Helen Pluckrose had multiple hoax papers accepted by other peer-reviewed journals. Like Sokal, their hoax showed that some journals will publish utter nonsense as long as the nonsense sounds progressive. Gross and Levitt, *Higher Superstitions: The Academic Left and Its Quarrels with Science* (Baltimore: Johns Hopkins University Press, 1998).

115. I used Project MUSE to conduct a keyword search on June 14, 2022.

116. Nel, *Was the Cat in the Hat Black?*, 135.

117. Mark Edmundson, *Nightmare on Main Street: Angels, Sadomasochism, and the Culture of the Gothic* (Cambridge, MA: Harvard University Press, 1997), 36.

118. Elizabeth Levy Paluck and Donald P. Green, "Prejudice Reduction: What Works? A Review and Assessment of Research and Practice," *Annual Review of Psychology* 60 (January 2009): 339–367, https://doi.org/10.1146/annurev.psych.60.110707.163607.

119. Colin Jerolmack and Shamus Khan, "Talk Is Cheap: Ethnography and the Attitudinal Fallacy," *Sociological Methods and Research* 43, no. 2 (March 2014): 178, https://doi.org/10.1177/0049124114523396.

120. Nel, *Was the Cat in the Hat Black?*, 225.

121. Nel, 1, 235.

122. Adrienne Westenfeld, "A Dr. Seuss Expert Cuts Through the Noise on the Cancel Culture Controversy" (interview by Adrienne Westenfeld of Philip Nel), *Esquire*, March 5, 2021, https://www.esquire.com/entertainment/books/a35738910/dr-seuss-racism-books-cancel-culture-interview/.

123. Paluck and Green, "Prejudice Reduction," 360.

124. James M. Glaser and Timothy J. Ryan, *Changing Minds, If Not Hearts: Political Remedies for Racial Conflict* (Philadelphia: University of Pennsylvania Press, 2013).

125. Paluck and Green, "Prejudice Reduction," 343.

126. John Milton, "Areopagitica," in *John Milton: The Major Works*, edited by Stephen Orgel and Jonathan Goldberg (Oxford: Oxford University Press, 2008), 236–272. .

127. Material here and elsewhere was published in Adam Szetela, "When It Comes to Banning Books, Both Right and Left Are Guilty," *Newsweek*, April 7, 2022, https://www.newsweek.com/when-it-comes-banning-books-both-right-left-are-guilty-opinion-1696045.

128. Jon Simpson, "Finding Brand Success in the Digital World," *Forbes*, August 25, 2017, https://www.forbes.com/sites/forbesagencycouncil/2017/08/25/finding-brand-success-in-the-digital-world/; A. Gutmann, "U.S. Advertising Industry—Statistics & Facts," Statista, 2021, https://www.statista.com/topics/979/advertising-in-the-us/.

129. Joel Best, *Flavor of the Month: Why Smart People Fall for Fads* (Berkeley: University of California Press, 2006).

130. Arthur Miller, *The Crucible* (New York: Penguin Classics, 2003), 30–31, 34.

131. According to Joel Best, "many intellectuals are sensitive to criticism that they live in ivory towers, divorced from the real world." The term "scholar-activist" is one way they live with that cognitive dissonance. Joel Best, *Is That True? Critical Thinking for Sociologists* (Berkeley: University of California Press, 2021), 57.

132. Eric Cheyfitz, "The End of Academia," in *The Future of American Studies*, edited by Donald E. Pease and Robyn Wiegman (Durham, NC: Duke University Press, 2002), 514.

133. Stanley Fish, *Professional Correctness: Literary Studies and Political Change* (Oxford: Oxford University Press, 1995), 133.

134. For critical takes on clicktivism, I recommend Amber A'Lee Frost, "The Poisoned Chalice of Hashtag Activism," *Catalyst: A Journal of Theory and Strategy* 4, no. 2 (Summer 2020); 228–247, and Jen Schradie, *The Revolution That Wasn't: How Digital Activism Favors Conservatives* (Cambridge, MA: Harvard University Press, 2019).

135. For the classic study of cleanliness, see Mary Douglas, *Purity and Danger: An Analysis of Concepts of Pollution and Taboo* (New York: Routledge, 2002).

136. Quoted in Sternheimer, *Pop Culture Panics*, 81, 92.

137. Quoted in Nyberg, *Seal of Approval*, 28.

138. "Place for Wolves."

139. Nel, *Was the Cat in the Hat Black?*, 73, 20, 72–73, 89, 67.

140. Moral panics often resemble disease panics. Writing in the *New England Journal of Medicine*, John F. Burnum, MD, explains: "We are predisposed to diagnose, and our patients to worry about, the diseases that are in the news, popularized,

and impressed on our minds. As an accompanying phenomenon, entrepreneurial specialists in and clinics for the various bandwagon diseases often spring up to capitalize on medical chic. . . . Cousins to diseases of fashion are media-sown disease panics; for example, fear of saccharin, of reserpine, or of coffee's causing cancer." Today, specialists in literature and their counterparts in the news media are diagnosing problems in books, popularizing these problems, and creating an increasingly irrational climate of concern. Burnum, "Medical Practice a la Mode," *New England Journal of Medicine* 317, no. 19 (November 1987): 1220–1222, https://www.nejm.org /doi/abs/10.1056/NEJM198711053171910.

141. For a discussion of concept creep and its implications, I recommend Nick Haslam, "Concept Creep: Psychology's Expanding Concepts of Harm and Pathology," *Psychological Inquiry* 27, no.1 (2016): 1–17, and the responses in that issue. For a discussion of the expansion of concepts like "trigger," "safety," and "danger," I recommend Keith E. Whittington, *Speak Freely: Why Universities Must Defend Free Speech* (Princeton, NJ: Princeton University Press, 2018), 57–77, and Bradley Campbell and Jason Manning, *The Rise of Victimhood Culture: Microaggressions, Safe Spaces, and the New Culture Wars* (London: Palgrave Macmillan, 2018), 71–105. As Campbell and Manning explain, "words and concepts affect what people talk about, what they pay attention to, how they understand problems, and how they try to solve them." When concepts related to harm are used to describe anything that someone dislikes, it raises the "crying wolf" problem. It also raises the problem of people being socialized to see themselves as fragile and weak, a problem explored in Lukianoff and Haidt, *Coddling.*

142. Quoted in Kate Eichhorn, *The End of Forgetting: Growing Up with Social Media* (Cambridge, MA: Harvard University Press, 2019), 7.

143. Quoted in Sternheimer, *Pop Culture Panics*, 90.

144. Waldman, "Is My Novel Offensive?"

145. Ibram X. Kendi and Ashley Lukashevsky, *Antiracist Baby* (New York: Penguin Random House, 2020), 17–18.

146. Anastasia Higginbotham, *Not My Idea: A Book about Whiteness* (New York: Dottir Press, 2018), 59.

147. Paul Kengor, "Our First 'Red Diaper Baby' President?," Accuracy in Academia, October 23, 2012, https://www.academia.org/our-first-red-diaper-baby-president/.

148. M. O. Grenby, "Moral and Instructive Children's Literature," *British Library*, 2014, https://www.britishlibrary.cn/en/articles/moral-and-instructive-childrens-literature/.

149. Mason, *Queer Anxieties*, 11.

150. Franco Moretti, "The Slaughterhouse of Literature," *MLQ: Modern Language Quarterly* 61, no. 1 (March 2000): 207–227, https://muse.jhu.edu/article/22852.

151. "Chuck Palahniuk's Crazy Stories (Compilation)—Joe Rogan Experience," YouTube video, 19:27, October 20, 2018, https://youtu.be/cvPQjL4wDIY.

152. Ellie Diaz, "Spotlight on Censorship: 'Make Something Up,'" American Library Association Intellectual Freedom Blog, April 12, 2017, https://www.oif.ala.org/spotlight-censorship-make-something/.

153. Chuck Palahniuk, *Consider This: Moments in My Writing Life After Which Everything Was Different* (New York: Grand Central Publishing, 2020), 118.

154. Bret Easton Ellis, *White* (New York: Penguin Random House, 2019), 116.

155. Summer Edward, "Caribbean Children's Literature, Where's Our Diversity Jedi?" *diuk dina papangge*, 2018, URL no longer available.

156. Debbie Reese (@debreese), "1) Oh my goodness! On Nov 2, 2015, @CynLeitichSmith coined the #DiversityJedi hashtag for those of us who were pushing hard on the status quo . . ." X, June 5, 2018, https://x.com/debreese/status/1004138034881851392. Perhaps there is a child or teenager among the dozens of Jedi listed by Reese. Though, as far as I can tell, this is a cabal of adults.

157. Debbie Reese, "Words Matter: About Meg Rosoff's 'Debbie Reese Crimes Against Diversity Stormtroopers' Remark," American Indians in Children's Literature, November 2, 2015, https://americanindiansinchildrensliterature.blogspot.com/2015/11/words-matter-about-meg-rosoffs-debbie.html.

158. Reese (@debreese), "Oh my goodness!"

159. Miller, *The Crucible*, 89.

160. Reese (@debreese), "Oh my goodness!"

161. The ribbon affair harkens to mind the process of "thinging." As psychologist Philippe Rochat describes it, "In the social realm, thinging is the basic process by which we compulsively objectify our alliances and we mark our social distinction at both the individual and group level." According to him, because "a reputation exists only in relation to other reputations," from this "competitive and comparison context derives the natural inclination to cultivate contempt as well as an inflated sense of superiority or inferiority toward others." Rochat, *Moral Acrobatics*, 87, 106.

162. Lakoff and Johnsen, *Metaphors*.

163. Vicky Smith, "The Diversity Jedi," *Kirkus Reviews*, April 4, 2019, https://www.kirkusreviews.com/news-and-features/articles/diversity-jedi/.

164. For a recent overview of the Stanford Prison Experiment and related studies, see Hubert J. M. Hermans, *Inner Democracy: Empowering the Mind Against a Polarizing Society* (Oxford: Oxford University Press, 2020).

165. Mina Cikara and Jay J. Van Bavel, "The Neuroscience of Intergroup Relations: An Integrative Review," *Perspectives on Psychological Science* 9, no. 3 (May 2014): 260, https://doi.org/10.1177/1745691614527464.

166. Rupert Brown, "The Origins of the Minimal Group Paradigm," *History of Psychology* 23, no. 4 (2020): 371–382, https://doi.org/10.1037/hop0000164.

167. Sunstein, *Conformity*, 35.

168. Mia Bloom and Sophia Moskalenko, *Pastels and Pedophiles: Inside the Mind of QAnon* (Redwood City, CA: Stanford University Press, 2021), 130.

169. Best, *Flavor of the Month*, 68.

170. Matthew J. Salganik, Peter Sheridan Dodds, and Duncan J. Watts, "Experimental Study of Inequality and Unpredictability in an Artificial Cultural Market," *Science* 311, no. 5762 (February 2006); 854–856, https://doi.org/10.1126/science.1121066.

171. Salganik, Dodds, and Watts, "Artificial Cultural Market," 855. For the follow-up experiment, in which the true popularity of songs was inverted, see Matthew J. Salganik and Duncan J. Watts, "Leading the Herd Astray: An Experimental Study of Self-fulfilling Prophecies in an Artificial Cultural Market," *Social Psychology Quarterly* 4, no. 4 (Fall 2008), https://doi.org/10.1177%2F019027250807100404.

172. Michael Macy et al., "Opinion Cascades and the Unpredictability of Partisan Polarization," *Science Advances* 5, no. 8 (2019), https://doi.org/10.1126/sciadv.aax0754.

173. Erin Overbey, "Eighty-Five from the Archive: Shirley Jackson," *New Yorker*, May 24, 2010, https://www.newyorker.com/books/double-take/eighty-five-from-the-archive-shirley-jackson.

174. Robb Willer, Ko Kuwabara, and Michael W. Macy, "The False Enforcement of Unpopular Norms," *American Journal of Sociology* 115, no. 2 (September 2009): 451, https://doi.org/10.1086/599250.

175. Damon Centola, Robb Willer, and Michael Macy, "The Emperor's Dilemma: A Computational Model of Self-Enforcing Norms," *American Journal of Sociology* 110, no. 4 (January 2005), 1011.

176. In the psychological literature, "impression management" denotes "the process by which individuals attempt to control the impressions others form of them." This process does not have to revolve around punishment. But, in moral panics, punishment is a useful tool in the impression management toolbox. Mark R. Leary and Robin M. Kowalski, "Impression Management: A Literature Review and Two Component Model," *Psychological Bulletin* 107, no. 1 (1990): 34, https://doi.org/10.1037/0033-2909.107.1.34.

177. For the classic experiment, see Solomon Asch, "Effects of Group Pressure Upon the Modification and Distortion of Judgments," in *Groups, Leadership and Men:*

Research in Human Relations, edited by H. Guetzkow (Pittsburgh: Carnegie Press, 1951), 177–190. As Cass R. Sunstein reflects, "Conformity experiments of this kind have produced more than 130 sets of results from seventeen countries . . . it is fair to say that [Asch's] basic conclusions hold up." Sunstein, *Conformity*, 16–17. For even more empirical research that lends support to Asch's conclusions, see Cass R. Sunstein, *On Rumors* and *Going to Extremes: How Like Minds Unite and Divide* (Oxford: Oxford University Press, 2011).

178. Christopher Bigsby, "Foreword," in Miller, *The Crucible*, xxv.

179. Bigsby, "Foreword," xxv.

180. Chris Bail, *Breaking the Social Media Prism: How to Make Our Platforms Less Polarizing* (Princeton, NJ: Princeton University Press, 2021), 56.

181. David Morgan calls this phenomenon "snobbery of position." As he describes it, "The idea of the servant who derives prestige from the status of his employer is a theme with comic—and sometimes less comic—possibilities that runs through the ages and through different cultures." Just as moral panics include guilt by association, they also include status by association. Morgan, *Snobbery* (Bristol: Bristol University Press, 2019) 14.

182. Quoted in Rosenfield, "Toxic Drama."

183. Not one to miss another opportunity for public self-flagellation, English professor Perry Nodelman commented: "You raise important concerns here, Debby—ones that are constantly on my mind these days as I continue to think about and write about children's literature. I recently became painfully aware of my own unconscious expression of white privilege." Debbie Reese, "Dear Philip Nel," American Indians in Children's Literature, December 5, 2015, https://americanindiansinchildrens literature.blogspot.com/2015/12/dear-philip-nel-some-questions-about.html.

184. By way of historical comparison, consider this observation by Kenneth W. Warren in *What Was African American Literature?*: "'The Literature of the Negro,' to quote the subtitle of an article by Alain Locke in the first number of *Phylon's* 1950 volume, was just as likely to include fiction by white writers who wrote with sensitivity about race, even on an international scale." Warren, *What Was African American Literature?*, 57.

185. For Russell Hardin, "a politically extreme view is likely to be a norm of exclusion that is self-enforcing, even self-strengthening. Norms of exclusion define groups to which those with the right views or with the right characteristics are admitted and from which others are excluded. Under the force of such norms of exclusion, the less intensely committed members of a group depart while extremists remain." Russell Hardin, "The Crippled Epistemology of Extremism," in *Political Extremism and Rationality*, edited by Albert Breton et. al (Cambridge: Cambridge University Press, 2014), 9.

186. Eli Pariser, *The Filter Bubble: How the New Personalized Web Is Changing What We Read and How We Think* (New York: Penguin Publishing Group, 2012).

187. Cass R. Sunstein, *Infotopia: How Many Minds Produce Knowledge* (Oxford: Oxford University Press, 2006), 9.

188. According to one study of Twitter, there "are asymmetries in individuals' willingness to venture into cross-cutting spaces, with conservatives more likely to follow media and political accounts classified as left-leaning than the reverse." Gregory Eady et al., "How Many People Live in Political Bubbles on Social Media? Evidence From Linked Survey and Twitter Data," *Sage Open* 9, no. 1 (2019), https://doi.org /10.1177/2158244019832705.

189. Jonathan Haidt, *The Righteous Mind: Why Good People Are Divided by Politics and Religion* (New York: Vintage Books, 2013), 219.

190. Spencer Baculi, "YA Author Jessica Cluess Denounced and Dropped by Agent for 'Personal Attacks' Against Lorena Germán," *Bounding into Comics*, December 5, 2020, https://boundingintocomics.com/2020/12/05/ya-author-jessica-cluess-denounced -as-racist-and-dropped-by-agent-for-personal-attacks-against-lorena-german/.

191. Lorena's Baby Sol is here! (nenagerman), "What's interesting to me is how I present a position on an academic point, and yet this 55%er decides to attack me personally over and over again . . ." X, November 30, 2020, https://archive.is/Y9q0q.

192. To better understand the dramaturgical aspects of allyship theater, I recommend Erving Goffman, *The Presentation of Self in Everyday Life* (New York: Anchor Books, 1959).

193. Mia Wenjen, "#OwnVoices Controversy," Pragmatic Mom, June 6, 2018, https://www.pragmaticmom.com/2018/06/ownvoices-controversy/.

194. Tosi and Warmke, *Grandstanding*, 51.

195. Sunstein, *Going to Extremes*, 3.

196. Quoted in Tunku Varadarajan, "A Challenger of the Woke 'Company Policy,'" *Wall Street Journal*, July 10, 2020, https://www.wsj.com/articles/a-challenger-of-the -woke-company-policy-11594405846.

Also see Glenn Loury, "Self-Censorship in Public Discourse: A Theory of 'Political Correctness' and Related Phenomena," *Rationality and Society* 6, no. 4 (October 1994): 428–461, https://doi.org/10.1177/1043463194006004002.

197. Miller, *The Crucible*, 50, 68.

198. In Lois Lowry's classic YA dystopian novel, children spend their time "learning to fit in, to standardize [their] behavior, to curb any impulse that might set [them] apart from the group." In this world, "corrections and apologies are very prompt." Lois Lowry, *The Giver* (Boston: Houghton Mifflin, 1993), 65, 69.

199. Lowry, *The Giver*, 70.

200. Orwell, *1984*, 253.

201. Jesse Singal (@JesseSingal), https://x.com, URL no longer available (post presumably deleted).

202. Bromwich, *Politics By Other Means*, 6.

203. Miller, *The Crucible*, 50.

204. Miller.

205. Mark Fisher, "Exiting the Vampire Castle," *openDemocracy*, November 24, 2013, https://www.opendemocracy.net/en/opendemocracyuk/exiting-vampire-castle/.

206. Jack Halberstam, "You Are Triggering Me! The Neo-Liberal Rhetoric of Harm, Danger and Trauma," *Bully Bloggers*, July 5, 2014, https://bullybloggers.wordpress.com/2014/07/05/you-are-triggering-me-the-neo-liberal-rhetoric-of-harm-danger-and-trauma/.

207. Ken Warren, "The Poetics and Politics of Black Lives Matter," *Nonsite*, September 10, 2020, https://nonsite.org/the-poetics-and-politics-of-black-lives-matter/.

208. "In general, the tendency for stigma to spread from the stigmatized individual to his close connections provides a reason for why such relations tend either to be avoided or to be terminated where existing," writes Erving Goffman. Goffman, *Stigma*, 30; Caley Tapp et al., "The Essence of Crime: Contagious Transmission from Those Who Have Committed Moral Transgressions," *British Journal of Social Psychology* 55, no. 4 (December 2016); 756–772, https://doi.org/10.1111/bjso.12153; Jie Liu et al., "Moral Contagion: Devaluation Effect of Immorality on Hypothetical Judgments of Economic Value," *Human Brain Mapping* 40, no. 7 (May 2019): 2076–2088, https://doi.org/10.1002%2Fhbm.24508.

209. Willer, Kuwabara, and Macy, "False Enforcement," 480.

210. Brooks Sherman (@byobrooks), "I hold myself to certain personal and professional standards for the values I support. I no longer represent Jessica Cluess. Her tweets against Lorena Germán . . ." X, December 3, 2020, https://archive.md/tPJY3.

211. Quoted in Jessica Bennett, "What If Instead of Calling People Out, We Called Them In?" *New York Times*, November 19, 2020, https://www.nytimes.com/2020/11/19/style/loretta-ross-smith-college-cancel-culture.html.

212. In his book on polarization, Hubert J. M. Hermans defends "inner diversity" as one buffer to extremism. Just as we should permit a multitude of perspectives in public life, we should also permit a multitude of perspectives within ourselves. Hermans, *Inner Democracy*, 7–8.

213. Anthony Burgess, *1985* (London: Serpent's Tail, 2013), 152.

214. Albert Bandura, *Moral Disengagement: How People Do Harm and Live With Themselves* (New York: Worth Publishers, 2016), 53.

215. Perhaps Cluess will return. But, years later, she has not published a novel since her agent dropped her. By contrast, she churned out novels in 2016, 2017, 2018, and just months before the #DisruptTexts blowout.

216. As Tage Shakti Rai and Alan Page Fiske put it, "Intentionally harming others will be perceived as more or less acceptable, and even morally praiseworthy depending on the social-relational context within which it occurs," especially "if the victim is perceived as potential threat or contaminant to the in-group." Rai and Fiske, "Moral Psychology Is Relationship Regulation: Moral Motives for Unity, Hierarchy, Equality, and Proportionality," *Psychological Review* 118, no. 1 (2011): 65.

217. Bandura, *Moral Disengagement*, 54.

218. Charles Mackay, *Extraordinary Popular Delusions and the Madness of Crowds* (New York: Start Publishing, 2012).

219. Quoted in Bennett, "Calling People Out."

220. Nicholas Tavuchis, *Mea Culpa: A Sociology of Apology and Reconciliation* (Redwood City, CA: Stanford University Press, 1991), 51.

221. "New Study: 55% of YA Books Bought by Adults," *Publishers Weekly*, September 13, 2012, https://www.publishersweekly.com/pw/by-topic/childrens/childrens-industry -news/article/53937-new-study-55-of-ya-books-bought-by-adults.html.

222. Valerie Peterson, quoted in "Diversity in Young Adult Literature: Young Adult Literature," *University of North Carolina-Greensboro Library Guide*, 2021.

223. Quoted in Rosenfield, "Toxic Drama."

224. Quoted in Rosenfield, "Toxic Drama."

225. "Diversity Resources," Cooperative Children's Book Center, https://ccbc.educa tion.wisc.edu/literature-resources/diversity-resources-multicultural-literature/.

226. There are exceptions to the trend. For example, the Young Adult Library Services Association publishes a Teens Top 10 list. "Nominators are members of teen book groups in fifteen school and public libraries around the country. Nominations are posted on the Thursday of National Library Week, and teens across the country vote on their favorite titles each year." "Teens' Top Ten," Young Adult Library Services Association, https://www.ala.org/yalsa/teenstopten.

227. Zhao (@ameliewenzhao), "To The Book Community."

228. Alter, "Online Outrage."

229. "Note from the Editor."

230. Lila Shapiro, "Can You Revise a Book to Make It More Woke?" *Vulture*, February 18, 2018, https://www.vulture.com/2018/02/keira-drake-the-continent.html.

231. Thomas, *The Hate U Give*, 447.

232. Paul Boyer and Stephen Nissenbaum. *Salem Possessed: The Social Origins of Witchcraft* (Cambridge, MA: Harvard University Press, 2011), 32.

233. Quoted in Rosenfield, "Toxic Drama."

234. Zerubavel, *Social Mindscapes*, 34.

235. Nolan, "J.K. Rowling."

236. Spencer Baculi, "Daily Dot Social Media Editor Anna Maria Asks Why Harry Potter Creator J. K. Rowling Has 'Not Gotten Jumped Yet,' Wishes She Gets Punched in the Face," *Bounding Into Comics*, September 18, 2020, URL no longer available.

237. Quoted in Julia Alexander, "A History of Harry Potter Books Being Burned— And J. K. Rowling's Perfect Responses," *Polygon*, February 1, 2017, https://www.polygon.com/2017/2/1/14474054/harry-potter-books-burning-jk-rowling-twitter.

238. Reese, "Words Matter."

239. adrienne maree brown, "On Cancel Culture, Accountability, and Transformative Justice," *Lit Hub*, January 25, 2021, https://lithub.com/on-cancel-culture-accountability-and-transformative-justice/; Burton, "Cancel Culture Is Real."

240. Katy Faust and Stacy Manning, *Them Before Us*, Post Hill Press, https://posthillpress.com/book/them-before-us-why-we-need-a-global-childrens-rights-movement.

Chapter 3

1. Both quotes were reprinted in Bertrand Cooper, "Who Actually Gets to Create Black Pop Culture?" *Current Affairs*, July 25, 2021, https://www.currentaffairs.org/news/2021/07/who-actually-gets-to-create-black-pop-culture.

2. Jason Allen, "The Working Poor in the Hamptons," *Salon*, May 4, 2019, https://www.salon.com/2019/05/04/the-working-poor-in-the-hamptons-i-cleaned-a-rich-authors-swimming-pool-while-writing-my-own-novel/.

3. Ian Wojcik-Andrews, "Introduction: Notes toward a Theory of Class in Children's Literature," *Lion and the Unicorn* 17, no. 2 (December 1993): 114, https://doi.org/10.1353/uni.0.0224.

4. Angela E. Hubler, *Little Red Readings: Historical Materialist Perspectives on Children's Literature* (Jackson: University Press of Mississippi, 2014), x.

5. Copyright © 2023 Children's Literature Association. Material from this paragraph and elsewhere first appeared in Adam Szetela, "Small Acts of Kindness in an Unequal

World: Picture Books During and After the Great Recession," *Children's Literature Association Quarterly* 48, no. 4 (Winter 2023): 395–411. Published by Johns Hopkins University Press.

6. I used ProjectMuse to conduct this search on May 18, 2021.

7. Pat Pinsent, *Children's Literature* (London: Palgrave Macmillan, 2016).

8. Carrie Hintz and Eric L. Tribunella, *Reading Children's Literature: A Critical Introduction* (Peterborough, ON: Broadview Press, 2019).

9. "CCBC Diversity Statistics FAQs," Cooperative Children's Book Center, University of Wisconsin–Madison, last updated April 3, 2024, https://ccbc.education.wisc .edu/category/diversity-stats-faqs/.

10. Crag Hill and Janine J. Darragh, "From Bootstraps to Hands-Up: A Multicultural Content Analysis of the Depiction of Poverty in Young Adult Literature," *Study and Scrutiny: Research in Young Adult Literature* 1, no. 2 (2016): 32, https://doi.org /10.15763/issn.2376-5275.2015.1.2.31-63.

11. Hill and Darragh, "Bootstraps to Hands-Up," 31.

12. Walter Benn Michaels, *The Trouble with Diversity: How We Learned to Love Identity and Ignore Inequality* (New York: Picador, 2016).

13. Michaels, *Trouble with Diversity*, 17.

14. MLA Job List, Modern Language Association, https://joblist.mla.org/jobs/?kw =american+literature. I conducted this search on September 23, 2022.

15. "Assistant Professor of American Literatures," MLA Job List, Modern Language Association, September 15, 2022, https://joblist.mla.org/job-details/6236/assistant -professor-of-american-literatures/?porder=Literature%2c+American&ix=7#top -pagination.

16. Nisi Shawl and Cynthia Ward, *Writing the Other: A Practical Approach* (Seattle: Aqueduct Press, 2005).

17. "About Us," The Fold, accessed November 5, 2024, https://thefoldcanada.org /about-us/.

18. "About Us," We Need Diverse Books, accessed November 5, 2024, https:// diversebooks.org/about-wndb/.

19. Smith, "Unmaking the White Default."

20. "The Hate U Give," *Kirkus Reviews*, review posted online on December 5, 2016, https://www.kirkusreviews.com/book-reviews/angie-thomas/hate-u-give/.

21. Smith, "Unmaking the White Default."

22. Amanda Michelle Gomez, "Politics and Prose Bookstore Employees Move to Unionize," *DCist*, December 14, 2021, https://dcist.com/story/21/12/14/politics-prose -bookstore-employees-unionize/.

23. Lee Fang, "Amazon Hired Koch-Backed Anti-Union Consultant to Fight Alabama Warehouse Organizing," *Intercept*, February 10, 2021, https://theintercept.com /2021/02/10/amazon-alabama-union-busting-koch/.

24. Adrian Liang, "Must-Read Books by Black Authors in Fall 2020," Amazon, July 10, 2020, https://www.amazon.com/amazonbookreview/read/B08CRZ9NS3.

25. Nel, *Was the Cat in the Hat Black?*, 229.

26. See under "Philip Nel" in "Kansas State Employees," Open the Books, 2023, https://www.openthebooks.com/kansas-state-employees/?F_Name_S=philip&F _OrderBy_S=Ascending&F_FieldName_S=name&pg=3; see under "Karin Westman," in "Kansas State Employees," Open the Books, 2023, https://www.openthebooks .com/kansas-state-employees/?F_Name_S=westman&Year_S=0. Accessed November 29, 2024.

27. Victor Wallis, "Intersectionality's Binding Agent: The Political Primacy of Class," *New Political Science* 37, no. 4 (November 2015): 604–619, https://doi.org/10.1080 /07393148.2015.1089032.

28. Michaels, *The Trouble with Diversity*, 17.

29. Erin Cooley et al., "Complex Intersections of Race and Class: Among Social Liberals, Learning about White Privilege Reduces Sympathy, Increases Blame, and Decreases External Attributions for White People Struggling With Poverty," *Journal of Experimental Psychology: General* 148, no. 12 (2019): 2218–2228, https://doi.org /10.1037/xge0000605. For the quotation from Cooley, see Zaid Jilani, "Telling Liberals about 'White Privilege' Doesn't Make Them More Empathetic," *National Review*, May 29, 2019, https://www.nationalreview.com/2019/05/study-telling-liberals-about -white-privilege-reduces-empathy-poor-whites/.

30. "Submit," *New Orleans Review*, accessed November 5, 2024, https://www.newor leansreview.org/submit/.

31. "Submit," *Portland Review*, accessed November 5, 2024, https://portlandreview .org/submit/.

32. "General Submissions (PRINT)," *Black Warrior Review*, accessed November 5, 2024, https://bwr.ua.edu/submit/guidelines/.

33. "How to Submit to *SHR*," *Southern Humanities Review*, accessed November 5, 2024, http://www.southernhumanitiesreview.com/submit.html; "Submit," *Hayden's Ferry Review*, accessed November 5, 2024, http://haydensferryreview.com/submit.

34. Stephanie Jones, "Grass Houses: Representations and Reinventions of Social Class Through Children's Literature," *Journal of Language and Literacy Education* 4, no. 2 (2008): 43, available at http://jolle.coe.uga.edu/archive/2008/representations.pdf.

35. "Kait Feldmann," Manuscript Wish List, accessed November 5, 2024, https://www.manuscriptwishlist.com/mswl-post/kait-feldmann/.

36. Cooper, "Black Pop Culture?"

37. For the classic study, see Richard Sennett and Jonathan Cobb, *The Hidden Injuries of Class* (New York: Knopf, 1972).

38. Rob Henderson, "'Luxury Beliefs' Are the Latest Status Symbol for Rich Americans," *New York Post*, August 17, 2019, https://nypost.com/2019/08/17/luxury-beliefs-are-the-latest-status-symbol-for-rich-americans/.

39. "Writing, Editing, and Publishing Indigenous Stories," University of Alberta Library, April 8, 2024, https://guides.library.ualberta.ca/c.php?g=708820&p=5049650.

40. Shapiro, "Sensitivity Reader."

41. Shapiro, "Sensitivity Reader."

42. James Tilton, "Sensitivity Readers! What Are They Good For? (A Lot.)," *Publishers Weekly*, August 10, 2018, https://www.publishersweekly.com/pw/by-topic/columns-and-blogs/soapbox/article/77726-sensitivity-readers-what-are-they-good-for-a-lot.html.

43. Pierre Bourdieu, "The Forms of Capital," in *Cultural Theory: An Anthology*, edited by Imre Szeman and Timothy Kaposy (Hoboken, NJ: Wiley-Blackwell, 2011), 89. For a longer discussion, see Pierre Bourdieu, *Distinction: A Social Critique of the Judgement of Taste*, translated by Richard Nice (Cambridge, MA: Harvard University Press, 1987).

44. Allan and Burridge, *Forbidden Words*, 37.

45. Here, I use the title listed on Google. Kristen Lopez, "'The Stand': CBS All Access Series Highlights Stephen King's Disability Stereotypes," *IndieWire*, December 30, 2020, https://www.indiewire.com/features/general/the-stand-ableism-stephen-king1234607039/.

46. Mya Nunnally, "There's a Weird, Sexist Problem in Fantasy That We Need to Talk About," *Book Riot*, January 21, 2019, https://bookriot.com/sexist-problem-in-fantasy/.

47. For a much deeper dive into the sociology of snobbery, and its intersections with the various forms of capital, I recommend Morgan, *Snobbery*, 4, 56, 66. As Morgan puts it, snobbery "is one of the ways in which class differences are expressed and reproduced," and "in the discussion of cultural capital, issues of moral capital

are rarely far behind." Given the fetish for "authenticity" in the Sensitivity Era, it is interesting that Morgan believes "the feeling that you, unlike some others, are being 'authentic' is one of the hallmarks of contemporary snobbery."

48. Catherine Lieu, *Virtue Hoarders: The Case against the Professional Managerial Class* (Minneapolis: University of Minnesota Press, 2021), 2, 75.

49. "Submit," *Folio*, accessed November 5, 2024, https://foliolitjournal.submittable .com/submit.

50. Jessica Pressman, *Bookishness: Loving Books in a Digital Age* (New York: Columbia University Press, 2020), 12.

51. For the classic study, see Goffman, *The Presentation of Self*.

52. Sternheimer, *Pop Culture Panics*, 7.

53. Shapiro, "Sensitivity Reader."

54. Quoted in Keeanga-Yamahtta Taylor, *From #BlackLivesMatter to Black Liberation* (Chicago: Haymarket Books, 2016), 75.

55. Rakesh Kochhar and Anthony Cilluffo "Income Inequality in the U.S. Is Rising Most Rapidly among Asians," Pew Research Center, July 12, 2018, https://www .pewresearch.org/social-trends/2018/07/12/income-inequality-in-the-u-s-is-rising -most-rapidly-among-asians/.

56. Musa al-Gharbi, "White Men Swung to Biden. Trump Made Gains with Black and Latino Voters. Why?" *Guardian*, November 14, 2020, https://www.theguardian .com/commentisfree/2020/nov/14/joe-biden-trump-black-latino-republicans.

57. Quoted in Eric Bradner, Sarah Mucha and Arlette Saenz, "Biden: 'If You Have a Problem Figuring Out Whether You're for Me or Trump, Then You Ain't Black,'" *CNN*, May 22, 2020, https://www.cnn.com/2020/05/22/politics/biden-charlamagne -tha-god-you-aint-black/index.html.

58. Paul Gilroy, *The Black Atlantic: Modernity and Double Consciousness* (Cambridge, MA: Harvard University Press, 1993), 32–33.

59. Paul Gilroy, *Against Race: Imagining Political Culture Beyond the Color Line* (Cambridge, MA: Harvard University Press, 2000), 214.

60. Cooper, "Black Pop Culture?"

61. Constance Grady, "Do the Soaring Sales of Anti-Racism Books Signal a True Cultural Shift?," *Vox*, June 11, 2020, https://www.vox.com/culture/2020/6/11/21288021 /anti-racism-books-reading-list-sales-figures.

62. Maria Bustillos, "Billion-Dollar Book Companies Are Ripping Off Public Schools," *New Republic*, December 22, 2020, https://newrepublic.com/article/160649 /book-companies-follett-overcharge-public-schools.

63. "Black Lives Matter," Penguin Random House Canada, accessed November 5, 2024, https://www.penguinrandomhouse.ca/news/1788/black-lives-matter-our-anti-racism-action-and-accountability-plan.

64. Nate Hochman, "Ibram X. Kendi Made about $541 a Minute for a Speech at the University of Virginia," *National Review*, February 9, 2022, https://www.nationalre view.com/corner/ibram-x-kendi-made-about-541-a-minute-for-a-speech-at-the -university-of-virginia/.

65. Akilah Johnson, "That Was No Typo: The Median Net Worth of Black Bostonians Really Is $8," *Boston Globe*, December 11, 2017, https://www.bostonglobe.com /metro/2017/12/11/that-was-typo-the-median-net-worth-black-bostonians-really /ze5kxC1jJelx24M3pugFFN/story.html.

66. "Ibram X Kendi Tickets," vividseats, accessed November 5, 2024, https://www .vividseats.com/ibram-x-kendi-tickets-boston-wilbur-theatre-6-27-2022--theater-public -speaking/production/3938260.

67. Z. Z. Packer, "Preacher of the New Antiracist Gospel," *GQ*, August 20, 2020, https://www.gq.com/story/ibram-x-kendi-antiracism-scholar-profile.

68. Packer, "Preacher."

69. Bruce A. Dixon, "Made Man in a Blue Vest," *Black Agenda Report*, July 6, 2016, https://blackagendareport.com/made-man-in-blue-vest.

70. McWhorter, *Woke Racism*. 33.

71. Gilroy, *Against Race*, 214.

72. bell hooks, *Where We Stand: Class Matters* (New York: Routledge, 2000), 119.

73. Quoted in Adolph Reed Jr., "*Django Unchained*, or, *The Help*: How 'Cultural Politics' Is Worse Than No Politics at All, and Why," *nonsite*, February 25, 2013, https:// nonsite.org/django-unchained-or-the-help-how-cultural-politics-is-worse-than-no -politics-at-all-and-why/.

74. Mark McGurl, *The Program Era: Postwar Fiction and the Rise of Creative Writing* (Cambridge, MA: Harvard University Press, 2011), 167.

75. Paul Elie, "How Racist Was Flannery O'Connor?" *New Yorker*, June 15, 2020, https://www.newyorker.com/magazine/2020/06/22/how-racist-was-flannery-oconnor.

76. Miller, *Impostors*, 25, 28.

77. bell hooks, *Where We Stand*, 94.

78. Shamus Khan, *Privilege: The Making of an Adolescent Elite at St. Paul's School* (Princeton, NJ: Princeton University Press, 2013), 195.

79. Michael Billig, *Learn to Write Badly: How to Succeed in the Social Sciences* (Cambridge: Cambridge University Press, 2013), 13, 26.

80. Nel, *Was the Cat in the Hat Black?*, 218.

81. Quoted in Meghan McCarty Carino, "Implicit Bias Training for Police Officers Is Big Business," *Marketplace*, June 2, 2020, https://www.marketplace.org/2020/06/02/police-officers-implicit-bias-training/.

82. Elisa Gall, "Being a 'Person of One's Time' in 2020," *Reading While White*, May 31, 2020, http://readingwhilewhite.blogspot.com/2020/05/being-person-of-ones-time-in-2020.html.

83. For a critical discussion of scholarship on "whiteness," see *International Labor and Working-Class History*, issue 60, which includes contributions from Eric Arnesen, Eric Foner, Victoria C. Hattam, and others. As historian Judith Stein puts it, "*ILWCH* decided to examine whiteness because we thought that the body of work associated with the idea had not been critically assessed." Judith Stein, "Whiteness and United States History: An Assessment," *International Labor and Working-Class History* 60 (Fall 2021): 1–2, https://www.jstor.org/stable/27672731. See also Cedric Johnson, "The Wages of Roediger: Why Three Decades of Whiteness Studies Has Not Produced the Left We Need," *nonsite*, September 9, 2019, https://nonsite.org/the-wages-of-roediger-why-three-decades-of-whiteness-studies-has-not-produced-the-left-we-need/.

84. "Friends of the Center," Center for Teaching Through Children's Books, accessed November 5, 2024, http://cttcb.org/partners.

85. For more on academia in the era of Twitter, I recommend Gordon Fraser, "The Twitterization of the Academic Mind," *Chronicle of Higher Education*, March 22, 2019, https://www.chronicle.com/article/the-twitterization-of-the-academic-mind/.

86. Melissa Chen (@MsMelChen), "The irony is that the people who decry the 'centering of whiteness' are precisely the ones centering whiteness because they see white supremacy/privilege . . ." X, March 12, 2021, https://x.com/MsMelChen/status/1370508761182302210.

87. Cedrick-Michael Simmons, "How Do We Make Sure That Black Students Matter?" Substack, 2020 and "I'm Black and Afraid of 'White Fragility,'" *Bellows*, 2020, https://thebellows.org/im-black-and-afraid-of-white-fragility-the-bellows-3/.

88. Westenfeld, "Dr. Seuss Expert."

89. Amélie Wen Zhao, *Blood Heir* (New York: Delacorte Press, 2019), inside cover, and Amélie Wen Zhao, *Red Tigress* (New York: Delacorte Press, 2021), inside cover.

90. For a related discussion, see Carl Rhodes, *Woke Capitalism: How Corporate Morality Is Sabotaging Democracy* (Bristol: Bristol University Press, 2022), 29–30. In his chapter "The Woke Reversal," Rhodes looks at the etymology of "woke." Although there is a "long tradition of African American culture that has used the metaphor of being awake to signal a general awareness of one's sociopolitical context," "woke" is now used as "a putdown aimed at a vapid politically correct morality."

91. Boyer and Nissenbaum, *Salem Possessed*.

92. Elizabeth Holden (@ElizabethH_WI), "I don't typically tweet about agents' rejections (as I also don't tweet about requests). But I received a rejection on a full today . . ." X, February 17, 2022, https://x.com/ElizabethH_WI/status/149446595 8961950720.

93. Evelyn Silver (@EternalEvelyn), "As a bi woman who is married to a man and who also writes queer romance, this makes me irrationally angry. Nonsense like this makes me feel the need to scream . . ." X, February 18, 2022, https://x.com /EternalEvelyn/status/1494734888091758602.

94. Lauren Spieller (@laurenspieller), "I really, really hate that we're in a moment that involves demanding people share their personal business/ identity/ trauma as a way of defending their rights . . ." X, February 1, 2020, https://x.com/laurenspieller /status/1223742438759596034.

95. JRE, "Open Letter to Haymarket Books and the Poetry Community," *Medium*, April 8, 2021, https://riceevans.medium.com/open-letter-to-haymarket-books-and -the-poetry-community-d0863dde9d9c.

96. John Loeppky, "Haymarket Anthology 'Against Ableism' Comes Under Scrutiny," *Publishers Weekly*, April 13, 2021, https://www.publishersweekly.com/pw/by -topic/industry-news/publisher-news/article/86068-haymarket-anthology-against -ableism-comes-under-scrutiny.html.

97. Shoshana Zuboff, *The Age of Surveillance Capitalism: The Fight for a Human Future at the New Frontier of Power* (New York: Hachette, 2019).

98. "FAQs," *Reading While White*, accessed November 5, 2024, http://readingwhile white.blogspot.com/p/faq.html.

99. For a related discussion, see Cooper, "Black Pop Culture?"

100. Nancy Fraser, *Fortunes of Feminism: From State-Managed Capitalism to Neoliberal Crisis* (New York: Verso Books, 2013), 162–171.

101. For a related discussion see Jesse Singal, *The Quick Fix: Why Fad Psychology Can't Cure Our Social Ills* (New York: Farrar, Straus and Giroux, 2021), 173–210.

102. hooks, *Where We Stand*, 7.

103. Keeanga-Yamahtta Taylor, "No Time for Despair," *Jacobin*, January 28, 2017, https://jacobin.com/2017/01/trump-black-lives-racism-sexism-anti-inauguration.

104. "Roxane Gay on Financial Independence: 'The Most Important Thing a Woman Can Do for Herself,'" *Wealthsimple Magazine*, September 28, 2018, https:// www.wealthsimple.com/en-ca/magazine/roxane-gay.

105. Charlotte Alter, "Secrets of Super Siblings," *Time*, August 25, 2016, https:// time.com/magazine/us/4465719/september-5th-2016-vol-188-no-9-u-s/.

106. Todd Gitlin, *The Twilight of Common Dreams: Why America Is Wracked by Culture Wars* (New York: Metropolitan Books, 1995), 126.

107. Karl Marx, "The Eighteenth Brumaire of Louis Bonaparte," in *Karl Marx: Selected Writings*, 2nd ed., edited by David McLellan (Oxford: Oxford University Press, 2003), 329.

108. Kevin McCarthy (@SpeakerMcCarthy), "I still like Dr. Seuss, so I decided to read Green Eggs and Ham. RT if you still like him too!" X, March 5, 2021, https://x .com/SpeakerMcCarthy/status/1368011754425483265.

109. Ted Cruz (@tedcruz), "Could Biden try to ban my book next? One Vote Away was the #1 Bestseller on Amazon a couple of months ago . . . maybe Joe could get it back there? GET it HERE: http://onevoteaway.com," X, March 3, 2021, https://x .com/tedcruz/status/1367148211169857541.

110. Ariel Shapiro, "How Much Have the Culture Wars Earned Dr. Seuss This Year? As It Turns Out, A 'Whole Awful Lot,'" *Forbes*, April 8, 2021, https://www.forbes.com /sites/arielshapiro/2021/04/08/how-much-have-the-culture-wars-earned-dr-seuss -this-year-as-it-turns-out-a-whole-awful-lot.

111. Representative John Joyce, MD, "Joyce Introduces GRINCH Act to Safeguard Students, Cherished Books from Cancel Culture," US House of Representatives, https://johnjoyce.house.gov/media/press-releases/joyce-introduces-grinch-act-safe guard-students-cherished-books-cancel-culture.

112. Joseph Wulfsohn, "Fox News Reaches Highest Viewership in Network's History, Topping MSNBC, CNN in 2020," *Fox News*, February 25, 2020, https://www .foxnews.com/media/highest-viewership-network-history-msnbc-cnn-2020.

113. Alex Pareene, "The Case for More Canceling," *New Republic*, April 9, 2021, https://newrepublic.com/article/161999/cancel-culture-conservatives-seuss.

114. Chris Riotta, "Fox News' Dr Seuss Obsession Enters Week Three with Warning That America Is 'Going Down a Dark Road,'" *Independent*, March 5, 2021, https://www .the-independent.com/news/world/americas/us-politics/fox-news-dr-seuss-cancel -culture-republicans-priorities-b1817601.html.

115. Lucian Gideon Conway III, Meredith A. Repke, and Shannon C. Houck, "Donald Trump as a Cultural Revolt Against Perceived Communication Restriction: Priming Political Correctness Norms Causes More Trump Support," *Journal of Social and Political Psychology* 5, no. 1 (May 2017): 244–259, https://doi.org/10.5964/jspp .v5i1.732.

116. Conway et al., "Donald Trump," 244.

117. Conway et al.

118. Conway et al., 250.

119. Harry Enten, "Why the GOP's Cancel Culture Pitch Is Good Politics," *CNN*, March 13, 2021, https://www.cnn.com/2021/03/13/politics/gop-cancel-culture-analysis /index.html.

120. Stephen Hawkins et al., *Hidden Tribes: A Study of America's Polarized Landscape* (New York: More in Common, 2018), 98, https://hiddentribes.us/media/qfpekz4g /hidden_tribes_report.pdf.

121. "Monthly Harvard-Harris Poll: February 2021," Harvard's Center for American Political Studies and Harris Insights and Analytics, February 3, 2021, https://harvard harrispoll.com/wp-content/uploads/2021/03/February2021_HHP_Topline_RV.pdf; Declan Garvey, "'How Is That Conservative?'" *Dispatch*, May 4, 2021, https://thedis patch.com/article/how-is-that-conservative/.

122. "Monthly Harvard-Harris Poll."

123. Editorial Board, "America Has a Free Speech Problem," *New York Times*, March 8, 2022, https://www.nytimes.com/2022/03/18/opinion/cancel-culture-free-speech -poll.html.

124. "2020 College Free Speech Rankings," College Pulse, 2020, https://marketplace .collegepulse.com/img/2020_college_free_speech_rankings.pdf.

125. "2021 College Free Speech Rankings," College Pulse, Foundation for Individual Rights and Expression, and RealClear Education, 2021, https://reports.collegepulse .com/college-free-speech-rankings-2021.
   Interestingly, "two thirds of students (66%) say it is acceptable to shout down a speaker to prevent them from speaking on campus, and almost one in four (23%) say it is acceptable to use violence to stop a campus speech."

126. "2020 College Free Speech Rankings," Foundation for Individual Rights in Education, College Pulse, and RealClearEducation, 2020, https://www.thefire.org /research-learn/2020-college-free-speech-rankings.

127. Rosenfield, "Toxic Drama."

128. Ryan Holiday, *Trust Me, I'm Lying: Confessions of a Media Manipulator* (New York: Penguin, 2017), 19.

129. Arlie Russell Hochschild, *Strangers in Their Own Land: Anger and Mourning on the American Right* (New York: New Press, 2018), 227.

130. Quoted in Molly Schwartz, "Roxane Gay Says Cancel Culture Does Not Exist," *Mother Jones*, March 5, 2021, https://www.motherjones.com/media/2021/03/roxane -gay-says-cancel-culture-does-not-exist/.

131. Philip Nel, "Breaking Up with Your Favorite Racist Childhood Classic Books," *Washington Post*, May 16, 2021, https://www.washingtonpost.com/education/2021 /05/16/breaking-up-with-racist-childrens-books/.

132. Dubréuil, "Nonconforming."

133. Orwell, *1984*, 51–52.

134. J. M. Coetzee, *Giving Offense: Essays on Censorship* (Chicago: University of Chicago Press, 1996), 34.

135. Eli Yokley, "More Gen Zers Have Negative Views about Capitalism Than of Critical Race Theory," July 8, 2021, Morning Consult, https://morningconsult.com /2021/07/08/gen-z-critical-race-theory-polling/.

136. The Learning Network, "What Students Are Saying about Cancel Culture, Friendly Celebrity Battles and Finding Escape," *New York Times*, November 19, 2020, https://www.nytimes.com/2020/11/19/learning/what-students-are-saying-about -cancel-culture-friendly-celebrity-battles-and-finding-escape.html.

137. Yokley, "More Gen Zers."

138. Aliza Vigderman, "5 Shocking Cyberbullying Facts That Every Parent Should Know," Security, September 12, 2022, https://www.security.org/digital-safety/cyber bullying-covid/#references.

139. "UNICEF Poll: More Than a Third Of Young People in 30 Countries Report Being a Victim of Online Bullying," UNICEF, September 3, 2019, https://www.unicef .org/press-releases/unicef-poll-more-third-young-people-30-countries-report-being -victim-online-bullying.

140. Sierra Elmore, quoted in Rosenfield, "Toxic Drama."

141. Jamie Ballard, "Most Americans Say Cancel Culture Is a Big Problem," YouGov, July 28, 2020, https://today.yougov.com/topics/entertainment/articles-reports/2020 /07/28/cancel-culture-yahoo-news-poll-data.

142. Quoted in Garvey, "'How Is That Conservative?'"

143. Robby Soave, *Panic Attack: Young Radicals in the Age of Trump* (New York: All Point Books, 2019), 240.

144. Angela Nagle, *Kill All Normies: Online Culture Wars from 4Chan and Tumblr to Trump and the Alt-Right* (Alresford, UK: Zero Books, 2017), 73.

145. Nagle, *Kill All Normies*, 9.

146. Nagle.

147. Quoted in Whitney Phillips, *This Is Why We Can't Have Nice Things: Mapping the Relationship Between Online Trolling and Mainstream Culture* (Cambridge, MA: MIT Press, 2015), 61.

148. Richard Fausset, "A Voice of Hate in America's Heartland," *New York Times*, November 25, 2017, https://www.nytimes.com/2017/11/25/us/ohio-hovater-white -nationalist.html.

149. "4Chan.Org," SimilarWeb, accessed November 6, 2024, https://www.similar web.com/website/4chan.org/#overview.

150. Becca Lewis and Alice E. Marwick, "Media Manipulation and Disinformation Online," Data & Society, May 15, 2017, https://datasociety.net/library/media -manipulation-and-disinfo-online/.

151. Amber A'Lee Frost, "The Necessity of Political Vulgarity," *Current Affairs*, August 25, 2016, https://www.currentaffairs.org/news/2016/08/the-necessity-of-poli tical-vulgarity.

152. Michael Brooks, *Against the Web: A Cosmopolitan Answer to the New Right* (Alresford, UK: Zero Books, 2020). Jia Tolentino, "What Will Become of the Dirtbag Left," *New Yorker*, November 18, 2016, https://www.newyorker.com/culture/persons-of -interest/what-will-become-of-the-dirtbag-left. For an example of this style of left humor, I recommend *The Michael Brooks Show*, as seen on "Re-living Joe Rogan's Incredulity at Jordan Peterson's Cider Trauma," YouTube video, 9:24, October 3, 2018, https://youtu.be/p1WNrnsfb44.

153. Matt Miller, "Have We Finally Grown Out of Thinking *Fight Club* Is a Good Movie?," *Esquire*, October 15, 2019, https://www.esquire.com/entertainment/movies /a29463962/fight-club-bad-20th-anniversary-analysis-essay/.

154. Nagle, *Kill All Normies*, 19.

155. Nagle.

156. Hochschild, *Strangers*, 227; Conway et al., "Donald Trump," 244; Nagle, *Kill All Normies*, 5.

157. Matt Sienkiewicz and Nick Marx, *That's Not Funny: How the Right Makes Comedy Work for Them* (Berkeley: University of California Press, 2022), 2.

158. Nagle, *Kill All Normies*, 80.

159. Conway et al., "Donald Trump," 245.

160. Conway et al.

161. In more ways than one, Andrew Doyle is the successor to a satirical tradition in English letters that dates back to the Martin Marprelate tracts of the late sixteenth century. Martin, another pseudonymous writer, also used direct address, racy insinuations, taunts, and wordplay as he ridiculed the opposition. Like Jonathan Swift, Lord Byron, and other satirists, Martin recognized the import of irreverence. By contrast, PC might be considered the antipode of this tradition. Joseph L. Black, "The Marprelate Controversy," in *The Oxford Handbook of English Prose 1500–1640*, edited by Andrew Hadfield (Oxford: Oxford University Press, 2013), 544–559.

162. Titania McGrath, *Woke: A Guide to Social Justice* (London: Constable, 2019), 2, 7.

163. Osita Nwanevu, "The 'Cancel Culture' Con," *New Republic*, September 23, 2019, https://newrepublic.com/article/155141/cancel-culture-con-dave-chappelle-shane -gillis.

164. Garvey, "'How Is That Conservative?'"

165. For empirical research on the relationship between conservatism and nostalgia, see Joris Lammers and Matt Baldwin, "Past-Focused Temporal Communication Overcomes Conservatives' Resistance to Liberal Political Ideas," *Journal of Personality and Social Psychology* 14, no. 4 (April 2018): 599. As these researchers argue, "Conservatives are more prone to warm, affectionate, and nostalgic feelings for past society." By framing issues with a focus on the past, liberals can use this to their advantage.

166. American Library Association Office for Intellectual Freedom, https://www.ala .org/aboutala/offices/oif.

167. "Frequently Challenged Books Top 10," American Library Association, accessed November 5, 2024, http://www.ala.org/advocacy/bbooks/frequentlychallengedbooks /top10.

168. *Guardian News*, "Barack Obama Takes On 'Woke' Call-Out Culture: 'That's Not Activism,'" YouTube video, 1:53, October 30, 2019, https://youtu.be/qaHLd8de6nM.

169. In *Private Truths, Public Lies: The Social Consequences of Preference Falsification*, Timur Kuran examines what happens when people misrepresent their preferences in response to social pressure. One consequence of preference falsification is that it can grant a facade of stability to unstable norms. In particular, see Kuran's sixteenth chapter, "The Fall of Communism and Other Sudden Overturns," in which he argues that "systemic processes rooted in preference falsification kept us from foreseeing the uprisings of 1989." Kuran, *Private Truths, Public Lies: The Social Consequences of Preference Falsification* (Cambridge, MA: Harvard University Press, 1997), 262.

170. Khaleda Rahman, "Jordan Peterson's New Book Release Prompts Tears, Outcry Among Publisher's Staff," *Newsweek*, November 25, 2020, https://www.newsweek.com /jordan-peterson-book-prompts-tears-publishing-staff-1550114.

171. Quoted in Alison Flood, "Mike Pence's Publisher Refuses to Cancel Memoir After Staff Protest," *Guardian*, April 21, 2021, https://www.theguardian.com/books/2021 /apr/21/mike-pences-publisher-refuses-to-cancel-memoir-after-staff-protest.

172. Julia Marnin, "Josh Hawley's Book 'Tyranny of Big Tech' No. 1 Bestseller on Amazon in Three Categories," *Newsweek*, May 7, 2021, https://www.newsweek.com /josh-hawleys-book-tyranny-big-tech-no-1-bestseller-amazon-three-categories-1589677.

173. Robby Soave, "Antifa Demands Powell's Stop Selling Andy Ngo's Book, Forces Store to Close Early," *Reason*, January 11, 2021, https://reason.com/2021/01/11 /powells-books-antifa-andy-ngo-store-censorship/.

174. "Pen America Supports Powell's Decision to Continue Selling Controversial Book," PEN America, January 15, 2021, https://pen.org/press-release/pen-america -supports-powells-decision-to-continue-selling-controversial-book/.

175. Jim Edwards, "The 10 Biggest Lies Told by American Apparel's Top PR Man," *Business Insider*, August 2, 2012, https://www.businessinsider.com/the-10-biggest-lies -told-by-american-apparels-top-pr-man-2012-8.

176. Coetzee, *Giving Offense*, 43.

177. Coetzee, 44.

Chapter 4

1. I used Project MUSE to conduct this search on April 8, 2021.

2. I used Project MUSE to conduct this search on November 19, 2021.

3. Khalid and Snyder, "Poverty of the Imagination."

4. Philip Smith, "Paddington Bear and the Erasure of Difference," *Children's Literature Association Quarterly* 45, no. 1 (Spring 2020): 25–42, https://muse.jhu.edu/pub /1/article/749929.

5. To see what happens to scholars with unpopular positions, I recommend work by Eric Cheyfitz, Michael Burawoy, Michael Bérubé, and Alice Dreger. Just as debut novelists are the biggest targets in children's and YA literature, scholars without tenure are some of the biggest targets in academia. Often, their critics focus on minor mistakes of little to no consequence to the work's main arguments, who the work did not cite (as if there is a doctrinal literature that one must cite), and inflated accusations that a work causes "harm." Similarly, critics claim that misrepresentation has occurred in places where a scholar offered an interpretation they dislike. At this point, the criticism is so formulaic that an algorithm could produce it. Eric Cheyfitz, "Framing Ward Churchill: The Political Construction of Research Misconduct," *Works and Days* 26–27, nos. 51/52 and 53/54 (2008–2009): 231–252; Michael Burawoy, "Empiricism and Its Fallacies," *Contexts* 18, no. 1 (March 2019), https://doi.org/10.1177/1536504219830677; Michael Bérubé, "The Way We Review Now," *PMLA* 133, no. 1 (January 2018): 132–138, https://doi.org/10.1632 /pmla.2018.133.1.132; Alice Dreger, *Galileo's Middle Finger: Heretics, Activists, and One Scholar's Search for Justice* (New York: Penguin Books, 2016).

6. Quoted in Rosenfield, "Toxic Drama."

7. Rosenfield, "Toxic Drama."

8. McGurl, *The Program Era*, 24–25.

9. Poe Ballantine, "Free Rent at the Totalitarian Hotel," in *The Best American Essays 2013*, edited by Cheryl Strayed (Boston: Houghton Mifflin Harcourt, 2013), 9.

10. Lukianoff and Haidt, *Coddling*, 5–6.

11. Lukianoff and Haidt, 24.

12. For example, at the University of California, diversity-related administration expanded amid a recession and state-budget cuts. See Campbell and Manning, *Rise of Victimhood Culture*, 261; Jason Brennan and Phillip Magness, *Cracks in the Ivory Tower: The Moral Mess of Higher Education* (Oxford: Oxford University Press, 2019), 39–41, 233–234.

13. Emma Whitford, "At Williams, a Play in Part about Race Called Off Before Opening Night," *Inside Higher Ed*, December 6, 2018, https://www.insidehighered.com/news/2018/12/07/williams-college-cancels-new-play-after-students-express-concerns-about-content.

14. Misha Chowdhury, "Dear Beast Thing cast and creative team," Facebook, November 12, 2018, https://web.archive.org/web/20200601041948/https:/www.facebook.com/notes/misha-chowdhury/dear-beast-thing-cast-and-creative-team/10104224214182713/.

15. Quoted in Darragh Roche, "College Music Professor Steps Down after Showing Students 'Blackface' Othello," *Newsweek*, October 9, 2021, https://www.newsweek.com/college-music-professor-steps-down-students-blackface-othello-1637274.

16. Schapiro and Morson, *Minds Wide Shut*, 203.

17. Deborah Appleman, "Triggers, Texts, and Changing Times: Teaching Literature in the 21st Century," *Research in the Teaching of English* 54, no. 1 (August 2019): 82, https://www.jstor.org/stable/26802773.

18. Troy Closson et al., "Addressing The Daily's coverage of Sessions Protests," *Daily Northwestern*, November 11, 2019, https://dailynorthwestern.com/2019/11/10/opinion/addressing-the-dailys-coverage-of-sessions-protests/.

19. Nico Perrino, "Laura Kipnis' Second 'Title IX Inquisition,'" Foundation for Individual Rights and Expression, September 20, 2017, https://www.thefire.org/news/laura-kipnis-second-title-ix-inquisition.

20. "Faculty Letter," Google Docs, July 4, 2020, https://docs.google.com/forms/d/e/1FAIpQLSfPmfeDKBi25_7rUTKkhZ3cyMICQicp05ReVaeBpEdYUCkyIA/viewform.

21. Maddy Foley, "Why Joyce Carol Oates's Comments about 'Sensitivity Readers' Are So Wrong," *Bustle*, December 28, 2017, https://www.bustle.com/p/joyce-carol-oatess-comments-on-sensitivity-readers-reveal-a-deep-misunderstanding-in-the-literary-community-7701607.

22. Jo, "Discussion: My Thoughts on Sensitivity Readers and the Censorship Argument," Once Upon a Bookcase, January, 2018, http://www.onceuponabookcase.co.uk/2018/01/my-thoughts-on-sensitivity-readers-and.html.

23. Quoted in Paige Allen, "Magazine Editor Resigns Over Dickman's Controversial Poem, as U. Community Weighs In," *The Daily Princetonian*, August 17, 2020, https:// www.dailyprincetonian.com/article/2020/08/princeton-michael-dickman-scholls -ferry-rd-poetry.

24. Quoted in McGurl, *The Program Era*, 24.

25. Jack Halberstam, "Jack Halberstam: Queers Create Better Models of Success," interview by Sinclair Sexsmith, Lambda Literary, February 1, 2012, https://lambda literary.org/2012/02/jack-halberstam-queers-create-better-models-of-success/.

26. Halberstam, "You Are Triggering Me!".

27. Irvine, *Slap in the Face*, ix.

28. McWhorter, *Woke Racism*, xiv.

29. Ken Kesey, *One Flew over the Cuckoo's Nest* (New York: Penguin Putnam Inc, 2002), 51. For a discussion of Kesey's time at Stanford, particularly his antagonistic relationship with the creative writing program's founder, Wallace Stegner, see McGurl, *The Program Era*.

30. Meghan Daum, "Who Killed Creative Writing?" Substack, October 16, 2022, https://meghandaum.substack.com/p/who-killed-creative-writing.

31. Vladimir Nabokov, *Strong Opinions* (New York: Knopf, 1990), 114.

32. Quoted in Rachel Johnson, "Would Any Publisher Dare to Print *Lolita* Now?" *Spectator Australia*, March 7, 2019, https://www.spectator.com.au/2019/03/would -any-publisher-dare-to-print-lolita-now/.

33. "Contests," *Hunger Mountain Review*, accessed November 5, 2024, https://hun germtn.org/contests/.

34. "Submit," *Redivider*, accessed November 5, 2024, https://redivider.submittable .com/submit.

35. "Submit," *Denver Quarterly*, accessed November 5, 2024, https://denverquarterly .submittable.com/submit.

36. "Submit," *Passages North*, accessed November 5, 2024, https://passagesnorth .submittable.com/submit.

37. Naomi Toftness, *School Library Journal*, February 2023, 95.

38. Payton J. Jones, Benjamin W. Bellet, and Richard J. McNally, "Helping or Harming? The Effect of Trigger Warnings on Individuals with Trauma Histories," *Clinical Psychological Science* 8, no. 5 (June 2020): 905, https://doi.org/10.1177/216770262 0921341.

39. Lukianoff and Haidt, *Coddling*, 29.

40. "About Us," Consumer Product Safety Commission, accessed November 5, 2024, https://www.cpsc.gov/About-CPSC.

41. William J. Brady et al., "An Ideological Asymmetry in the Diffusion of Moralized Content on Social Media Among Political Leaders," *Journal of Experimental Psychology* 148, no. 10 (October 2019): 1802–1813, https://doi.org/10.1037/xge0000532. For related research, see C. Heath, C. Bell, and E. Sternberg, "Emotional Selection in Memes: The Case of Urban Legends," *Journal of Personality and Social Psychology* 81, no. 6 (2001): 1028–1041, https://doi.org/10.1037/0022-3514.81.6.1028.

42. Sternheimer, *Pop Culture Panics*, 136.

43. Quoted in Childress, *Under the Cover*, 173.

44. Bradbury, *Fahrenheit 451*, 85, 134.

45. David Sedaris, *The Best of Me* (Boston: Little, Brown and Company, 2020), 4.

46. In another example of people confusing fictional characters with their authors, people claimed that Burgess was in love with violence because his most famous work, *A Clockwork Orange*, is told from the perspective of a fictional character who is in love with violence. By this standard, one should assume Thomas Harris, who wrote *The Silence of the Lambs*, loves the taste of human flesh. Burgess, *1985*, 35, 80.

47. In *Fahrenheit 451*, the classics are "cut to fifteen-minute radio shows, then cut again to fill a two-minute book column, winding up at last as a ten- or twelve-line dictionary resume." "Life is immediate," and this "flings off all unnecessary, time-wasting thought!" Above all, it eliminates "conflicting theory and thought." Bradbury, *Fahrenheit 451*, 52 53, 59.

48. Alter, "Debut Book."

49. Orwell, *1984*, 40.

50. Fernando M. Pinguelo and Timothy D. Cedrone, "Morals? Who Cares About Morals? An Examination of Morals Clauses in Talent Contracts and What Talent Needs to Know," *Journal of Sports and Entertainment Law* 19, no. 2 (2009), 354–355, https://papers.ssrn.com/sol3/papers.cfm?abstract_id=1471031.

51. Quoted in Rachel Kaufman, "Are You a Moral Author? HarperCollins Hopes So," *Adweek*, January 18, 2011, https://www.adweek.com/performance-marketing/are-you-a-moral-author-harpercollins-hopes-so/?itm_source=related_articles&itm_medium=position2.

52. Shulevitz, "Must Writers Be Moral?"

53. Quoted in Sian Pattenden, "Children's Writers, Don't Misbehave," *Guardian*, August 1, 2008, https://www.theguardian.com/books/booksblog/2008/aug/01/childrenswritersdontmisbeha.

54. https://www.societyofauthors.org/About-Us/Dignity-respect.

55. Nyberg, *Seal of Approval*, 37.

56. Greenwald, "New York Times Guild."

57. Quoted in Pamela B. Paresky, "The Apocalyptic Psychology of Mobs—and Media," *Psychology Today*, June 26, 2020, https://www.psychologytoday.com/us /blog/happiness-and-the-pursuit-leadership/202006/the-apocalyptic-psychology -mobs-and-media.

58. Hu, "Gut Check"; Colleen Flaherty, "Retracting a Bad Take on Female Mentor-ship," *Inside Higher Ed*, December 21, 2020, https://www.insidehighered.com/news /2020/12/22/retracting-bad-take-female-mentorship.

59. Quoted in Shulevitz, "Must Writers Be Moral?"

60. For an in-depth, insightful, and provocative discussion of news media, I recom-mend Batya Ungar-Sargon, *Bad News: How Woke Media Is Undermining Democracy* (New York: Encounter Books, 2021).

61. The Authors Guild, "Why We Oppose Morals Clauses in Book Contracts," *Authors Guild Bulletin* (Winter 2018–Spring 2019), 25.

62. Richard Curtis, "Are Morality Clauses Immoral? An Agent's Perspective," *Authors Guild Bulletin*, Winter 2018–Spring 2019: 26.

63. Quoted in Garvey, "'How Is That Conservative?'"

64. Nadine Strossen, *HATE: Why We Should Resist It With Free Speech, Not Censorship* (Oxford: Oxford University Press, 2020), 87.

65. Adrian L. Jawort, "The Dangers of the Appropriation Critique" *Los Angeles Review of Books*, October 5, 2019, https://lareviewofbooks.org/article/the-dangers-of-the -appropriation-critique.

66. Quoted in Jawort, "Dangers of the Appropriation Critique."

67. Sternheimer, *Pop Culture Panics*, 49.

68. Quoted in Sternheimer, *Pop Culture Panics*, 57.

69. Joel Best, *Everyone's a Winner: Life in Our Congratulatory Culture* (Berkeley: Uni-versity of California Press, 2011), 122.

70. Paula Backscheider, *Daniel Defoe: His Life* (Baltimore: Johns Hopkins University Press, 1989), 116.

71. Electric Company Theatre, "Carmen Aguirre Video Essay Commissioned for the PuSh International Performing Arts Festival's Rally," YouTube video, 28:58, January 23, 2021, https://youtu.be/pht0zlyQj8w.

72. Presente.Org (@PresenteOrg), "Today, #DignidadLiteraria & @PresenteOrg won an unprecedented commitment from the leadership of @macmillanbooks to transform their publishing practices . . ." X, February 3, 2020, https://x.com/PresenteOrg/status/1224479038506291201.

73. David Bowles, "'American Dirt' Is Proof the Publishing Industry Is Broken," *New York Times*, January 27, 2020, https://www.nytimes.com/2020/01/27/opinion/american-dirt-book.html.

74. Jesse Singal, "David Bowles' Criticism of 'American Dirt' Is Riddled with Unfair Inaccuracies and Distortions," *Medium*, February 9, 2020, https://medium.com/@jesse.singal/david-bowles-criticism-of-american-dirt-is-riddled-with-unfair-inaccuracies-and-distortions-e40071cdf646.

75. "Dear Oprah Winfrey: 142 Writers Ask You to Reconsider *American Dirt*," *Literary Hub*, January 29, 2020, https://lithub.com/dear-oprah-winfrey-82-writers-ask-you-to-reconsider-american-dirt/.

76. Christian Toto, "American Dirt: 'Cancel Culture' Embraces Book Burning in the Digital Age," *The Hill*, February 3, 2020, https://thehill.com/opinion/technology/481147-american-dirt-cancel-culture-embraces-book-burning-in-the-digital-age/.

77. Richard Ovenden, *Burning the Books: A History of the Deliberate Destruction of Knowledge* (Cambridge, MA: Harvard University Press, 2020), 232.

78. Elizabeth Redden, "German University to Paint Over 'Sexist' Poem," *Inside Higher Ed*, January 25, 2018, https://www.insidehighered.com/quicktakes/2018/01/25/german-university-paint-over-sexist-poem.

79. Quoted in Armitstead, "Morality Clauses."

80. *The New Yorker*, "Chimamanda Ngozi Adichie on Liberal Cannibalism | The New Yorker Festival," YouTube video, 8:45, October 9, 2017, https://youtu.be/fo3OZWPOa3g.

81. Quoted in Lisa Allardice, "Chimamanda Ngozi Adichie: 'America Under Trump Felt Like a Personal Loss,'" *Guardian*, November 14, 2020, https://www.theguardian.com/books/2020/nov/14/chimamanda-ngozi-adichie-america-under-trump-felt-like-a-personal-loss.

82. Anis Shivani, "Notes on the Ascendency of Identity Politics in Literary Writing." *Subtropics* 23 (2017): 93–94, 78, 106.

83. George L. Kelling and James Q. Wilson, "Broken Windows: The Police and Neighborhood Safety," *Atlantic*, March 1, 1982, https://www.theatlantic.com/magazine/archive/1982/03/broken-windows/304465/.

84. Baculi, "YA Author Jessica Cluess."

85. The word "fundamentalism" "can be traced to American pamphlets, published between 1910 and 1915, in a series called 'The Fundamentals,'" financed by Lyman and Milton Stewart. "Fundamentalist" was coined in 1920 by Curtis Lee Laws, the editor of the *Watchman Examiner*. Schapiro and Morson, *Minds Wide Shut*, 13–14.

86. George Lakoff, *Don't Think of an Elephant! Know Your Values and Frame the Debate* (White River Junction, VT: Chelsea Green Publishing, 2014), 108–109.

87. Lakoff, *Don't Think of an Elephant!*, 164.

88. Orwell, *1984*, 210.

89. Quoted in Lila Shapiro, "Famous Authors Drag Student in Surreal YA Twitter Controversy," *Vulture*, November 16, 2019, https://www.vulture.com/2019/11/famous -authors-drag-student-in-ya-twitter-controversy.html.

90. Ruth Graham, "The 2017 College Grad Who Got Attacked by a Horde of YA Authors Had No Idea What She Was Getting Into," *Slate*, November 15, 2019, https://slate.com/culture/2019/11/sarah-dessen-ya-books-authors-brooke-nelson -social-media-attack.html.

91. Quoted in Graham, "Horde of YA Authors."

92. Quoted in Shapiro, "Famous Authors Drag Student."

93. Lewis Carroll, *Through the Looking Glass, And What Alice Found There* (Philadelphia: Henry Altemus Company, 1897), 123.

94. Thorstein Veblen, *The Theory of the Leisure Class* (Oxford: Oxford University Press, 2007).

95. Graham, "Horde of YA Authors."

96. Eichhorn, *End of Forgetting*, 143.

97. Orwell, *1984*, 133.

98. Bail, *Social Media Prism*.

99. For research on "selective disclosure," a phenomenon in which people are reluctant to voice disagreement, see Sarah K. Cowan and Delia Baldassarri, "'It Could Turn Ugly': Selective Disclosure of Attitudes in Political Discussion Networks," *Social Networks* 52 (January 2018): 1–17, https://doi.org/10.1016/j.socnet.2017.04.002.

For a discussion of "pluralistic ignorance," a potential consequence of selective disclosure, see Nathaniel Geiger and Janet K. Swim, "Climate of Silence: Pluralistic Ignorance as a Barrier to Climate Change," *Journal of Environmental Psychology* 47 (September 2016): 79–90, https://doi.org/10.1016/j.jenvp.2016.05.002.

Although neither of these papers concern the moral crusade over literature, their conclusions are pertinent to understanding the social dynamics and consequences of bystander silence. One consequence, pluralistic ignorance, suggests that people who disdain these degradation ceremonies might not be aware that so many other people disdain them, too.

100. Quoted in Blgsby, "Foreword," xx.

101. Quoted in Shapiro, "Famous Authors Drag Student."

102. Mia Wenjen, "Sarah Dessen: Cyberbully and Her Posse of Mean Girls," Pragmatic Mom, November 20, 2019, https://www.pragmaticmom.com/2019/11/sarah-dessen -cyberbully-and-her-posse-of-mean-girls/.

103. Philippe Rochat, *Moral Acrobatics*, 13.

104. Leon Festinger, *A Theory of Cognitive Dissonance* (Redwood City, CA: Stanford University Press, 1957).

105. Social media companies can take action to reduce this kind of behavior on their platforms, too, and that action does not have to revolve around censorship. For example, Instagram experimented "with its 'like' button, allowing users in some countries to see the number of likes their posts received but not displaying the information to others. The company learned that this change might discourage status seeking or bullying on the platform." Bail, *Social Media Prism*, 122.

106. For years, Dan Kahan has produced some of the best research in this area. Kahan, "The Politically Motivated Reasoning Paradigm, Part 1: What Politically Motivated Reasoning Is and How to Measure It," in *Emerging Trends in the Social and Behavioral Sciences*, edited by Robert Scott and Stephen Kosslyn (Hoboken, NJ: John Wiley, 2016), 1–16. Dan Kahan et al., "Biased Assimilation, Polarization, and Cultural Credibility· An Experimental Study of Nanotechnology Risk Perceptions," Harvard Law School Program on Risk Regulation Research Paper No. 08–25 (February 2008), https://papers.ssrn.com/sol3/papers.cfm?abstract_id=1090044; Kahan, "Fixing the Communications Failure," *Nature* 463 (January 2010): 296–297, https://doi.org /10.1038/463296a.

107. Sunstein, *Conformity*, 26.

108. Jonathan Rauch, *Kindly Inquisitors: The New Attacks on Free Thought* (Chicago: University of Chicago Press, 1994), 159.

109. Bradbury, *Fahrenheit 451*, 78.

110. Stuart Hall, "Some 'Politically Incorrect' Pathways through PC," in *War of the Words*, edited by Sarah Dunant (London: Virago, 1994), 168.

111. Hall, "'Politically Incorrect' Pathways," 183.

112. Hall, 173.

113. Sternheimer, *Pop Culture Panics*, 7.

114. Smith, "Fascinated to Presume."

Acknowledgments

1. David Belinski, *Newton's Gift: How Sir Isaac Newton Unlocked the System of the World* (New York: The Free Press, 2000), 84.

2. Adam Szetela and Shiyu Ji, "Move Over, New York Times Bestseller List. Joe Rogan Is the New Kingmaker for Authors," *Newsweek*, December 21, 2023, https://www.newsweek.com/move-over-new-york-times-bestseller-list-joe-rogan-new-kingmaker-authors-opinion-1853508.

3. Shamus Khan, "Shamus Khan's AMA," Sociology Job Market Rumors, 2015, https://www.socjobrumors.com/topic/shamus-khans-ama.

4. Morrison, "Introduction," 160.

5. Adam Szetela, "Remembering Erik Olin Wright," *Dissent*, January 23, 2019, https://www.dissentmagazine.org/blog/remembering-erik-olin-wright/.

6. John McWhorter, "The Performative Antiracism of Black Students at the U. of Wisconsin," *New York Times*, August 24, 2021, https://www.nytimes.com/2021/08/24/opinion/antiracism-university-wisconsin-rock.html.

7. Hunter S. Thompson, "Fear and Loathing at the Super Bowl," *Rolling Stone*, February 28, 1974, https://www.rollingstone.com/feature/fear-and-loathing-at-the-super-bowl-37345/2/.

8. Dan Gable, "Once You've Wrestled, Life is Easier," YouTube video, 0:02, August 20, 2021, https://youtu.be/npTHFXV_61s.

9. Matthew Alford, "Chomsky Cracks Me Up," *Guardian*, January 21, 2008, https://www.theguardian.com/books/booksblog/2008/jan/21/chomskycracksmeup.

10. "Episode 93: The Thinking Mind," *Ram Dass: Here and Now* (podcast), March 7, 2016, https://www.ramdass.org/ep-93-the-thinking-mind/.

11. Quoted in Walter Kauffman, *Tragedy and Philosophy* (Princeton, NJ: Princeton University Press, 1992), 268.

12. Alexandra Alter and Erica Ackerberg, "Writer's Best Friend," *New York Times*, April 9, 2021, https://www.nytimes.com/interactive/2021/04/09/books/author-writer-national-pet-day.html.

13. Karl Marx, "The Eighteenth Brumaire of Louis Bonaparte," in *Karl Marx: Selected Writings*, 2nd ed., edited by David McLellan (Oxford: Oxford University Press, 2003), 329.

Index